shadowboxing in shanghai

Available from *tgl books*

Translated from the Chinese by Andrea Mary Falk
Jiang Rongqiao's Baguazhang
Li Tianji's The Skill of Xingyiquan
Yan Dehua's Bagua Applications
Di Guoyong on Xingyiquan: Volume I, Foundations
Di Guoyong on Xingyiquan: Volume II, Forms and Ideas
Di Guoyong on Xingyiquan: Volume III, Weapons
Zhang Wenguang's Chaquan

Researched and written by Andrea Mary Falk
A Shadow on Fallen Blossoms: The 36 and 48 Traditional Verses of Baguazhang
Falk's Dictionary of Chinese Martial Arts
Beijing Bittersweet
Shadowboxing in Shanghai

 www.thewushucentre.ca

Shadowboxing in Shanghai

A Memoir,
And a Guide to the
Traditional Chen Taijiquan
From Dragon Park

Written by Andrea Mary Falk
Copyright © Andrea Mary Falk, 2023
ISBN 978-1-989468-29-6

All right reserved.
Cover art by Marco Gagnon

This book or any portion thereof may not be reproduced or used in any manner whatsoever without the express written permission of the publisher except for the use of brief quotations in a book review or scholarly work.
First printing: 2023
Published by tgl books, Québec, Canada.
tgl books logo by Carol Rae

Library and Archives Canada Cataloguing in Publication
Canadian CIP data is no longer done ahead of publication time for small publishers such as tgl books.
The library number is assigned after legal deposit of the published book.

The techniques described in this book are intended for experienced martial artists. The author, translator, and publishers are not responsible for any injury that may occur while trying out these techniques. Please do not apply these techniques on anyone without their consent and cooperation.

tgl books is based in Canada. Its publications are available through www.thewushucentre.ca

"Tradition is not the worship of ashes,
but the preservation of fire."

Gustav Mahler

Dedicated to the memory of my sifu,
Huan Dahai, 1926-2015.

And for my parents, William André and Mary Elliott.
With me. Always.

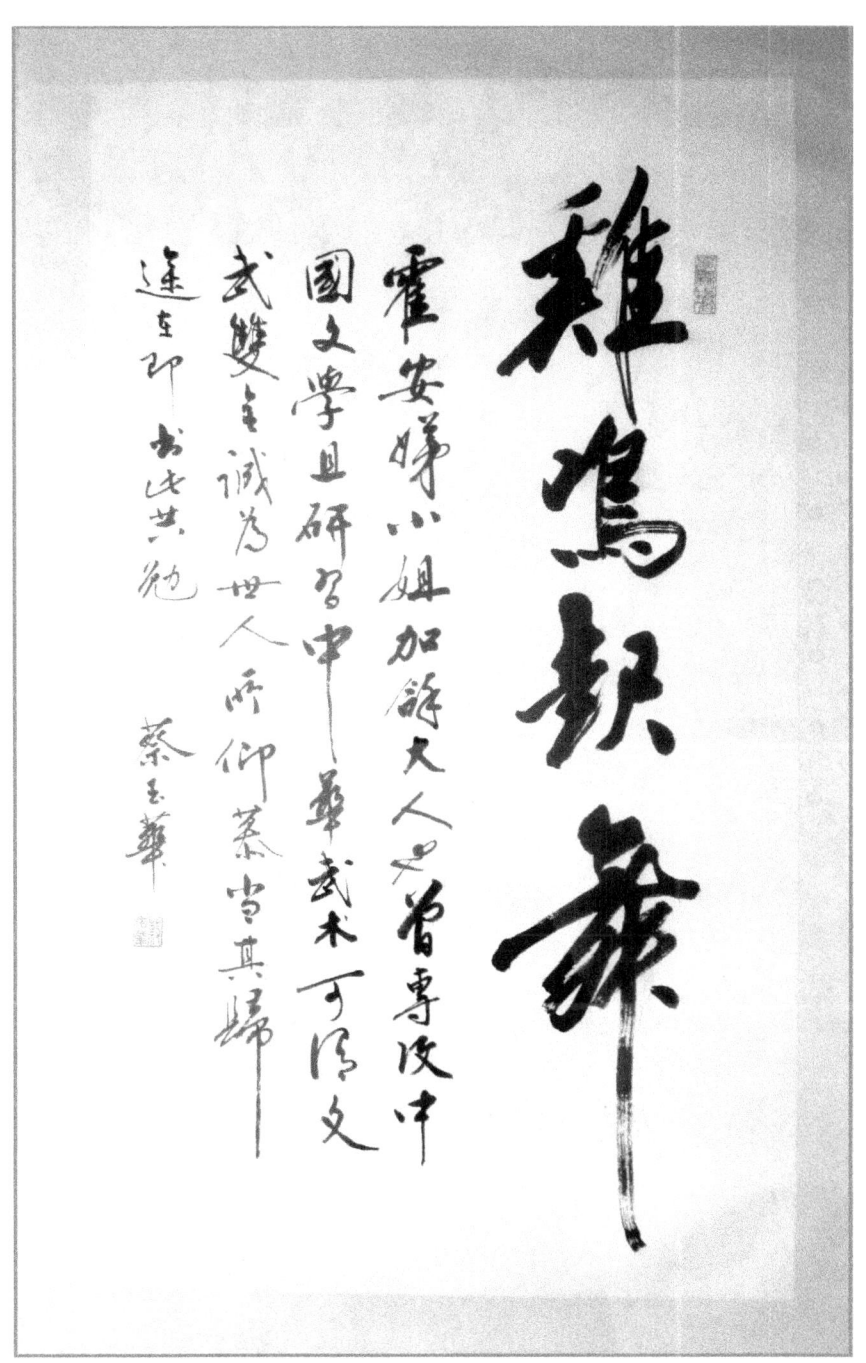

"Get up and train when the swan calls."
Calligraphy from Cai Yuhua, 1983.

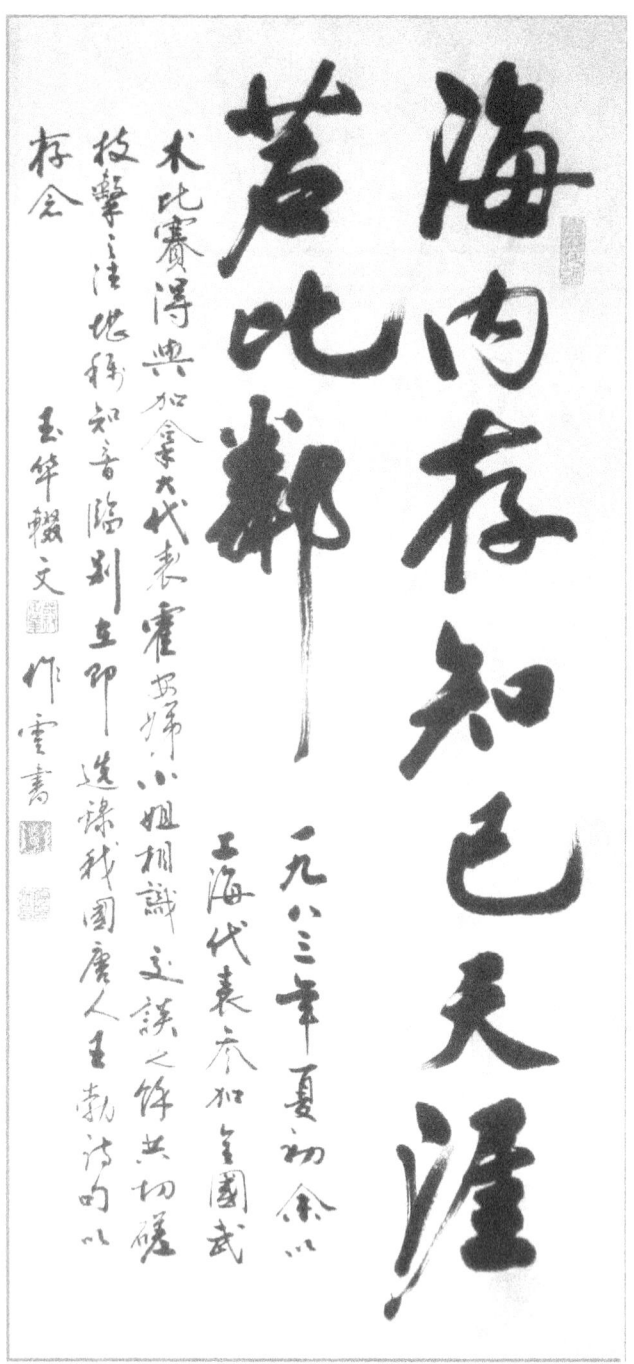

"When you have a good friend within the four seas,
then even when separated, far away feels like next door."
Calligraphy from Cai Yuhua, 1983.

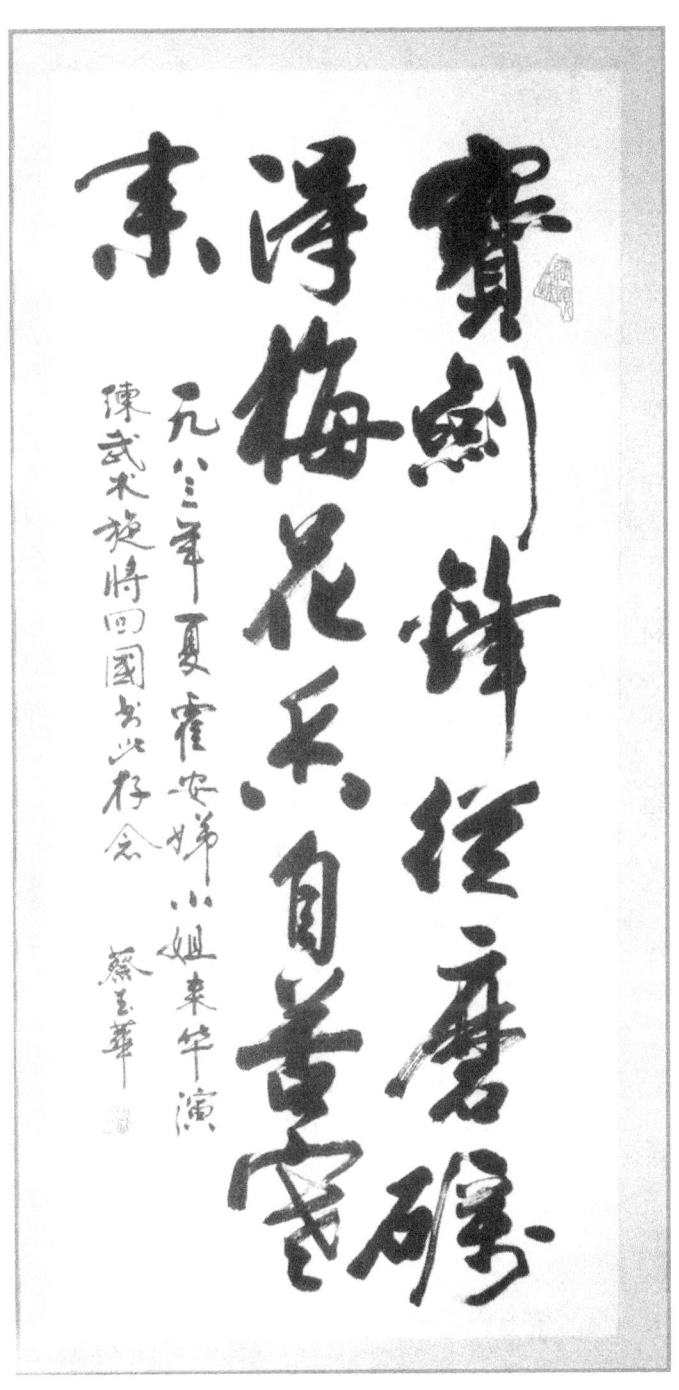

"The sharpness of a precious sword is honed on the whetstone;
The fragrance of a plum blossom is grown during the winter's bitter cold."
Calligraphy from Cai Yuhua, 1983.

This photo of the Bund, published in a 1970s wushu booklet, is titled "The Shanghai waterfront at dawn." Every morning all the residents downtown dress up in the same outfits and take part in mass, synchronized, exercise. As if. This is the Bund as it appeared, once, for this photo. My book, in addition to describing the Taijiquan that I learned, is about actual training in Shanghai.

(Photo from Wushu, A Traditional Chinese Sport, China's Sports, People's Sports Publishing House, Peking, China, undated, c.1974)

CONTENTS

CALLIGRAPHY OF CAI YUHUA, 1983

PREFACE xiii
A NOTE ON REFERENCES xiv
ACKNOWLEDGEMENTS xv

LINEAGE OF DRAGON PARK CHEN TAIJIQUAN 1

YILU: THE FIRST FORM
    NAMES OF MOVEMENTS OF YILU 7
    DESCRIPTION OF MOVEMENTS OF YILU 11

SANLU: THE THIRD FORM
    NAMES OF MOVEMENTS OF SANLU 297
    DESCRIPTION OF MOVEMENTS OF SANLU 298

SOME TERMS IN CHINESE 319
PRONUNCIATION GUIDE FOR PINYIN 321
ABOUT THE AUTHOR 325

INSERTS ABOUT SHANGHAI
INTRODUCTION TO SHANGHAI xvii
19TH CENTURY SHANGHAI 40
THE SHANGHAI CLIMATE 76
EARLY 20TH CENTURY SHANGHAI 111
THE LONGHUA CORNER OF SHANGHAI 148
LATE 20TH CENTURY SHANGHAI 188
21ST CENTURY SHANGHAI 221
NOSTALGIA AND PRESERVATION 247
SHANGHAIHUA, A LANGUAGE OF THE WU KINGDOM 283
SHANGHAI IN THE FUTURE? 315

MAPS

CENTRAL SHANGHAI, 1991 .... xviii - xix
THE CHINESE CITY AND SETTLEMENT, 1843 AND 1853 43
GREATER SHANGHAI, 1920'S 115
OUR NEIGHBOURHOOD, 1990 150
DOWNTOWN SHANGHAI WITH OLD STREET NAMES, DESIGNATED HISTORICAL
    AREAS, AND PROTECTED STREETS (C. 2017) 250-251
THE OLD CHINESE CITY (C. 2017) 316

Preface

I started out writing up this Chen Taijiquan form in English to reduce the chances of it becoming a lost form. I ended up including principles, conversations with my sifu, training experiences, and whatever came to mind relating to my time spent learning this very traditional Taijiquan in Shanghai. I have interspersed these stories into the text, instead of keeping everything all tidy and separate. I learned this Chen Taijiquan and Jiang Rongqiao's Baguazhang and Taiji Changquan in Shanghai during the late 1980s and through the 1990s. I have been going back to Shanghai for checkups since 2015.

I have noticed that in many books that describe martial arts forms the important concepts are introduced at the beginning and then the form is presented, getting sketchier towards the end as the repetitions wear down the author. Naturally the reader also starts to skim. This is the equivalent of paying attention at the beginning of practise of a form and getting distracted towards the end. I have tried to avoid this. I purposefully mixed up theory, practice, and relevant and irrelevant things in the text. I may or may not repeat important concepts. Something written in one repetition of a move applies to all repetitions of that move, and often to other moves, whether or not I mention it, to give that 'just like training with sifu' touch. I often say something that is so obvious as to not need saying. I enjoy seeing comments like that in books I read. Sometimes they make you think about the obvious in a slightly different way.

The Guide to Yilu is the main text with the technique photos.

> Extra performance, training, teaching, concepts, and advice notes that apply to more than the move in which they appear are in plain white boxes with a solid border.

The Memoir, which is comments about daily life, or other, non-training, non-educational details, is in grey boxes with no border.

I have also scattered throughout this book bits of the history and feel of Shanghai. Shanghai refuses to be a backdrop. It imposes itself, it demands to be heard. It is also the only city in China where a foreigner feels a part of its history and future. When I was there in the 1980s and 90s I was mostly in a proscribed round of training and home, or going around with Cai Yuhua. I think I got lost every time I went downtown alone. I have since expanded my range and enjoyment of the city, so am quite happy now to offer it here for you.

> Comments about Shanghai are in gradient shaded boxes with a solid border.

If you find this method of writing confusing or distracting, then I have succeeded in giving you a little of the feel of living in Shanghai and trying to learn and train.

I have kept away from theory as much as possible. Taijiquan is an art learned intuitively and kinesthetically, and the intellect can play tricks on you. You can only learn by being taught by someone who can do it and deeply understands it with their body and heart/mind. In Chinese there is a different word for knowing intellectually (知 *zhi*) with the intelligent mind (意 *yi*) and comprehending in your heart and body (悟 *wu*) with your heart/mind (心 *xin*). Martial arts are learned and known with your heart/mind/body. All the knowledge in the world is no use if you can't do the moves. I realise that saying this, you are going to ask why I bothered to write a book. My sifu, Huan Dahai, wanted me to write up his Chen style Taijiquan. He told me that I had the best background to do this work, as I was his youngest inner apprentice, the only foreigner, the best educated, and the most specialized in martial arts.

I regret not having photos or film of myself in the 1990s. I did film the form once then – a student filmed me and promised a copy – but I never did get it. The filming here was done in 2010, when my beautiful stances were no more. We did not plan the video to be used except as a reference, so did not pay attention to the backdrop, but that is when I started to write up the form more completely, and in English. When those images were unclear or from the wrong angle, I asked my apprentice James to film them (in 2022 as I was preparing the book). My book is meant to add to the material available on this traditional branch of Chen style Taijiquan that comes from Chen Yanxi when he taught outside his hometown. I am sorry that my knowledge and skill is so limited. I am sorry that the writing took so long, but here it is.

A Note on References

I referred to many books, but do not have references at the back because writing this book has been a gradual process over many years. I cannot list everything I have ever read. I have called on papers about Shanghai that I wrote at university in the 1990s, which had pages of references. I have also updated my knowledge of Shanghai with many more recent books. When I actually quote someone, I give the reference within the text, and I try to credit each photo not taken by me.

One book that I quote often is Chen Xin, *Chenshi Taijiquan Tushuo*, Illustrated Book on Chen family Taijiquan, Shanghai Shudian Publishing House, Shanghai, 1986. This is the reprint from the original, from 1921, and the page numbers correspond to the 1986 edition. Cai Yuhua gave me this book as soon as it was re-published, in 1986. In the past I often used this book, on old small frame, as reference, as it is the only book that describes movements a bit similar to ours (although ours is not small frame). Many readers of his book feel his illustrations and comments are peculiar, but that is only because this way of doing Chen style is not common. There is a translation, *The Illustrated Canon of Chen Family Taijiquan,* published in 2007, that is excellent, especially in the theoretical parts.

> Chen Xin's comments, and my comments about his book, are in white boxes with dot-dash lines.

Acknowledgements

Thanks most especially to Cai Yuhua, without whom none of this would have happened. He gives so much for nothing in return. I also thank him for giving his permission for me to write anything I wanted to say about our time together.

Thanks to Kate Baur in Switzerland, for getting me back in contact with Cai Yuhua and for the extra lineage information.

Thanks to Deb Chen, for helping me find Cheng Jiefeng in 2015, twenty years after he taught me the Taiji Changquan.

Thanks to Elena Camesi for the video footage that the Yinianzhai Qigong and Taijiquan school posted online. The photos of Cai Yuhua are clipped from this footage, filmed in 1995 and posted in 2020. It was filmed by his Swiss friends at his home in Shanghai. The photos are given here with Cai Yuhua's and the Yinianzhai school's permission.

Thanks to Patrick Kelly, who taught me the moves of Yilu, and gave permission to include photos of, and comments about, him.

Thanks to James Saper for helping with the details on the internal linkages, for a great job of copy editing and suggestions for improvement of this book, and for filming some moves for use in this book.

Thanks to Neil Bates for the final proof reading, and especially for his thoughts in discussions that helped me finalize the book.

Thanks to David Cliff for filming me doing the form and transferring the high resolution files to me in 2010.

Thanks to Tam Davage for giving his permission to publish some photos he took of some of us in Playfair Park, back in Victoria in the 1990s.

Thanks to Byron Jacobs for cleaning up some of the old photos.

Thanks again to Marco Gagnon, for another great book cover.

Thanks to my husband, Gilbert Ethier, for giving his permission for the photo of him in Playfair Park. And for the occasional apt comment during the long writing process, which often led to a lot of work, but did improve the book.

The Yinianzhai Qigong and Taijiquan school in Switzerland would like me to say for them, "Since 1996 Cai Yuhua has contributed greatly to its achievements, through his teachings of Taijiquan, Baguazhang, Tuina and traditional Chinese painting and through his personality that has made him the most appreciated Chinese teacher and friend of the Yinianzhai school."

I hope you enjoy this book, and I hope that you see its imperfections as part of its charm.

Andrea Mary Falk

aka Huo Andi 霍安娣

February 2010 to February 2023

Morin-Heights and Québec City, Québec, Canada

When Shanghai is part of a book, it takes it over. Like London, when it is used as a backdrop in novels, it insists on being one of the characters.

Shanghai has been a cosmopolitan city since 1843, with many cosmopolitan citizens. When I was there in late 20th century Socialist China, Shanghainese saw themselves as a cut above the countrified Beijingers. Well, to tell the truth, Shanghainese – the Chinese residents of Shanghai (distinct in that they speak the Shanghai dialect, *Zånghewo*, thus calling themselves *Zånghenin* and everyone else Outlanders, or *Ñadinin*) – see themselves as a cut above everyone else. This, while it should be annoying, is part of their appeal. They have been called 'wily' and 'blasé.' I prefer 'urbane' and 'irreverent.' What I especially like is their confidence of identity, which means that they can treat foreigners as people, too.

Shanghai is one city in China where foreign residents played a key role. Foreigners are part of the city, integrated into the history and culture. Shanghailanders – long term foreign residents – were never just privileged rich English expats. Middle class and poor foreigners from many countries worked and made their lives there, and still do.

I have seen Shanghai called an 'urban aberration,' growing as it did on farmland beside a walled city – a forced treaty port won in opium wars. It was always a mess to administer, and especially between the two world wars, was one of the most boisterous places on earth, where people partied while war in China loomed, and the Sino-Japanese war, though officially 1937-1945, started being felt by 1932 in Shanghai.

In 2020, the Shanghai population of 28 million included 150,000 foreigners, which was about a quarter of all foreigners in China. Because of this shared history, and because Shanghainese treat everyone not born in the city or not speaking their language as 'Outlanders,' I feel more comfortable with my foreign-ness in Shanghai than in Beijing. Somehow both 'more' and 'less' foreign. I usually also am aware of being not as well-dressed as the locals.

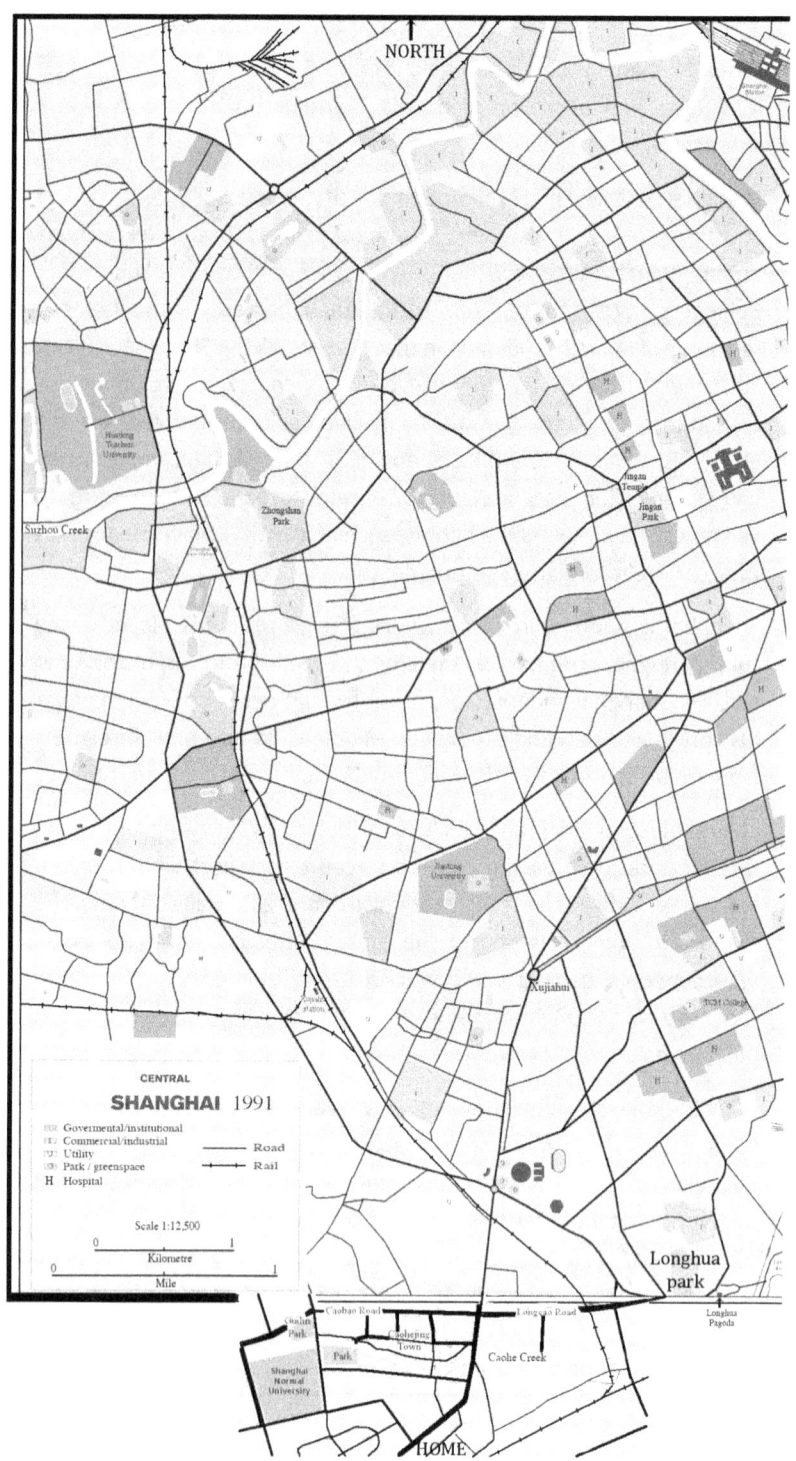

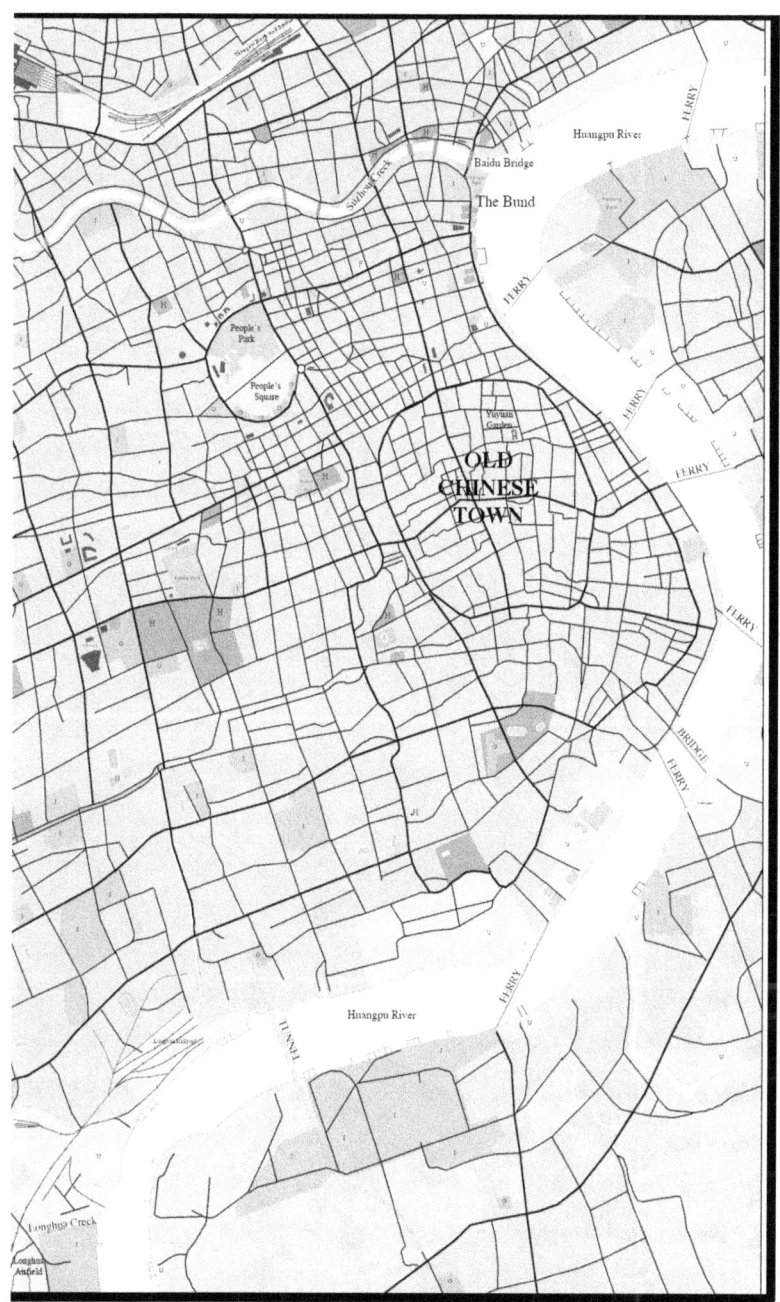

Central Shanghai, 1991
With our neighbourhood added by hand on the bottom left, because it was off the map. You have to feel for me, coming from Beijing, with its long, straight, north-south, east-west roads.

Lineage Introduction

We sometimes call our branch of Chen style Taijiquan 'Dragon Park' Chen style, after the park where Huan Dahai taught for years in Shanghai. He normally called it called old style, or 'real' old style.

Our lineage starts the same as most Taijiquan, with stories. From Wang Zongyue 王宗岳, Jiang Fa 蒋发, and Chen Wangting 陈王廷 (c. 1600-1680), and through the generations within Chenjiagou village. The more researchable part of our lineage starts from Chen Yanxi:

Chen Yanxi 陈延熙 (1848-1929)

Yuan Keding 袁克定 (1878-1958), possibly with influence from Li Ruidong 李瑞东, and Hu Yuchun 胡玉春.

monk Zhai Hui'an 翟慧庵

Huan Dahai 宦大海 (1926-2015)

Cheng Jiefeng 程杰峰 (1945-), Cai Yuhua 蔡玉华 (1951-), Andrea Falk 霍安娣 (1954-), and others.

Most branches of Chen style Taijiquan hold in common some variation of the lineage up to Chen Yanxi. Many branches start with Chen Wangting, putting Wang Zongyue into the realm of legend, and I am fine with that. Chen Wangting is the first actual, most likely to be real, source of Chen's kungfu with Taijiquan characteristics. Some lineages give place to Jiang Fa as co-creator, as a friend of Chen Wangting. Some even put Jiang Fa as teacher of Chen Wangting. Images from the time, with Jiang Fa standing behind and Chen Wangting sitting indicate that the relationship is with Chen Wangting as senior. Then again, were the images made at the time, or later, with the desire to place Chen Wangting higher in status? Or were they equals martially, and Chen placed in higher status because of his social standing in the village?

Although Chen Yanxi is a focal starting point for a number of Chen Taijiquan branches, many of them are filtered through his son Chen Fake (1887-1957). Chen Fake is thought to have changed the style when he moved to Beijing, so any lineage coming through him would necessarily be different from ours. Chen Fake was born later in Chen Yanxi's life, and Chen Yanxi travelled a great deal to teach, so Chen Fake's development was more through uncles than his father. Distinctions between 'new' and 'old' branches were developed later, by others. A more useful distinction is 'large' and 'small,' but even with that, our lineage is hard to categorize.

Huan Dahai referred to our style as 'old.' It bears little resemblance to either what is called old frame or new frame nowadays. In some ways it looks similar to what is now called small frame. It is very likely that our lineage, directly from Chen Yanxi, has developed on its own. Modern performance of small frame does not look quite like us, though the use of relatively tight circles within the body to perform relatively large movements is similar. We have also looked at the Zhao Bao style, out of interest, and it is clearly different. Zhaobao, a village 2.5 kilometres from Chen village, has a style that came from Chen Qingping (1795-1868).

I have researched the people in our lineage, but not all were famous enough to be in historical reference materials.

Huan Dahai was reluctant to give me our lineage chart, as it includes Yuan Keding, the son of Yuan Shikai. Yuan Shikai (1859-1916), was the minister of the Beiyang region (Liaoning, Hebei, and Shandong provinces) in the early 1900s, and the first president of the Republic of China, ruling from 1912 to 1916. This makes him one of the major warlords of the time, and he also wanted to become the next emperor, so he is generally considered one of the 'bad guys' in Chinese modern history. In his position, he was able to seek out the best martial arts instructors and bring them to teach his family and soldiers at his bases. He was interested in martial arts himself, not just in training the army to deal with modern warfare.

Other sources confirm that Chen Yanxi was hired by Yuan Shikai to teach his children in addition to his troops. Davidine Siaw-Voon Sim and David Gaffney, in *Chen Style Taijiquan: The Source of Taiji Boxing* (North Atlantic Books, Berkeley, California, 2002) noted that Chen Yanxi taught martial arts in Yuan Shikai's household. Lin Chaozhen, in *Fu Zhen Song's Dragon Bagua Zhang* (Blue Snake Books, Berkeley, California, 2010, page 19), wrote that Fu Zhensong learned old frame Chen Taijiquan from Chen Yanxi, who had been hired at his village to teach. Fu started learning from Chen Yanxi in 1888, and it is not known for how long he trained with him, just "a number of years." This book states that after Chen Yanxi left Fu's village he most likely went on to become the private martial tutor to the children of Yuan Shikai. That means that Yuan Keding would have been at least thirteen when Chen arrived, and most likely older.

Lineage Introduction

C.P. Ong, in *Taijiquan: Cultivating Inner Strength* (Bagua Press, Charleston, SC, 2013, page 42), wrote that Chen Yanxi was "treated as a prized acquisition as he defeated all the famous martial artists that came his way," and he suggested that perhaps Yanxi wasted his time, that "Taijiquan was more admired than pursued." But, Chen Yanxi taught in Yuan Shikai's household for six years, during the time that Yuan Shikai was governor of Shandong. C.P. Ong suggested that he did not teach much, but who really knows? Yuan Keding very likely did learn directly from Chen Yanxi, as our lineage claims.

Yuan Keding, one of Yuan Shikai's many sons, was born in Henan, and lived, probably, in Shandong, Tianjin, Beijing, and again in Henan. He followed his father in gaining government positions, through which he rose fairly high up while his father was in office. Yuan Keding worked for his father in a variety of positions and places, and was often around martial artists. He had so little real influence that I could find no information on him after his father died. One interesting thing about him were some fairly disparaging remarks about his character, or lack of it, from contemporaries, some of whom wrote that he was dependent on his father's influence for advancement, and did not have a strong character of his own. Another interpretation, though, is, seeing that he had many friends in the fine arts world of painting and calligraphy, perhaps he was not really interested in politics. This perceived lack of character might simply have been lack of interest. He is known to have been skilled at art, so it is quite reasonable that he loved Taijiquan, too. He most certainly received good martial arts instruction. He lived to eighty years old, which suggests the good health of a Taijiquan player.

Li Ruidong, a name listed in our lineage as a possible influence, came from Wuqing county in Hebei province. He worked for Yuan Shikai as a martial arts instructor, and taught at the army's martial academy. He was known for his Shaolin, Taijiquan, weapons, and wrestling. He learned from Yang Luchan, among others. It is likely that he had contact with Yuan Keding, possibly Hu Yuchun, and probably Chen Yanxi directly. He would at least have been a steadying influence on Yuan Keding, and possibly learned Chen Yanxi's Taijiquan and played a part in passing on the style. As a martial arts instructor in the household, he would have been senior to Yuan Keding in the martial world.

One other household where Chen Yanxi taught was Du Yan's. Du Yan was a government official in charge of the county where Chenjiagou village is situated. Adam Hsu, *Lone Sword Against the Cold Cold Sky* (2006), says that

Du Yuze was a student of Chen Yanxi when Chen was hired as a bodyguard for Du's father, Du Yan. C.P. Ong (page 93) also mentions this, though neither give dates. Huan Dahai often told me that there was someone named Du teaching a Chen Taijiquan in Taiwan that he heard was similar to what we did. This is most certainly Du Yuze (1896-1990). His style is also notably different from that taught by Chen Yanxi's son Chen Fake. This is similar to our situation with Yuan Keding – Chen Yanxi working for a warlord or official privately, outside of his village. Du Yuze moved to Taiwan in 1949. In 1987 Adam Hsu visited Chenjiagou village and found that a few of the older people still did something similar to his style. Someone in our lineage also visited, with the same result. It looks very much that there is indeed a branch of Chen style, spread by Chen Yanxi, that developed separately from what would become the officially recognized style of the village.

My sifu Huan Dahai learned from his friend, a monk called Zhai Hui'an, and also from his martial uncle Hu Yuchun. Aside from our story that Zhai Hui'an learned from Yuan Keding, I could find no information about him. Neither have I found information about Hu Yuchun. Hu Chunyun may have had more responsibility in the lineage that we are aware, being the senior 'uncle.'

Chen Xin (1849-1929) aka Chen Pinsan, described an old version of Taijiquan in his book, *Illustrated Book on Chen Family Taijiquan*. Chen Xin was of the same generation as Chen Yanxi. Chen Xin was Chen Zhongshen's son, and learned from him, though his father made him study more than train, and made his brother, Chen Yao, train more than study. Proper study of Chinese literature and arts is rigorous, so it was hard to be accomplished at both. Chen Xin decided to use his skill to write a book about Taijiquan, the first to come out of Chen village. It took him from 1908 to 1919 to write. I understand that it was dated as 1921, but some say it was not published until 1933.

Our branch preserves the seven forms that are claimed to exist in the early Chen style, five of which have been largely lost in the standard branches. The first form follows the basic route of most versions of the Chen Yilu (First Form), though with more, and more variety of, moves. The second form, *Paochui* (Pounding Fists), is also recognizable as similar to the standard *Paochui*. The third, *Dasi Taochui* (Big Four Sets of Pounding), is a short form that emphasizes elbow, shoulder, and knee techniques. One person in our lineage showed it to someone from Chenjiagou village, who recognized it as similar to one practiced by an old lady in the village, but little practiced by others. The fourth is called *Hongquan* (Flooding Fists), so that may indicate some Shaolinquan influence. I have not seen the form to compare it with Shaolin's *Little Hongquan* and *Big Hongquan*. The fifth and sixth I do not know, and have never seen. I am not even sure that Huan Dahai remembered them, so saying that we preserved them is a bit of a stretch.

What sifu called the seventh form is the *Taiji Changquan* (Taiji Long Fist). It does not move in the same manner as the other forms. It rolls like a grand river, gracefully and powerfully without interruption. It combines elements of Baguazhang, Xingyiquan, Taijiquan, and even moves familiar from Chaquan. It may be a later form influenced by other styles, an early form that influenced other styles, or a form that happened to have similar techniques to other styles in the area in which it was practiced. This form was actually learned within Jiang Rongqiao's lineage, so it isn't really the seventh form. Both Huan Dahai and Cheng Jiefeng learned it directly from Jiang Rongqiao, and they taught it to me. I have no idea why sifu said it was the seventh form.

Generational categories and linkages can be confusing in lineage lines. I learned from Huan Dahai, Cai Yuhua and Cheng Jiefeng. If I had not been accepted as an inner apprentice of Huan Dahai, I would have been considered as the next generation after Cheng and Cai, even though we are close to the same age and even if I had received instruction from Huan. But since I was accepted, and most of my instruction was from Huan Dahai, I am considered to be of their generation.

My friend and martial brother, Cai Yuhua, was a factory worker who was selected many times to the Shanghai Municipal Team for national wushu exchange meets, the venue for traditional stylists and amateurs. He had a good background in traditional Changquan, Shaolinquan, and Xinyiquan before he met Huan Dahai in 1970, and started this traditional Chen Taijiquan, Xingyiquan, and Baguazhang with him. As if this weren't enough, he also excels at Chinese *tuina* therapy, *qigong*, and painting and calligraphy, and has studied with well-known practitioners and artists in those fields. This photo shows a young Huan Dahai (on the left) and Cai Yuhua in 1970.

To continue the lineage, my apprentice James Saper, as a doctor of traditional Chinese medicine, will continue the style in his own way. I have also taught him the Taiji Changquan. I have taught these forms to a few others, but not many. I am known as a Baguazhang and Xingyiquan teacher, which is my profession. Yilu and Taiji Changquan are more personal to me, and I do not teach them in public classes. This book is the first writeup of this particular Yilu of which I am aware.

The value of this branch of Chen Taijiquan, whatever it is and wherever it came from, is undisputed to those who practice it. Its intricate coiling and recoiling movements show a true balance, support, and interaction of *yin* and *yang*; its practical applications are clear and effective; and it directly stimulates the internal system in a way that renders irrelevant any additional practice of *qigong*. Performing this Yilu allows you realise that time and space are not as separate as they seem.

Yilu, The First Form yī lù 一路

	Names of the Movements of Yilu		Page
1.	预备式	Preparation	11
2.	无极式	Position Of Chaos	14
3.	太极式	Position Of Order	14
4.	金刚捣碓	Temple Guard Pounds with The Pestle	19
5.	懒扎衣	Tuck In The Robe Casually	25
6.	如封似闭	Seal Off, Shut Down	31
7.	丹变	Dantian Transforms	36
8.	金刚捣碓	Temple Guard Pounds With The Pestle (2nd time)	44
9.	白鹅亮翅	White Goose Flashes Its Wings	47
10.	搂膝拗步	Brush Knee Counter Stance	52
11.	初收	Initial Gathering	56
12.	左右斜行	Left And Right Diagonal Stepping (2nd and 3rd times, alternate version of Brush Knee)	59
13.	搂膝拗步	Brush Knee Counter Stance (4th time, alternate)	62
14.	再收	Gather In Again	64
15.	斜行拗步	Diagonal Stepping To Counter Stance	67
16.	抛架子	Cast The Frame	68
17.	前堂拗步	Front Hall Counter Stance (5th time, alternate)	71
18.	掩手肱捶	Hide The Hand And Punch	73
19.	金刚捣碓	Temple Guard Pounds With The Pestle (3rd time, alternate version)	78
20.	三盘落地	Three Basins Lower To The Ground	79
21.	七寸靠	Seven-Inch Body Strike	80
22.	伏虎式	Ambush The Tiger	82
23.	错骨分筋	Dislocate Bones And Separate Tendons	84
24.	背折靠	Bend And Hit With The Back	88

25.	急三捶	Three Urgent Hits	91
26.	窝里炮	Punch Into The Dens	93
27.	青龙出水	Green Dragon Shoots Out Of The Water	95
28.	撇身捶	Cast Away And Hit	97
29.	双推手	Double Push	99
30.	肘底看拳	See the Fist Under The Elbow	101
31.	倒念肱(捻)	Backup Twisting The Arms	103
32.	白鹅亮翅	White Goose Flashes Its Wings (2nd time)	107
33.	搂膝拗步	Brush Knee Counter Stance (6th time)	110
34.	海底针	Needle At Sea Bottom	116
35.	三通背	Three Through The Back	118
36.	掩手肱捶	Hide the Hand And Punch (2nd time, alternate)	120
37.	懒扎衣	Tuck In The Robe Casually (2nd time, alternate entry)	122
38.	如封似闭	Seal Off, Shut Down (2nd time)	125
39.	丹变	Dantian Transforms (2nd time)	127
40.	中运手	Middle Travelling Hands	129
41.	高探马	High Pat On Horse	134
42.	右插脚	Right Stab The Foot	137
43.	左盘插脚	Left Coil And Stab The Foot	139
44.	左蹬一跟	Left Thrust A Heel	141
45.	裹边炮	Inside Hits	144
46.	击鼓炮	Hit The Drum	146
47.	倒插势	Stab Backwards	151
48.	翻江倒海	Overturn Rivers And Reverse The Seas	152
49.	搂膝栽捶	Brush The Knee And Plant A Punch	154
50.	翻身二起	Roll Over And Two Rises	157
51.	左兽头式	Beast's Head (left)	160
52.	右打虎	Hit The Tiger (right)	162
53.	右兽头式	Beast's Head (2nd time, right side)	163
54.	左打虎	Hit The Tiger (2nd time, left side)	164

55.	右踩一掌	Right Stomp With A Palm	165
56.	旋风腿	Whirlwind Kick	167
57.	倒蹬一跟	Thrust A Heel Behind	169
58.	搴旗出鼓	Capture The Flag And Go Forth With The Drums	171
59.	架梁肱捶	Brace The Roofbeam To Punch	173
60.	下击掌	Palm Strike Below	175
61.	迎面手	Greet the Face With The Hand	176
62.	小擒打	Little Grapple And Hit	178
63.	抱头推山	Carry The Head And Push A Mountain	180
64.	三换掌	Triple Palm Exchange	182
65.	连珠炮	String Of Pearls Strikes	184
66.	单鞭	Single Whip (3rd time, alternate version)	186
67.	前招	Forward Beckoning	194
68.	后招	Backward Beckoning	196
69.	野马分鬃	Wild Horse Tosses Its Mane	197
70.	六封四闭	Six Sealings, Four Closings (3rd time, alternate)	200
71.	丹变	Dantian Transforms (4th time)	202
72.	双劈掌	Double Chop	203
73.	玉女穿梭	Jade Maiden Throws The Shuttle	205
74.	懒扎衣	Tuck In The Robe Casually (3rd time)	207
75.	如封似闭	Seal Off, Shut Down (4th time)	208
76.	丹变	Dantian Transforms (5th time)	210
77.	上运手	Upper Travelling Hands (2nd time, alternate)	212
78.	双摆莲	Double Swaying Lotus	215
79.	跃岑	Leap The Mountain Peak	217
80.	扫胫炮	Sweep The Shin And Double Strike	219
81.	金鸡独立	Golden Rooster Stands On One Leg	224
82.	朝天蹬	Heel Faces The Sky	226
83.	倒捻肱	Backup Twisting The Arms (2nd time)	228
84.	白鹅亮翅	White Goose Flashes Its Wings (3rd time)	230

#	中文	English	Page
85.	搂膝拗步	Brush Knee Counter Stance (7th time)	232
86.	白蛇吐信	White Snake Spits Its Tongue	234
87.	闪通背	Dodge Through The Back (2nd time, alternate name and version)	236
88.	掩手肱棰	Hide The Hand And Punch (3rd time, alternate)	238
89.	懒扎衣	Tuck In The Robe Casually (4th time, alternate entry)	239
90.	如封似闭	Seal Off, Shut Down (5th time)	242
91.	丹变	Dantian Transforms (6th time)	245
92.	下运手	Lower Travelling Hands (3rd time, alternate)	252
93.	凤凰展翅	Phoenix Spreads Its Wings	256
94.	高探马	High Pat On Horse (2nd time, alternate version)	257
95.	十字腿	Crossed Kick	258
96.	指裆捶	Hit To The Groin	260
97.	野猿献果	Wild Ape Presents Fruit	261
98.	双撞棰	Double Ramming	263
99.	如封似闭	Seal Off, Shut Down (6th time)	264
100.	丹变	Dantian Transforms (7th time)	265
101.	铺地锦	Spread A Quilt On The Ground	266
102.	七星拳	Seven Stars Fists	269
103.	跨虎势	Ride The Tiger	271
104.	转身摆莲	Turning Swaying Lotus	273
105.	获心拳	Seize The Heart	275
106.	当头跑	Rap On The Head With Cannon-Balls	276
107.	金刚捣碓	Temple Guard Pounds With The Pestle (4th time)	279
108.	收式	Closing Posture	281

DESCRIPTION OF YILU, THE FIRST FORM

1. **Preparation** yù bèi shì 预备势

   or **Position Of Chaos** or **Nonpolarity** wú jí shì 无极势

Overall Movement: Stand quietly, relax your body, and empty your mind.

Footwork: Do not move the feet yet. Stand with the heels together, toes slightly apart (up to a fist's width) throughout this move.

Breakdown of Movement:

Part One: Stand with the knees straight but unlocked, lower back flat and the head raised. Let the arms hang naturally, palms in, armpits slightly opened. Settle the hips and shoulders. Pull up the Yang Men point (just in front of the anal sphincter) slightly, with no more force than it takes to close your eyes. Place the tongue on the palate, opposite the soft spot on the top of the skull. Look straight forward. Breathe into your *dantian*.

Part Two: When you feel ready to move, pull the belly (proximal segment) of the middle fingers slightly towards the palms, and touch the tip of the middle fingers and thumbs on the thighs. The middle fingers press the Feng Shi points on either side of the thighs. Photo 1.

Direction of Movements: Just for convenience in describing the form, start standing facing south. You don't have to do the form facing the same way all the time, just face in the way most practical to your training area, with room to move into on your left.

Possible Applications: Since you do not move, this position allows you to isolate the practices of mental focus and breath control. To be able to react quickly and effectively in a stressful self defense situation, an attentive, detached, and calm focus is needed. Practise this mindset first standing still, then throughout the form, then in applications, and finally in sparring.

The touch to the Feng Shi point is the first of a number of such touching, pressing, and passing by pressure points throughout the form. Each time you touch points on yourself you remind yourself where they are. The light touch you give yourself may help to unblock meridians, and knowledge of the points can be used to injure an opponent. Also, knowing the points, you can avoid unnecessary injury to an opponent.

Internal Connections: The beneficial effects of a quiet mind and breath control in basic *qigong* standing are well known. Stand until you feel that your mind is quiet and that your breathing is happening on its own.

Use reverse breathing – as you inhale, stop the lower abdomen from bulging and expand instead the lower ribs to the back. Then as you exhale, press with the diaphragm and lower abdomen without overly bulging out. Fill up into the whole torso without puffing up the front of the chest. This type of flank breathing is natural and gives more power to all movements, and especially to explosive moves. It also brings *qi* up the back of the body then settles it down into the *dantian*. It is best to practise breathing in this posture first, before applying it throughout the form.

This position makes a deliberate connection of the middle finger and thumb to the outer thigh. The tip of the middle finger accesses the hand's final-Yin pericardium (the membrane enclosing the heart) line. When the arms hang straight, the middle fingers naturally touch the Feng Shi points on the midline on the outside of the thighs. Feng Shi's overall action is to increase *qi* and blood circulation in the leg Shao Yang channel, strengthening and opening the joints of the lower limb.

An acupoint has a certain effect on the *qi* dynamic of a meridian. During acupuncture, a needle is inserted into an acupoint to cause a change that will affect a symptom or disease. When we put light pressure on an acupoint during Taijiquan, we may change the *qi* dynamic of its meridian. We should not think that we will cure this or that disease. In other words, pressing the Feng Shi may help heal knee joint pain, but the fleeting nature of the touch suggests probably not. At most, the pressure may help to release blockages of that particular meridian.

<u>About the Name</u>: Prior to starting the form, you are still unbalanced and disordered, and your mind may be on other things. The first task is thus to stand quietly, calm the mind and regulate the breathing, to prepare for the upcoming change from chaos to balance.

In one version of the names, this is called the Position Of Chaos, and the next move is Three Openings And Closings Of The Dantian. The process is blended smoothly, once you stand until you arrive in the balanced, differentiated, or Taiji, posture.

<u>Additional Comments</u>: Take your time in this position. Stand until you feel ready to start. Stand until you lose yourself and give in to the Taijiquan form on which you are about to embark. The initiation of movement should grow naturally from the stillness, as a plant starts growing from a seed. Do not think 'start' – let your body start itself.

Do not become sluggish while standing. Keep your eyes open and remain alert. Your *qi* should be circulating well even when standing, you don't want it to become slow, as this will result in the form starting sluggishly, and then you will struggle to bring energy to it. Close the lips, lightly touch the teeth together, and touch the tongue to the palate to allow *qi* to circulate throughout the body.

There is a tendency to space out a bit while standing and breathing. I find that before starting to move, when I touch the fingers to the legs, that my eyes become focused and brighter and I am ready to start the form with good energy.

If I have trouble remembering a form once it starts to get repetitious, I pretend I am where I learned it. I have often imagined a line of trees at my back, or a fountain in front of me, or 'the Go players' to my right. I then react to my body's memory of place rather than my brain's faulty memory of movement sequence, and know where I am in a form. Different people have different memory triggers, and I am one of those who remembers how to get to a place after I've been there only once, so this works for me, but might not work for you.

> My meeting with Cai Yuhua that resulted in my learning this branch of Chen style, living in Shanghai with his family, and making a lifelong friend, was out of character for both of us. I was observing a national friendship wushu meet in Nanchang in May 1983. From 1980 to 1983 I was a foreign-exchange scholarship student at the Beijing Physical Culture Institute. Part of my education was to be sent to watch the national wushu competitions, both professional and amateur. Cai Yuhua came up and introduced himself. He was a competitor in Taijiquan and Baguazhang, on the Shanghai team. He told me later, when we were friends, that he had never come up to a strange foreigner like that before. For my part, I usually brushed off people who did that, because the only Chinese people who came up to foreigners were those annoying and insistent ones wanting to practice their English or run a scam. I responded to his open face and clear honesty, and we practiced together in the mornings during the meet. At the meet, he helped me with a photo shoot with Zhang Tong, a Xingyiquan master who taught me in the mornings. We took some photos showing some applications of Xingyiquan.

Cai with Zhang Tong, 1983

2 to 3. Going from **Position Of Chaos** towards **Taiji**, or **Polarity Posture**
tài jí shì   太极势

or **Three Openings And Closings Of The Dantian**   dān tián sān
kāi hé   丹田三开合

<u>Overall Movement</u>: Fully open and close the articulations and spaces of the entire body, then settle to the middle way.

<u>Footwork</u>: At first, continue to stand without moving the feet. Bend the legs slightly in part four. From part five, bend the legs to sit down slightly and roll the hip joints to turn the toes out until the feet are almost ninety degrees to each other. During part six, roll the hip joints to close the knees, and push up to raise the heels (bend the knees, do not let the body rise) and land with the heels out, the feet again almost ninety degrees to each other. During part seven, lift the toes slightly to open them until the feet are parallel and settle into the short horse stance (*kaibu*).

Do not let the body rise and fall during the sequence. Be sure to open and close in the hip joints to move the knees and feet, so that the knees remain aligned with the feet. In the final position, the crotch area is rounded, the hip joints released, and the knees and toes aligned. In part eight, straighten the knees then settle again.

<u>Breakdown of Movement</u>:

Part One: Bend the arms slightly to raise the hands enough to make movement easy. Open and *shunchan* the chest, shoulders, and arms to rotate the palms to face forward. Continue to coil, circling the index fingers, hyper-extending the wrists on the thumb edge, pulling the hands quite far back to open up the chest. Circle the hands until the movement turns to *nichan* and the fingers point forward. At the end of the movement, the thumbs rest again on the thighs and the palms press down slightly. Photos 2a and 2b.

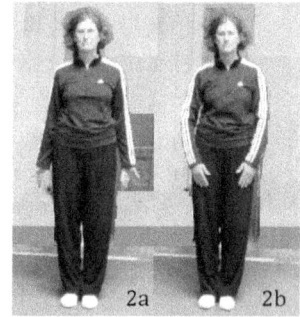

Part Two: *Nichan* until the palms face back, and circle them up and around to in front of the shoulders, closing the chest and gradually changing to *shunchan*. Breathe in and pull in the belly. When the hands arrive in front, touch the tip of the ring fingers together, then the tips of the little fingers. Continue to roll the hands together as they come closer to the body, touching the blade of the hands, around the edge to the thumbs, then the tips of the index fingers, and finally the middle fingers. Continue to rotate the arms while bringing the hands together, so by the end of the move the fingers point up.

Yilu: The First Form

The palms appear to be in a Buddhist salute, but the hollows of the palms are not touching. Breathe out and settle into the belly. (You may just touch the tips of the middle fingers and rotate to continue directly to part three, but you miss out on the Buddhist salute.). Photos 2c, 2d, and 2e.

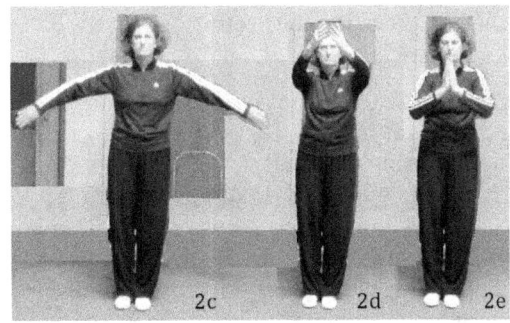

Part Three: Coil to turn the fingers to point to the chest, then push the palms away from the body and up, keeping contact with the tips of the middle fingers until the very last. When the fingertips arrive at head height, push well forward to open up the upper back, then separate the hands and open them out, continuing to *nichan* until the coiling becomes *shunchan* as the hands circle down and in, to in front of the body, palms facing each other. (You may circle the hands well back to open up the shoulders, or you may keep within more usual range.) Breathe in as you push out and breathe out as you lower the hands, lowering the *qi* and relaxing into the belly. Photo 2f.

Part Four: Close the chest and coil the hands in so that the palms first push forward, fingers down, at about waist height. Roll the belly in.

Part Five: Keep the wrists flat and continue to close the body in to *nichan* the arms to curl the palms in. Bring the thumbs in to touch the meridian points in the belly, palms down. Then slide the thumbs out to meridian points just above the hip bones, then out to the Feng Shi on the side of the thighs. Sit down and open the front of the hips, knees, and feet as the rest of the body settles and then opens. Photos 2g and 2h.

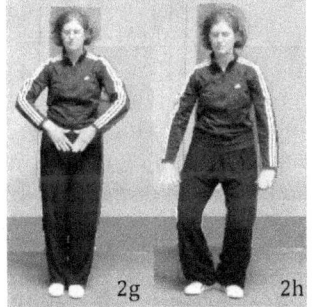

Part Six: Close the front of the hips and knees and roll the belly in and over. Keep the thumbs on the Feng Shi point, coiling the arms to turn the backs of the hands to each other. Continue to coil the hands until the palms are forward, so that they appear to be pushing forward at the side, but the pressure is in the backs of the hands. The thumbs release from the legs during

15

the roll. Push into the ground, roll up the back and open the heels as the backs of the hands press out. Photos 2i and 2j.

Part Seven: Close the body down again to roll the hands over and all the way around, so that the palms do almost a full circle facing up, then turn to face down. Get the thumbs back to the Feng Shi soon, and keep them on as the hands complete the circle. Open the feet to a small parallel stance (*kaibu*) once the thumbs are on the legs, to open as the hands open out. Settle the *qi* and relax the belly. This last position is Taiji Posture. Photos 2k and 2l.

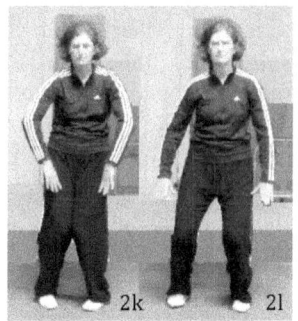

Part Eight (optional): Circle the palms out to the sides, then up to shoulder height, turning the palms up. Then lower them to in front of the stomach, palms facing out at first and gradually facing down. Bend the knees, settle the shoulders, press the head up, and settle the *qi*. This is the same position as taken in part seven, just a bit more settled. Photos 2m and 2n.

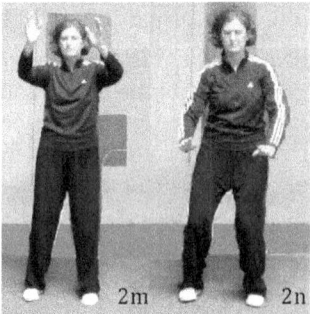

Direction of Movements: You are still facing south.

Possible Applications: It is possible to create a practical use for these moves (breaking a grip, pressing down to control), but is it necessary to do this for every single move of a form? These actions open the form and set every part of the body up for what will come. This style uses full completion of *shunchan* and *nichan* to blend one into the other just as *yin* and *yang* grow to fullness to blend into each other; uses opening and closing of the body; and uses the pushing into the ground and rotation in the hip joints.

The opening move develops this ability to open and close, and to *shunchan* and *nichan* the whole body. This type of movement will later be used in absorbing and releasing methods. This ability to fully roll from *yang* to *yin* and back without visible movement will also be used to readjust the body around a fixed point such as the wrist, so that when grabbed you can readjust and come back from a stronger position without giving away your intention.

Internal Connections: Let the opening and closing of the chest bring the breath in and out, rather than breathing in and out to open and close the chest. Bring *qi* up the back and down the front during part one. Lift the anal sphincter lightly, with no more effort than that of closing the eyes, as the hands circle back during part one.

Yilu: The First Form

During part two, contact is made on the final meridian points on the edges of both hands, completing the *qi* flow to both sides of the body. The order of the fingertips touching (ring, pinkie, thumb, index, then middle) pairs the channels according the six levels. There are three yang channels; Tai Yang (outer), Shao Yang (pivot) and Yang Ming (inner) and three Yin channels; Tai Yin (outer), Shao Yin (pivot), Jue Yin (inner). The fingertip order is Shao Yang, Shao Yin, Tai Yang, Tai Yin, Yang Ming, Jue Yin. This pairs channels that have a similar *qi* dynamic – Shao Yang and Shao Yin, Tai Yang and Tai Yin, Yang Ming and Jue Yin.

During part four and five, the thumbs touch the Guan Yuan point, but more importantly, connect to the lower *dantian* and then spread out and down to settle the *qi* out into the hip joints (the root of the thighs) and down into the legs. The thumbs come in to touch onto meridian points on the belly and then follow a line out, touching on the stomach meridian, to get back to the Feng Shi points on the thighs. This action can act as a reminder to release tension in the hip joints, called *song kua*. Being able to release excess hip tension is the key to all the stances and stepping in Chen Taijiquan and other internal styles. For power to come through the legs to the body core, and for the body to settle into the legs, the hip joints must be comfortable. The same goes for the shoulders. They must be settled and released so that power can flow to and from the body and the arms.

About the Name: Going from Position Of Chaos towards Taiji Posture, the actions take all parts of the body past their normal positions, then settle them into the smooth and released Taiji Posture. This makes Taiji Posture feel comfortable and natural. Instead of starting out by trying to sink into Taiji Posture directly, the Opening rotates the joints to each extreme so that they 'want' to settle into Taiji Posture. Also called Three Openings And Closings Of The Dantian, this reminds you to fully use the body to complete the opening and closing actions of the arms – do not simply move the arms. The movement of parts four to five is also called 'Full Yang And Full Yin Inside The Sleeves,' meaning that the hands change between palm up and palm down hidden within the long sleeves of a gown. The body must be able to coil within itself such that similar actions remain hidden within the body during the whole of the form.

Open and close fully, taking the joints past the normal positioning of Taijiquan. This movement over-cranks the joints, then replaces them into the position of Taijiquan – as if telling the body what its limits are to remind it how and why Taiji Posture, or the golden mean, is natural and comfortable. In addition, the opening and closing of the joints and body cavities causes expansion and compression of the synovial fluids. These fluids help keep the joints healthy. A dry joint is a painful joint.

> In our style, in our normal stances like *kaibu* and *mabu*, we open the space of the hip sockets by slightly rotating the femur inward (medial rotation), which creates more space within the joint for the head of the femur. Many other styles open the front of the hips (lateral rotation), which we see as closing the femur into the socket.
>
> This rotation action creates a natural rounding of the crotch. Do not force the loins to be 'round' or 'open,' as this would be unnatural, and would also probably open up the knees, putting you into a weak position.

For my apprenticeship ceremony in 1990, I paid for a feast with lots of meat for sifu's family and the other inside apprentices, at his home. No tea pouring, no incense, no bowing. Cai Yuhua said that if people really wanted to do a ceremony, they could do one for show, but they didn't themselves. This made me feel more like a real apprentice, as I was accepted in the real way that they had been.

The next morning, I got to call out "sîfu zo" (good morning, shifu) instead of "losî zo" (good morning, teacher) when he arrived at our training spot. We always called out when he arrived, instead of stopping our training. He got up at four am to train himself, then came along to the park at six thirty to teach us.

The teacher-apprentice relationship is cheapened in the West, where sifu seems to be used as a job title instead of a relationship. In China, you only call your own shifu 'shifu.' You call other people's teacher 'laoshi.' Because I was in Shanghai, it was 'sifu' (not see-foo, but si-fu with a short i, like sit. Especially not 'shir-fu' – with a Beijing accent, which comes across as affected.

Sifu with two inside apprentices.

Yilu: The First Form

4. **Temple Guard Pounds With The Pestle**   jīn gāng dǎo duì
   金刚捣碓

   or **Temple Guard Pounds Three Times With The Pestle**   jīn gāng sān dǎ duì
   金刚三打碓

Overall Movement: Catch to pull down to the side three times then step forward, coil three times, like grinding with a pestle.

Footwork: In part one, shift around using the *yin-yang* fish symbol (or infinity symbol ∞) action within the body and around the outer edges of the feet. In part two, as an extension of the already existing coiling of the legs, shift to the right leg and turn the left foot in, then shift to the left leg and turn the right out, then shift to the right leg and bring the left leg straight up, then across to the right, hooking to catch, then extend to the front, and bend the right leg to drop into low pouncing stance. In part three, shift forward to the left leg then bring the right leg forward under control to form an empty stance. In part four, dorsi-flex the right ankle then lift the leg straight in front, then bend the knee, pull in, and then lower the right foot to place the toes on the ground beside the left foot, about a foot apart. In part five, push into the right foot, keeping the weight between the feet. In part six, finally settle into the short horse stance (*kaibu*).

Breakdown of Movement:

Part One: Draw three clockwise circles – small, medium, and large. Keeping the palms within the basin of the *kaibu* (straight line from the right foot to the front, and heel line to the left side) at all times, first draw a small circle, almost with just the wrists, then a larger circle, and finally a circle that pulls all the way to the left side and back to the front at shoulder height. As the hands circle down towards the left, the left is *nichan* and the right is *shunchan*. As the hands circle back to the front, the right is *nichan* and the left is *shunchan*. Start these rotations in the legs and body, so the body shifts back to the left leg then forward to the right leg, going around the outside of the feet in an infinity symbol (∞) action. Make sure that the knees stay within the stance, don't circle them, but coil within the legs. Settle the shoulders at all times. Cai Yuhua does these more as coiling circles, rather than going well over to the side. Photos 4a, 4b, 4c, 4d, 4e, and 4f.

Part Two: On the last circle, continue to pull across to the right, coiling the hands over more as if catching and controlling. Shift to the right leg and turn the left foot forty-five degrees inward, then shift to the left leg and turn the right foot ninety degrees outward as you pull across. By the end of the pull your torso is facing the right and the hands are in front of it at the right. Settle onto the right leg and lift the left leg straight, bring it around to the right, then hook it in, and then extend it to the front as you sit onto the right leg into a low pouncing stance. Pull further back and down as you settle into the low pouncing stance (*pubu*), keeping the back straight and the shoulders settled. If you don't sit to the drop stance, step to a higher open stance and keep the weight more even between the legs. Photos 4g, 4h, 4i, and 4j.

Part Three: Shift forward to a bow stance (*gongbu*) on the left leg, drawing the left hand around the left knee, thumb pointing to the kneecap at the left side of the knee, palm down. Extend the right hand to the right side. (You may also bring both hands forward with the body as you shift to the bow stance, pulling down and then to the front). Settle on the left leg and bring the right foot forward slowly to an empty stance, rear leg weighted, placing the right foot flat but unweighted. Relax the right arm and bring it through fairly straight, with the shoulder relaxed. Place the right palm up at groin height, wrist slightly hyper extended, and bring the left hand palm down touching the right forearm. Place the inside tip of the left thumb on the inside right forearm, aligned along the elbow crease, and place the tip of the middle finger further down the forearm along the same line. Photos 4k (left hand not yet outside the knee) and 4l.

Part Four: Flex the right wrist and flex the right ankle as if the hand and foot were attached with a string. Lift the right leg straight in front with the foot dorsi-flexed. Lift the right arm slightly as if pulling the leg up on a string, wrist flexed, palm still facing up, but softly closed. Bring the right knee up to the right elbow, then flex the knee to pull in with the foot still hooked. Circle the right hand in front of the nose but fairly far away, palm still up, torso turning slightly to the right. Touch the right toes down, one foot distance to the right

Yilu: The First Form

of the left foot. Push the left hand forward with the little finger side on top, keeping the wrist fairly straight. When the left hand arrives out in front, the right palm is tucked in front of the nose. Continue the circle of both hands – the left circling around to the little finger side and then coming in with the palm facing right, keeping the wrist quite straight, staying on the left side of the body – the right circling on the spot, first tucking the thumb into the palm, then closing each finger as it circles past the nose. Then turn the left palm down as it coils in, slide the right thumb out, rubbing the middle and index fingers to form a fist, then thread the right hand forward, palm up. The arms and hands have drawn a *Taiji* fish, or infinity, shape during this movement. Photos 4m, 4n, 4o, 4p, and 4q.

Part Five: Coil again in the same way, but with slightly different timing. Push into the ground, lifting the right heel to apply force by lengthening the leg segment without pushing the body up. Transfer the power of the right leg through the body into the arms. This time the right hand forms a fist and keeps it as it moves forward. Photos 4r and 4s.

Part Six: Coil and push again in the same way, but keeping the right hand in a fist throughout. When the left hand is fully extended, reach the right fist out and settle it into the left palm. Sink the right heel into the ground and settle the hands down to the *dantian*. The left hand is like a piece of floating wood, and the right fist sits like a stone in the left palm. Relax and let the weight of the fist gradually take the left hand down. Settle into the *kaibu*, making sure the knees do not go past the toes. Press the head up, keep the body comfortably upright, settle the shoulders and elbows. Don't look at the hands when they lower, look ahead. Photos 4t and 4u.

<u>Direction of Movements</u>: You are still facing south.

Possible Applications: Part two practises controlling the power transfer through the body to pull an opponent down to the side, to pass by your body. Catch any part of the opponent that you can and drop him down and to the side. The circles within your body keep you in balance as you control the opponent in either direction.

In part three, grab the opponent and pull him to the side, hooking your foot around him or in between his legs, then kick one leg out from under him, still not releasing your grip above. This can be an entry technique if you are not close enough to hook and sweep.

In part four, block aside and/or grab with the left hand and come through to groin strike with the right, placing the right foot ready to kick if need be. Part five, can be a knee groin strike, then swing the leg up to off balance the opponent, then stomp on the instep.

In part five, grab and control the opponent's arm, twisting his face, placing his neck in an awkward position to control him.

In part six, control the opponent with the left hand and punch to the face with the right fist, then take down.

Internal Connections: In part two, this is the first time you roll around the feet, drawing the infinity sign in the legs. This moves from the Yin Bai on the big toe, the Da Dun on the second toe, the Li Dui on the third toe, the Qiao Yin on the fourth toe, the Zhi Yin on the little toe, the Tong Gu then the Da Zhong on the outside of the foot. This rolling from one foot to the other by rolling in the legs is a constant throughout the form. Be careful to not just roll in a circle. And be careful to roll in both the legs and the feet.

In part three, the radial side of the thumb of the left hand tucks along the crease of the elbow, along the Heart line. At the end of part three, the left middle fingertip (the end of a short branch of the Pericardium line, the Triple Burner Meridian) presses on the middle of the forearm making the connection of the Pericardium line through the upper body (the placement of the thumb is to help the middle finger find the correct point). The middle finger touches Xi Men, the cleft point on the Jue Yin Pericardium channel. This has the function of unblocking the flow of *qi* and blood in the chest, which has the effect of calming the mind.

In part six, the foot point Yong Quan is massaged with the pressing movement of the right leg. Yong Quan is the well point of the Shao Yin Kidney channel. Stimulating this point has the effect of enhancing this channel's functions of regulating the Ming Men fire.

Settle into a high horse stance, so be sure to keep the loins rounded and open, with the meaning of 'open' being what I described back in move 2-3, the femur rotated inward. The high horse stance allows the pelvis to remain in a natural position, releasing in the hip joints and keeping the knees in.

Yilu: The First Form

<u>About the Name</u>: The grinding action of the whole body, and of the hands three times in front of the body, is like the grinding of a pestle (a rod for crushing) into a mortar (a thick bowl). In many styles of Chen, this is done in one single pounding action, so the name is normally called Pound With The Pestle. In our branch the action is done with the foot touching the ground, coiling and pushing three times, like grinding the pestle within the mortar. It feels like a grinding action through the body, not like an up and down action, and the hands follow the inside of the mortar, pressing out into its walls. The back is connected to this action, so that it seems like the mortar surrounds the whole body, or, indeed, is the body.

Jingang is the name of one of the four warrior attendants that guard the Buddha. Their large and terrifying statues are placed at each side of temple entrances throughout China, so if you have visited them you do not need a great imagination to obtain the powerful feeling to the movement – as if you are grinding up evil doers in hell.

<u>Additional Comments</u>: Be sure to touch down the right foot to *kaibu* width, don't put the right foot down too close to the left foot. You need to be able to push directly into the body, so the feet should be hip width apart. When pushing into the right foot, be sure to keep the body at the same height and to keep the weight on both legs. This causes a power transfer from the right foot into both hands. If you shift weight or rise, the power will dissipate into the left leg or into the body.

You can turn a fair bit while coiling the arms. Keep the right elbow down. Keep pressure in the palms away from the centre of the infinity symbol (∞)

> The pouncing stance should sit down onto the right thigh, to the full extent that you can. Keep the knee tracking with the toes to prevent its twisting. This form calls for a fair degree of suppleness, with the idea that it is better to be supple than not. If you are not supple or strong enough, or have problems that prevent you from sitting down, keep your back straight and sit as far as you can. Do not lean forward to force yourself into an awkward position.

that each hand is drawing, so the hands are working on a *yin-yang* fish shape in front of the body. The right hand draws a small *yin-yang* fish circle within the left hand's larger circle.

> Chen Xin's illustration of Jin Gang Dao Dui makes perfect sense when you do the move as we do. To other branches of Chen, where the right fist is simply picked up and set down on the left hand, this diagram is a mystery.
>
>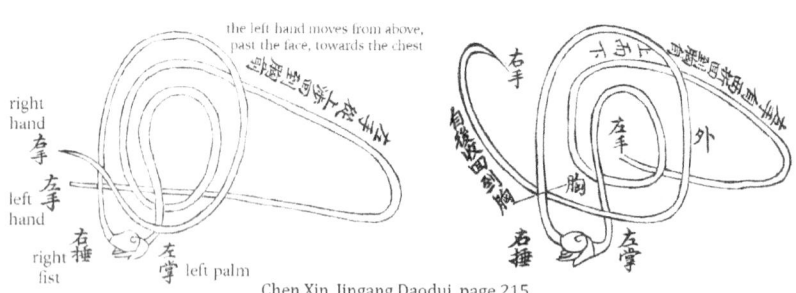
>
> Chen Xin, Jingang Daodui, page 215.
>
> The work with the meridian lines and acupoints is completely natural, and the effects will occur whether you are aware of them or not. If you focus on them, rather than on performing the move right, you can cause problems. If you perform the moves correctly, you will not cause problems. Even Chen Xin, who puts a lot of effort into describing the meridians and acupoints in the moves, says, "There are many writings on this, but I think it is better to clear the mind and reduce desires, to cultivate one's original *qi*, thus becoming stronger." (Chen Xin page 117)

I have the dubious distinction of learning Yilu from an external stylist. I dropped off Patrick Kelly, one of my 'Winnipeg boys,' with Cai Yuhua's family in 1988. He trained with a wushu team and learned Qingping sword, Yilu, and colloquial Shanghaihua. Cai Yuhua hooked him into the Taijiquan by doing this move – the shine in Patrick's eyes when he saw the twisting, swirling moves of parts four and five was all I needed to know I was leaving him in good hands.

I had worked on Baguazhang with Yuhua up until then, and had not yet learned Yilu. I learned the whole form from Patrick during a summer visit in Montreal in 1989. Patrick's eye for detail meant that the moves were all correct. If I he didn't quite understand the power yet, I knew intuitively how they should be done. I was ready for detailed corrections from sifu when I went in 1990. Learning the form in Shanghai the traditional way would have taken a lot longer.

Yilu: The First Form

5.   **Tuck In The Robe Casually**   lǎn zhā yī   懒扎衣

<u>Overall Movement</u>: Coil within the body, then coil larger, finally setting into the characteristic horse/bow stance of Chen style, as if casually tucking a robe into your belt to get ready to fight.

<u>Footwork</u>: First roll within the *kaibu*, then step twice to settle into the Chen horse stance, which sometimes called a bow stance, and is actually something in between the two. Step the left foot in a backward arc to the left, then step the right foot to a larger stance in a frontward arc to the right. In this way the feet continue to follow the infinity symbol, coiling as they step.

<u>Breakdown of Movement</u>:

Part One: Roll twice inside the body. Circle power up the left abdomen from the right leg then down the right abdomen into the left leg. Circle and roll the hands up the left side of the abdomen and down the right, keeping the back of the right fist in the left palm. Roll the right fist over so that it is under the left palm at the solar plexus, then is back on top by the time it comes back to the lower belly. On the second roll, the right fist can finish under the left palm or on top. Photos 5a, 5b, 5c, 5d, 5e, and 5f.

Part Two: Thread and *nichan* the right hand out to the left and open the arms, the right reaching forward and up, the left reaching down and a bit rightwards, also *nichan*. Sit on the right leg and push into the left foot to lift the left heel with the left palm near the left knee, fingers down. The right hand is facing out at head height, pointing to the left. Photo 5g.

Part Three: Step the left foot to the left, drawing a circle behind. Reach the left palm to the left, palm still facing out. Open the right arm, palm turned out. Bring the right foot in to touch down near the left, turning the left hand to protect the face/shoulder and bring the right hand across to catch. Gradually cross the forearms, the right pressing forward and the left guarding above, both having gradually changed to *shunchan*. Photos 5h and 5i.

Part Four: Step the right foot to the right, drawing a front arc. Coil the arms together with distinct and separate circles. Shift towards the right leg and draw the right arm across to the right as you *nichan* to above the right thigh at shoulder height. Keep the left hand on the right forearm, palm up, slide it along to the right shoulder, then draw the palm edge diagonally across the body. Photos 5j, 5k, and 5l.

Part Five: Settle into the Chen style bow/horse stance (usually about sixty percent on the right leg, though this posture may also be done rear weighted, settling into the left leg and not opening the body out so much), settle the right elbow and *shunchan* through the right arm to the middle finger. Coil the left palm down onto the pelvic crest, fingers in front and thumb behind. The left foot is turned in and the right foot slightly out (be sure not to leave the left foot open). To coil the left hand, tuck the wrist down and curl the fingers up then tuck the wrist back up to the front, then drop back to the pelvic crest, tucking the elbow in front of the body. Keep the hip joints open, the loins rounded, the left foot closed, and the right foot open. Settle the shoulders, press the head up and look at the middle finger of the right hand, which is at shoulder height. Make sure that the right wrist is not bent too much, but allow the *qi* to flow smoothly through it. Photos 5m, 5n, and 5o.

Yilu: The First Form

Direction of Movements: The left foot takes a small step to the east, the right foot steps to the west and the stance is completed facing south.

Possible Applications: This is too early in the form to think about applications, and the application to this move is obvious and one of the most common take downs. At this point you need to focus on your lines of energy, power, connections, and structure. This is a vital movement in terms of internal linkages, structural lines in the body, application of the power lines, and stepping with the circular pathway. This move is repeated later in the form, don't worry.

Internal Connections: This move takes the coiling that up until now you have been doing in a small stance out into stepping and the larger horse stance. The feet and legs must continue in the same infinity symbol (∞) action both within the body and in the outer appearance of the stepping.

In part one, the edge of the left palm and the edge of the right fist massage the abdomen up the left side and down the right side, mostly on the Stomach and Liver meridian lines. In part four, the left hand is in contact with the body the whole time, touching the Greater-Yin Lung and Pericardium lines of the right arm for much of the move, then cuts across the chest towards the top of the pelvis. In part five, the left hand covers the acupoints in front of the hip.

This is the first time you adjust within the body in a larger stance in the form. The four *yin-yang* fish circles you draw in the legs and send out to the arms give you an opportunity to feel what is going on inside the body and establish the pattern for the rest of the form. You must focus on this changing and find how it develops a soft but persistent power. The changing inside the body is the *chansi*, or coiling silk, power. *Chansi* power is like you are the silk worm, twisting and coiling, creating the silk from inside your body and forming it outside your body. Each move completes itself then coils back inside the body, where it changes and coils out as another move without any break in power. You do not 'do' the moves of the form, you allow them to transform inside your body and change from one to the next spontaneously.

Some consider the coiling silk as reeling silk, coiling the silken cords onto a reel like a fishing rod. This definition also gives the idea of a power that displaces as it rotates, so also works as an image, though it is not quite so deep an image.

About the Name: Chen Xin called this move Trap And Rub The Clothes 揽擦衣 *lan ca yi*. *Lan* is a trapping action with the forearm. The *cayi* means to rub along the clothes. This rubbing means to stick so close to the opponent as to slide along the clothing. The name has gradually changed, perhaps due to pronunciation of the characters.

Just about everyone calls the move *lan zha yi* now. The whole movement is like drawing up a long silk robe and tucking it into your belt in preparation for a fight. If you were wearing a long robe, you would need to scoop up one side and tuck it into your belt to be able to continue comfortably with the form. This action would be needed prior to fighting, especially if you wanted to kick. The word '*lan*' (lazy) suggests that the movement should be done in a relaxed and casual way as if you could hardly be bothered, so as to show full confidence in your abilities. Of course, to be truly confident you need to be truly comfortable, not just pretend. The original name was probably not lazy, anyway.

Additional Comments: In part one, hardly turn the waist. Roll the power inside the body instead. If you turn, the power will dissipate. Also in part one, the fist is fire and the palm is water, if the fist finishes underneath the fire is extinguished and the spirit is calm. If you want to stay a bit keener for the form you can leave the fire unextinguished (the fist on top) on completion of the second roll.

In part four, be sure to stay upright and in control when you take the larger step. Build the habit now of maintaining the torso upright in all cases except for when it specifically leans forward (such as Needle At Sea Bottom). The roots of the legs and arms (that is, the hips and shoulders) are partially blocked when the body leans, so you impede *qi* and blood circulation as well as making a movement awkward and unusable when you lean.

In part six, have the hip joints open and relaxed in the final stance, but not the feet. The crotch is rounded by opening the hip sockets in the back, which closes the thighs slightly in the front. This stance may be done back weighted or front weighted, but the power comes from rear leg the same either way. Be sure to tuck in the left elbow so that it remains within the stance and keeps power moving to the right arm.

The final stance is higher than that done in many branches, but we are not the only branch that sits into this higher stance. It is a practical stance, and the thighs are not parallel to the ground. This allows you to step naturally and easily, it keeps the groin area open but not over-open, and allows for smooth power transfer through the body. Sink into the legs and release the hip joints but do not force the body down. An open groin, or rounded loins area, means that it is rounded, not too pointed and not too flat. If you are in too high a stance it is pointed, if you are in too low a stance it is flat or opened out so much as to weaken you. As with anything, it is the intent that is important, not the degree. If you are conscious of the area you don't need to do much to effectively open it.

Here are four photos showing the detail of the rolling.

One time I was doing this move and asked sifu how high the right hand should be in the final posture, expecting the type of correction I would have gotten from my previous teachers. Something like 'fingers at shoulder height, wrist below, elbow dropped, shoulder settled, attention on the middle finger.' He said, "Try it out, where do you feel it should be?" He had me try a bit higher, a bit lower, a bit further out, a bit closer in, a bit more coiled, a bit less coiled, until my arm settled into its natural place. This happens to be with the fingers at about shoulder height, quite extended, and mid-coiled, what he would have said if he had told me. Needless to say, after years of being told exactly what to do, something clicked that I was now doing something that was fully traditional and personal at the same time.

You have to find the sweet spot for each final position on your own, within the Taijiquan principles. The final position will never have the limbs completely extended. If you extend fully you will feel that you cannot do coiling power in the limbs. Coiling needs some space to move. But you will never find a tightly bent posture comfortable either, as something will be blocked somewhere. Generally, the final placement is slightly bent, with a feeling of extension.

The posture and movement are specific to Chen Taijiquan, to best use the coiling transfer of power. There is a range of angles that will work, but the result should always look and feel like Chen Taijiquan. Other styles use different stances for the base and different methods for power transfer, so do not apply the same rules, and will not find the same angles. This searching is not to find where you 'like' the position, it is to apply the principles of Chen Taijiquan to your body in order to find the best fit.

> This book was developed by following my original notes, which were made after each training session, and were never erased or rewritten, just added to. I made a page for each movement so I could add new information or corrections to the movement as I learned and improved. Some of the pages got a little messy, especially because the names of the moves were given to me only after I was comfortable with the form. This is the traditional way of teaching. Students had to earn the right to the name list by performance of the form and proof of dedication.
>
> It took a long time to get a name list out of sifu. When I finally did, it had 108 moves. Cai Yuhua then showed me his list, from years before, with 106 moves. He thought sifu had changed names around so that we had the classic '108.' The performance of the moves is the same. Both versions have their own inconsistencies.

Cai Yuhua's house was his father's farmhouse with a dirt courtyard, a common dining room, and rooms to either side, one big room for his parents and one big room, with a split into a small work room, for his family. The kitchen was a separate room accessed from outside, because the coal briquettes created a black smoke that stung the eyes and lungs. I learned to cook Shanghai style watching from the doorway, but Yuhua wouldn't let me suffer the smoke, and didn't trust me with the fuel. The chickens had a little coop in the courtyard sheds, and were let out to wander with a string tied to a leg. We spent most of the time in the walled courtyard, partly because it is nicer to be outside, and partly because inside was lit by a twenty watt bulb. The dining room table was plain, dark, scratched rosewood, and the benches were like in kungfu movies. The other cool furniture was the scattering of tiny stools. We'd sit around in the courtyard on these low stools, chatting and busy with something in our hands – usually washing clothes or vegetables, or picking stones out of the rice or fleas off the cats. People think that when you live with your teacher you spend all your day training and talking about martial arts. In fact, you spend a lot of time shelling peas and trying to get the dirt out of spinach and the rocks out of rice.

Yilu: The First Form

6. **Seal Off, Shut Down** rú fēng sì bì 如封似闭

<u>Overall Movement</u>: Four coiling trapping actions moving into a controlling downward and away push (*an*).

<u>Footwork</u>: Draw infinity symbols within the horse stance, then step forward to the corner in a front weighted empty stance.

<u>Breakdown of Movement</u>:

Part One: Coil into the body, moving all the joints of the legs and within the torso, shifting the weight slightly but not shifting the feet at all. Coil the right arm, *shunchan*, first pressing down, then pressing out with the palm up. Coil the left hand over on the spot, closing the body so that the left elbow comes around to the front when the right hand coils in. Photos 6a and 6b.

Part Two: Coil again the same way, shifting and coiling the body and legs. This time bring the left hand forward so that both forearms coil and press out, palms up, the left hand just behind the right elbow. Photos 6c and 6d.

Part Three: Coil again the same way with the body and legs. This time place the left fingertips on the right forearm as it coils in, then press out with the forearms together, the right on the outside, palm facing out, the left on the inside with the palm facing in. The wrists are touching. Photos 6e, 6f, and 6g.

Part Four: Hook the left hand over the right wrist, reach the right hand out, palm down. Bring both hands in, tucking the right behind the left and press out with the forearms again, this time with the left on the outside and both palms facing in. The arms are connected at the wrists. The legs and body coil again, but this time draw a bit more directly into the body and roll the energy up to the upper back and more directly straight into the arms. Photos 6h, 6i, and 6j.

Part Five: Follow through the action with the right hand, to reach out to the stance line as if hitting to the right with the back of the hand. Keep the left hand at the right elbow. Coil both hands over palms down, then pull down and back. Gradually change the left arm to a pressing action and turn to the left. Press up to shoulder height, still pulling with the right hand. As you move across to the left, allow all the joints in the legs to move, turn the right foot in, and shift to the left leg. Photos 6k and 6l.

Part Six: Coil both forearms, circling the hands, keeping power throughout, so that you are now doing the press out with the right forearm and a pull with the left hand. Shift across to the right in the same manner, but don't go as far. Complete the *peng* as you get in front of the right foot. Photos 6m and 6n.

Part Seven: Coil the arms and pluck (*cai*) back towards the left. As you get to the middle, curl the left hand to catch, keeping the wrist relaxed and the fingers hanging down. Tuck in the chest and bring the hands in fairly close and low. Bring the right foot in towards the left foot. Photos 6o and 6p.

Yilu: The First Form

Part Eight: Step the right foot to the forward right. Turn the body well to the left, open the hands, then bring the hands down close to the face, down as if stroking a beard, bending the arms but with an outward power. Shift forward and bring the left foot in behind the right foot, left heel up, hip open, feet fairly wide apart. Be sure to keep the right knee behind the toes, don't push too far forward, settle between the feet. Push out and down with the

elbows down, the thumbs and index fingers forming a diamond ('the tigers' mouths talking to each other'), extending quite far at just below rib height. Finish the downward press. Then continue to *nichan* the arms allowing the hands to rise, so that the little finger edges drive up almost to shoulder height. Be careful to keep the shoulders settled down when continuing the action of the arms. Press the head up. It also works very well to sit down more than I have in photos 6s and 6t, particularly to balance the push as it changes from down and forwards to upwards and away. Photos 6q, 6r, 6s, and 6t.

Possible Applications: This movement repeats four more times during the form, which gives you lots of opportunities later on to think about applications. Seek out the correct feelings in the body during this first performance. The final movement, especially, needs to find the closing power that puts energy outward.

If you are told applications, remember that they are only possibilities. If you don't have good bodywork, they won't work. Knowing applications without having the connections through the body and the right lines isn't much use. If the movement is correct and the body connection is solid, any move has a multitude of applications. If you think about one application you are limiting yourself and probably subtly altering the movement to fit your preconception. If you think of 'an application,' the move becomes too set.

Internal Connections: The back and forth shifting within the large stance makes the diagonal connections from the rear leg to the front arm in both directions. This must be done more as a power transfer than a weight shift, and must transfer through the centre of the body segments in an organic whole. To apply power it is best not to think so much of which leg is weighted and which is unweighted, but of which is giving the power. Often the power leg is more unweighted, but not always.

About the Name: *Rufeng* means 'like sealing' (an envelope), *sibi* means 'like closing' (a door). Many people take this in the sense of 'almost like' but the phrase '*ru – si –*', the two used together, is also used with the meaning of 'just like.' An example is *rulong sifeng* – 'like a dragon, like a phoenix' (calligraphy printed on the club sweatpants that James is wearing). This indicates that this movement is both defensive and offensive – it both seals off the opponent so that he cannot enter further, and shuts your own doorways of entry.

This movement is often called Six Sealings, Four Closings' (*liufeng sibi*). The two names are usually interchangeable, though not in our branch. The move Six Sealings, Four Closings occurs later in this form for a slightly different performance of the movement.

Additional Comments: Parts one through four are fairly big circles with the legs and body. In parts five and six, be careful to stay at the same height. Watch the middle finger of the hand that is doing the pull until it gets in front of the body, then watch the hand that is doing the press.

The final push (*an*) can be done with a *fajin* and stomping of the rear foot as it comes in, together with a 'ha' sound. *Fajin* is not used the first time this movement is done, but may be done later in the form. The first section of the form, up to the first Travelling Hands, and especially up to the third Temple Guard, is intended to develop the *qi* and blood circulation and establish the correct power flow in the body. There are few *fajin* movements, and the mind is not too occupied with possible applications. It is best to focus on the power flow and feeling inside the body. The rest of the form has more 'practical' actions, and the mind can shift its focus more towards power and application.

Chen Xin's book goes directly from *Lancayi* to *Danbian*, without a movement name in between. If you think about it, Seal Off, Shut Down can be seen as a transitional move.

In part eight, Cai Yuhua drops all the way down, but I never saw anyone else do this. He had to change the form slightly for competitions, so this may be one of the 'flashy' moves that he developed for competition.

Here are three photos from the side.

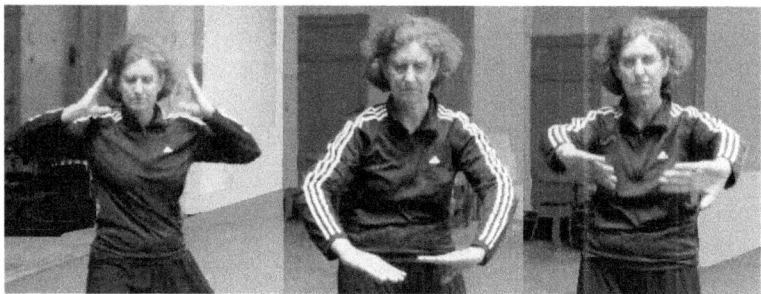

In our style we practice one *chansi* exercise that develops the ability to adjust the body around the arm, or the other way around, with the power and weight transfer. We have only the one exercise to train the complete *chansi*, not a variety to train specific directions.

Sitting in horse stance, maintain an infinity sign, or figure eight movement in the legs throughout the exercise. Make sure the legs are doing a figure eight '∞', going around the edges of the feet, never transferring directly back and forth 'o', or worse '–'. Sit fairly low, enough to work the legs. But the point of the exercise is to develop the *chansi* power diagonally through the body, so you want to be neither too low nor too high.

Moving to the right, lay out the right arm with a *shunchan*, palm up in line with the thigh at face height. Moving to the left, keep coiling the right arm back to the face with the palm up, this becomes a *nichan*. Moving to the right, lay out the right arm back to the same place with the palm down and out, to full *nichan*. The left index and middle fingertips sit in the dip under the right elbow throughout, feeling the rotation of the end of the two bones. The elbow has remained aligned with the thigh.

Moving to the left, coil the right hand in, palm up, and send the left hand out along the right arm, also palm up. You arrive at the left the same as you have done on the right, with the right hand touching under the left elbow, and continue the same movement on the left.

This trains the shifting and coiling in and out on both sides, both *shunchan* and *nichan*. When the coiling is connected through the arms, the arms are like a snake, in constant contact with each other.

If you have trouble with it, do just the legs and body for a while, then add the arms. The body needs to become balanced and comfortable with the action, combining all the qualities of Chen style within this one exercise (open and closed, upper and lower connected, released, rounded). Movement must be continuous, slow at first, and later either fast or slow.

7. **Dantian Transforms** dān biàn 丹变

Overall Movement: Draw and coil around at the right side, then shift across to draw the left arm to the left while controlling with the right hooked hand.

Footwork: Coil around the legs and feet, then step the left foot out and settle to a bow stance, then press the left heel up to roll to a Chen bow/horse stance.

Breakdown of Movement:

Part One: Push out the right hand, shift to the left leg, turn the left palm to push out and coil it in. Continue to coil and spiral the hands, both palms pressing out from the middle of a vertical cylinder in front of the right foot (like following the double helix model of a DNA molecule). Shift to the right foot. When the left hand arrives on top, thread the right palm over it. Photos 7a and 7b.

Part Two: Shift again to the left leg, then the right leg, keeping the coiling action going in the legs, which turns the right toes inward as they unweight in a natural action as the infinity sign continues. Close the right hand to hook, then place the tip of the hook on the left palm and circle the left hand on the spot, keeping the palm up. Photos 7c, 7d, and 7e.

Part Three: Step the left foot out to a bow stance distance, only stepping as far as you can control while remaining upright. Continue to strongly *nichan* through the arms so that they are almost upside down, left palm almost facing up and the right hook almost pointing up. Draw the left arm across to align with the left foot and put pressure in the right arm back to keep aligned with the right foot. Settle to a bow stance with the hips straight and the front toes turned slightly in, push the right heel back as the left arm draws across, keep sixty percent of the weight on the

rear leg, do not let the front knee go past the heel. *Shunchan* through the arms so that they settle, the left arm finishes directly above the left thigh at shoulder height and the right arm at ninety degrees to the torso at the same height. Relax the right wrist, do not pull the hook strongly down. Relax the left wrist, press down into the palm but do not bend the wrist too much, press into the third finger. Pay attention when stepping out to keep the stance narrow to facilitate the following action. Photos 7f and 7g.

Part Four: Press into the left foot to coil through the body, turning the heel out and rotating especially in the right hip and shoulder, to settle into a Chen style bow/horse stance with the arms aligned above the thighs. Press the head up. Power flows from the right hand to the left. This stance is weighted a bit towards the left leg. If you have stepped too widely or narrowly in part three, you will notice the bow/horse stance is awkward and misaligned. Photo 7h.

7h

Possible Applications: This move repeats four more times in the form, time enough to focus on the applications. During the first repetition, focus on the feelings inside. Your applications will never work if you are not comfortable in your own body and have not found the lines of power.

Internal Connections: In part three, feel the force of the right calf sending energy especially to the left hand, though both hands are connected. Make sure to keep the hook in the right hand, keeping the elbow down and not loosening off. When the left hand gets to the front, twist in to loosen up the back so that power can connect to the right heel. Don't just turn the hand, but twist the little finger and pull the elbow down. In part four, feel the force of the left foot push power to transfer throughout the body to achieve the readjustment.

The changing inside the body is the *chansi*, or coiling silk, power. *Chansi* power is like you are the silk worm, twisting and coiling, creating the silk from inside your body and forming it outside your body. Each move completes itself then coils back inside the body, where it changes and coils out as another move without any break in power. Allow the power to transform inside your body and change from one movement to the next spontaneously.

About the Name: This movement, *Danbian*, is usually called Single Whip (*dan* = single, *bian* = whip). The posture of Single Whip is like the posture taken by opera players 'riding a horse.' They hold a whip out to the side to show that they are riding, and hold the other arm out front to hold the reins. It has also been likened to the posture taken carrying a steel rod (which is called a *bian*) over the shoulders.

In our style, we differentiate between the two names, pronounced almost the same, but written differently. Part three of this movement is the Single Whip posture. Part four shifts to transform the *dan*, meaning that the *dantian* resettles as the stance changes. The meaning is '*dan*' from '*dantian*,' and '*bian*' meaning change or transform. The *dantian* changes while the rest of the body remains in place, so that the direction of power application shifts within the body without being apparent. This trains the ability to adjust the body around a fixed point (where you are attached to your opponent) without signaling the change to your opponent.

Additional Comments:

Here are photos of the action of parts one through to the beginning of three, showing details.

The hook hand is quite relaxed, with the fingers bent. The thumb touches the tip of the index finger, forming a circle, and the other fingers curl in to stay within that circle. Especially do not let the little finger stick out – this is not a tea party. The relaxed hook allows the wrist to stay relatively flat. Never break at the wrist.

Part three may be done as a *fajin*, whipping the left arm out by snapping the right heel back. Turn the right heel at the same time as you draw the left hand across. This is not usually done the first time the movement occurs in the form, but may be done later if the mood takes you. There are no rules as to when you *fajin* in the form, only habits. If the coiling power is correct you can *fajin* at any time.

The final move may also be done without the transitional bow stance, going directly into the more normal Chen style bow/horse stance.

When doing the shift from the bow stance to the bow/horse stance, be very careful that you stay upright and motionless, transferring power throughout the body to reposition all the segments relative to each other without travelling through space. You need to release and settle in the hip and shoulder joints.

Switching from the bow stance to the bow/horse stance, you must be aware of the placement of the pelvis and the greater trochanter of each femur (the root of the thigh). Throughout the form, the pelvis is sometimes slightly tucked under and sometimes slightly rolled out, depending on the stance and the depth of the stance. The exact placement of the pelvis facilitates the easy movement of the femur within it and the ability of the torso to rest

Yilu: The First Form

comfortably vertical in the pelvic basin. The key to silk coiling power is the ability to move inside the hips easily, transferring power directly from the legs to the body core. In a bow stance, the best position is usually tucked under, and in a bow/horse stance the best position is usually rolled out. Releasing the hips, or *songkua,* means to place the pelvis in the most advantageous position relative to what the thighs are doing, and releasing all tension to allow them to roll easily and transfer power.

Chen style emphasizes releasing the hip sockets (*song kua*) more than of tuck in the buttocks (*lian tun*) or tip the buttocks (*fan tun*), because *song kua* is the feeling, and the pelvis placements are postures that assist in achieving this feeling. Dantian Transforms works on the transfer from *lian tun* in a bow stance to *fan tun* in a bow/horse stance, and focuses on the difference between them, as that is essentially the only movement that is being done during part four.

The hand shape used throughout the form is a soft roof tile palm. The palm and fingers are soft, not tense, just enough power to maintain the shape. The hand maintains a slight coiling at all times, so that the base of the thumb is slightly tucked in and the fingers are offset like Chinese ceramic tiles. Not exaggerated – the index finger must stay with the other fingers – all fingers are together. The power in the fingers is extending, but they do not extend fully, they are slightly curved. The fingers are neither flexed nor extended, so that blood and *qi* can reach to the fingertips. This is a soft, small hand, useful for getting into small spaces without getting caught, smooth to allow for the flow of *qi*, aligned to coil power to circle the tip of the middle finger without breaking at the wrist.

In all instances of the bow stance, the power comes from pressing the rear calf back, which sends power up to the kidney area. It is important to not allow the leading knee to go past the heel. This stance uses a power transfer through the body, not a weight shift to apply force. If the weight shifts too far towards the forward leg then the power is dissipated and wasted into the forward leg. The hip joints must be released to allow the force to transfer, as must the shoulders. This finds and develops the natural spring in the rear ankle.

As a general rule, the hands range between the midline and in alignment with the knees. This can be quite a large action, depending on the stance. To take them further, such as across the midline, or past a knee, turn the torso.

19th Century Shanghai

Established in the kingdom of Wu around BC 513, the town's original name, Hudu, comes from the old name for the Suzhou river, the creek that comes through town to the Huangpu River. Hu 滬 (沪) is still the short name for Shanghai, used in telegrams and railway lines. A port off the main communication lines, it was less important as a commercial and cultural centre than Hangzhou, Suzhou, or Nanjing, more of a city for shipping of goods. It became a walled town in the 1530s to protect itself from Japanese pirates, and grew to a city of about 300,000 by the mid 19th century, when its life abruptly changed. The land beside it was ceded to foreign powers in 1843.

Not a colony, but an area where foreigners could live and follow their own laws within the boundaries (called extraterritoriality, often shortened to extrality). At first two separate British and American enclaves, it soon became a mixed International Settlement, with a French Concession to the south. The foreigners made themselves at home. The early days were very English, time off spent with tiffin, cricket, paper chases, and horse racing. A race course went in very early on, then a second and third, as the enclave moved outwards. The third race course with sports grounds inside, which became People's Park, was built in 1863.

Two Municipal Councils ran things with no Chinese representation on them. The foreigners needed to get permission from the Chinese government for much of what they did. The relationship between the Chinese and foreigners in Shanghai was not always smooth, to say the least. The patronizing attitude of the foreigners didn't help. The resistance of the Chinese government to any change also didn't help. Shanghai had a good port, but the Huangpu River had a sand bar at Wusong, where it met the Yangzi River, and larger ships needed to offload there. The Council wanted to build a railroad to Wusong, but ran into Chinese resistance. They snuck one in, in 1875, but it was shut down two years later, not being rebuilt for another twenty years. Similarly, the Chinese government was suspicious of telegraphs, but finally saw their use by about 1878, and allowed a line between Shanghai and Wusong.

By 1852 there were only about two hundred foreigners living in the foreign enclaves, and about 500,000 Chinese, mostly in the original walled city.

The Settlement and Concession remained neutral throughout all the revolts, civil wars, and revolutions in China though the late 1800s and early 1900s, and this is when the Chinese population started to grow outside the walled city. A volunteer self defense corps protected the enclaves, and foreign navy ships lay at anchor, ready if needed. Each episode of fighting in China brought a wave of refugees from the nearby area, which the Settlement had to find place for. The Tai Ping rebellion alone brought in 1,500,000 refugees. Many went home after its suppression in 1864, but with each influx of refugees, some stayed. That the Chinese people stayed after each event showed that there was something in the city that they liked. The draw of trade, commerce and industry, for both entrepreneurs and labourers, and the protection from rebellions and civil wars brought them to the International Settlement and the French Concession.

An 1865 census of the International Settlement, French Concession, and Hongkew found the Chinese population to be about 137,500, and the foreign population about 2,750, with a further 2,832 in the forces.

There was no urban planning when the International Settlement was built. The foreigners simply sent out feelers with roads and houses, taking more land where they could. The land allowed them in 1843 was not large enough, and applying for extensions was troublesome. The Settlement grew, with renters or the Municipal Councils building outside roads, putting in lighting and sewers, building houses along the roads, and then applying for a legal extension of the settlement. The old Chinese town remained as it was, the International Settlement and French Concession spread out from the river, and the Chinese municipality grew around the foreign enclaves, north and east in Chapei and Hongkew, south and west to the Longhua and Caohejing area.

Rickshaws arrived in 1874, from Japan, a fact for some reason always mentioned in history books. Perhaps because the image of the rickshaw puller and the moneyed passenger is a common image of the imperialism and oppression of the old society.

The Public Gardens on the Bund was built even as the Bund was just a row of bungalows along the Huangpu River. A mudflat, the land was filled in and the park and esplanade were completed by 1886. Although it is not apparently true that there was a sign posted at the Gardens gate 'no dogs or Chinese allowed,' Mr. Pott, an early historian, noted that on the esplanade extending from the Public Gardens, "All respectable and decently clad Chinese were admitted to them, but when it was found that coolies used the benches for siestas, notices were posted on the benches restricting their use to foreigners." (F.L. Hawks Pott, D.D., A Short History of Shanghai, Kelly & Walsh, Ltd., Shanghai, 1928, page 116.)

Trinity church was built early enough to have to be replaced in 1866-69 by a more permanent, and larger, red brick church, which was to become Holy Trinity Cathedral, the tallest building in the city. The University of Bristol has a remarkable set of ten panoramic photographs of the Settlement taken from the church tower. It wasn't designed with a spire, so one was built in 1893. You would think that the only reason to build a free standing bell tower with a spire would be to house a nice set of bells, but, although there is reference to a magnificent organ being shipped from Durham, I have never found any mention of change ringing bells or bell ringers in Shanghai.

Modern cotton mills were established as early as 1889, closely followed by more light industry, a larger Chinese population of workers, and an extension of the Settlement. The dredging of the Huangpu River's bed, particularly at the Wusong bar, in the early 1900s, helped the city grow, as larger ships were able to come in to the city harbour. Pudong gradually became a line of factories, warehouses, and docks – extensive, but mostly along the river's edge.

A downtown tramway and the first cars arrived in the early 1900s. By 1909, in looking for another extension, it was noted that 50,000 houses were owned by the Chinese in the Settlement, as opposed to 3,000 owned by foreigners. The surrounding Chinese municipality grew around the foreign enclaves, and the Chinese moved freely between them in everyday life. Foreigners tended to stay in their areas, where they could find everything they needed. It seems as though educated well-off Shanghainese were the cosmopolitan urbanites, and the Shanghailanders largely kept to their own groups.

Yilu: The First Form

Top map: G. Lanning, S. Couling. The History of Shanghai: Part I. Kelly & Walsh, Shanghai.
Bottom map: Pan Ling, In Search of Old Shanghai, Joint Publishing Co., Hong Kong, 1982. These first maps were drawn aligned with the Huangpu River, as if facing town from a boat, so the top is west. Later, maps were turned to the more usual alignment of north on top.

8. Temple Guard Pounds With The Pestle (for the second time)

jīn gāng dǎo duì (dì èr)　　　　　　　　　　金刚捣碓(第二)

Overall Movement: Turn left then right, coiling and sitting back to low pouncing stance (*pubu*). Then move forward and repeat the Temple Guard Pounds With The Pestle.

Footwork: Sit back to low pouncing stance then move through bow stance (*gongbu*) and high empty stance (*xubu*), to repeat the leg lift, placement, and pressing, finishing settling into *kaibu*.

Breakdown of Movement:

Part One: Shift the legs in the infinity symbol (∞) to circle both hands clockwise to the left and then right, coiling the hands to arrive in a position to *cai*. Use the upper back and shoulders to roll the arms. Photos 8a and 8b.

Part Two: Bring in the left leg and *cai* to the right. Reach out the left leg and sit into the right leg and pull down and back in the opposite direction. Photo 8c.

Part Three: Continue to *cai* across to the left and shift forward to bow stance, then bring the right foot forward to an empty stance with both feet flat on the ground. Photos 8d and 8e.

Yilu: The First Form

Part Four: Continue on the same as the first time through Pound With The Pestle (see move 4), but making two circles instead of three. Photos 8f, 8g, 8h, 8i, 8j, 8k, 8l.

Part Five: When the right fist is in the left hand, first start to slowly lower, then allow the hands to drop to the *dantian* and quickly settle the right foot into the ground. Maintain the vertical body and press up into the top of the head. Photos 8m and 8n.

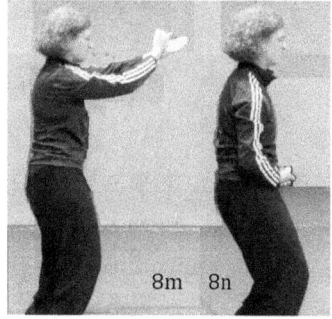

Direction of Movements: Since you started facing south, you are now facing east.

Possible Applications: Coiling around an opponent's arm to catch and control, or squirming out of a grip on your arm to catch and control. Then pulling across, kicking, and grappling.

Internal Connections: When switching from the settled position to movement, keep connected diagonally through the body, settling further in to start the movement. Settle well into Dantian Transforms, so that the initial impulse is to coil on release. Completion of the movement settles the *qi* into the lower *dantian* (located in the lower abdomen). It is important for *qi* to remain settled throughout the form so that the Heart is not stirred. If the *qi* remains settled then the breathing can remain even and the mind can remain calm.

In Taijiquan we sometimes refer to the *dantian*, sometimes to the Kidneys, and sometimes to the Ming Men, almost interchangeably. The Ming Men lies between the kidneys, and the lower *dantian* is usually considered to contain the Kidneys. Practically speaking, referring to any of the three refers to the place that is the source of *qi*, and where *qi* accumulates to build your power and health. The completion of each movement involves a natural return to the *dantian*, so that the following movement can grow naturally from there.

Shadowboxing in Shanghai

<u>Additional Comments</u>: Cai Yuhua shows the drop in part two. He also shows the leg lift in part four, with both knees quite bent, as the most practical way of using the leg technique. This is the same with all repetitions of this move.

This photo is from 1990, when I did a slow, controlled straight lift to shoulder height. We weren't really supposed to lift it that high or that straight, it is more practical to start to pull in earlier. It was my fun, for a show-off 'fancy' move.

This move displays very clearly the difference between coiling and rotating. Coiling is to wrap around something and follow along its length, like vine coiling around a tree to climb it. There is closing and expanding power, and forward movement, in coiling. This is much different from rotation, which is a simple turning of a body segment that involves neither another object nor different directional powers.

Yilu: The First Form

9. **White Goose Flashes Its Wings** bái é liàng chì   白鹅亮翅

<u>Overall Movement</u>: Control and step forward into a raised knee open position. Then elbow control and drop, stepping forward again into a throw down.

<u>Footwork</u>: Left and right circular steps to advance, then raise the left knee. Then lower on the right leg to touch the left toes down. Then stand up and do left and right circular steps to advance again, and finish in *kaibu* facing south.

The stepping in this form is almost always circular whether stepping forward, to the side, or to the rear. Draw the stepping foot in near the supporting foot and circle it forward or backward, following the coiling action that the legs are already doing within the stance. As an example, before the first step you are coiling into the right leg, so the left leg circles back to step out. The right foot then comes in to the left foot and continues to circle forward to set before the knee lift stance.

<u>Breakdown of Movement</u>:

Part One: Roll the left hand and right fist up the left side of the belly and down the right, as before, but just once this time. Finish with the right fist below. Photos 9a and 9b.

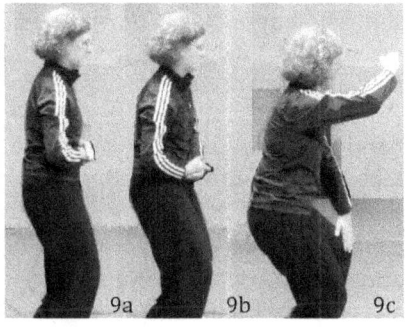

Part Two: Continue to shift in the legs and unclench the right hand and thread it out to the left from under the left hand. Circle both hands on opposite sides, to finish on the right leg with the left palm on the left knee and the right palm facing out by the right temple. Photo 9c.

Part Three: Step the left foot in a back circle, then the right foot in a front circle, circling the hands through to cross, so that the right does a slice up and the left protects at the right upper arm/shoulder. Coil the hands until the left palm is up and the right palm is down. Shift across to the right leg, standing up and raising the left knee, and draw the right arm across and up to finish with the right palm facing out above head height. Draw the left palm, facing

47

up, touching the body, across the right shoulder, diagonally across the ribs to the *dantian*, then out to the inside, then the back of the palm on the outside of the left thigh, and finally coil the hand around the knee to place the thumb on the outside of the knee and the index finger on the inside of the knee. Settle the right foot, grip with the toes, keep the left thigh open with the foot tucked in, breathe in and settle down. The thigh can be more open than in my photos, and the foot more tucked in (see the photos of Cai Yuhua in the additional comments). Photos 9d, 9e, 9f and 9g.

Part Four: Come down on the right leg, turning to the left and lowering the left foot to near the right foot. Keep the left hand on the left knee for as long as possible. If you are strong, first extend the left leg as you turn to the left, then tuck the foot in again before sitting down. Be sure to keep the hips level, don't lift one side to get the move done. Open the thigh further and loosely open the left foot out, rotating the knee slightly, so that the foot makes a circle. Keep the left knee bent and raised, and sit down on the right leg, so that the left foot touches down only at the completion of the sit. When the left foot touches down, keep the heel off the ground and sink further into the right leg. If you need to, you can reach towards the ground with the left foot early, to descend on both legs. *Shunchan* the right hand and bring it down with the forearm vertical, elbow leading the action. Breathe out. Photo 9h.

9h

Part Five: Turn to the right with the weight still on the right leg. Pull across to the right with the right hand and bring the left forearm around with it to help with a *cai* action. Then curl the left hand in around the face and throw a backhand out with the right. If you *fajin*, it is a light snap that does not break the continuity of the movement. As soon as you strike, coil the right hand over to release and prepare to pull. Photo 9i.

9i

Here are some extra photos of parts three, four, and five from the side, and part three from the front (at the Great Wall in 2004, in my mango coloured silks).

Part Six: Step the left foot in a back circle and step the right foot to the forward right. Pull with both hands down to the left knee then continue on to circle them both up to the right. Bring the left foot in beside the right and continue to bring the hands down to press (*an*) in front of the body. Photos 9i, 9j, and 9k.

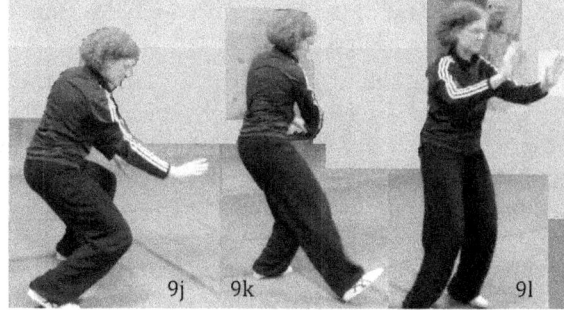

Part Seven: Continue to close the body, cross the arms, and settle the left foot. Palms at first face in, then coil to face out. Settle onto the right leg and place the left foot in a high empty stance. Open the arms out to either side, right a bit above shoulder height, left at shoulder height, settling the shoulders. Photos 9m and 9n.

Part Eight: Step the left foot a bit forward and settle the arms and shoulders a bit more, touching the left heel down. Photo 9o.

This 'step and settle' of part eight seems to be something that sifu had me do specially. For the others, the open arms went more directly into the following move.

Direction of Movements: You move generally easterly with zigzag stepping, and end up facing east.

Possible Applications: You will repeat this move two more times in the form. This first time, find the stability and continuation of the movements within the intricate stepping pattern, search out the large opening and closing of your body, and pass the left hand clearly along the points that it touches the body. If you want to think about something, you can ponder how unfortunate are the styles that do not have such a cool move, that just step straight into the last part.

Internal Connections: In part two, the little finger edge of the left hand touches on the body from the right shoulder, across the body, and then turns at the hip so that back of the hand touches along the outside of the left thigh. Then the left thumb sets on the outside of the left knee and the fingers curl around the front of the knee until the index finger presses the point on the other side of the knee.

During the sliding movement, the left hand touches four channels. It does not trace the complete route of any one channel, but touches from one to the other in a reverse sequence. The twelve channels of the body are linked forming a continuous circuit. The last two channels in the sequence are the Gallbladder and Liver channels. The first two are the Lung and Large Intestine channels. In this movement, the left hand contacts sections of these four as it passes along the forearm (Large Intestine channel), upper arm and chest (Lung channel), flank (Liver channel) and thigh (Gallbladder channel).

In the final raised knee position, the left index finger touches the Xue Hai point on the leg Taiyin Spleen channel. This point has the function of invigorating the blood. The left thumb touches the Liang Qiu point – the cleft point of the leg Yang Ming Stomach channel. The Yang Ming channels are the channels that are fullest in *qi* and blood. These are cleft points, which have the function of opening and unblocking their channel. Liang Qiu ensures the free-flow of this abundance of *qi* and blood. The index finger is the initial point of the Large Intestine channel – a Yang channel. The thumb is the terminal point of the Lung channel – a Yin channel. The hand position of this posture balances the Yang (index finger) with Yin (Xue Hai's position on the Tai Yin channel) and Yin (thumb) with Yang (Liang Qiu on the Yang Ming channel). You don't have to know all this, and certainly don't want to be thinking of it. If you do it, the effect is natural.

<u>About the Name</u>: Possibly because of oral transmission, this move is often called *bai he*, or white crane, but in our style, it is called *bai e*, or white goose, sometimes translated as swan. The name 'white goose' is also seen in Chen Xin's book. The whole continuum uses the connections of the upper arms / shoulders as the wings of a large bird, opening and closing repeatedly, it doesn't really matter which bird. The positions taken in parts two, three, and seven could be thought to resemble a large bird opening its wings.

The word flash, *liang*, means to open or beat the wings to show off to a potential mate, to perform a threatening display, or to dry the wings. It is a different word from that used to open the wings to fly. 'Flash' implies a lifting of the wings with strength at the upper arms, and usually implies an external rotation to present the bottom of the wings forward. When a bird opens or beats its wings to fly, the power application is down. When a bird flashes its wings for display, the power is both in the lift and in a beating action.

In some styles, the word *liang* in this name is written 晾, which means to dry in the sun. I have often seen mergansers sitting in the sun with their wings spread open to dry. With this word, the meaning is more descriptive of the final posture.

Yilu: The First Form

<u>Additional Comments</u>: Here is Cai Yuhua moving from part three to part four with clarity, opening the hip, going down on the right leg, and touching the toes down with the left knee up throughout.

This is the coiling action in part seven, in which the body opens and closes, sticking the *qi* to the upper back, from the front.

> White Goose Flashes Its Wings is made up of many parts, and shows many characteristic power applications: the snaky actions, the opening and closing actions, and the pressing into the leg. It also uses a full range of high and low stances.
>
> It particularly trains the ability to 'stick the *qi* to the upper back.' The power stretches from the upper back to the hands, rounding the upper back to exert power in both directions. If you only exert power in one direction, whether going in or out, the body is unstable. If you exert in both directions at all times, the body is stable, and the stance is automatically more solid.
>
> If you can master this move with power, then you will be able to do many other moves in the form.
>
> It is important to fully complete each portion of the move. Well, it is always important to complete what you are doing, but it seems particularly important when the move is a long and complicated one.

10. Brush Knee Counter Stance   lōu xī ào bù   搂膝拗步

Overall Movement: Step forward and coil, then open and throw or strike.

Footwork: Land the right foot, step the left, and coil within the stance to bring power to the principal arm, which comes through from the back.

All non-moving actions that coil within the stance roll around the edges of the feet. This creates the *chansi* power in the legs, which creates a vortex that coils power up the legs. It is harder to get the *chansi* power in the legs than in the arms, so you have to pay special attention to this. Roll around the knees and ankles without shifting the feet. Within each foot, in sequence, roll from the big toe to the little toe, around the outside of the foot to the heel, then back around the instep to the big toe. You should practise this very slowly to get the feeling in the legs. Later, when you do it faster, you will be able to keep the feeling. You will not be able to find it if you do the form fast all the time. Be sure that you are rolling around each foot, one after the other, drawing an infinity symbol (∞), not doing a circle around the feet as one unit (0). Be sure, also, that you are rolling inside the legs, at the depth of the bones, not around the outside.

Breakdown of Movement:

Part One: Land the left foot full and shift to the left leg, lifting the right knee in front. Bring both palms down and then up to lift and push at either side of the knee. Lower the right foot in a front cross step (or land it beside the left foot with a stamp, lifting the left foot by the right ankle) then step the left foot out into a horse stance, angled about thirty degrees to the northeast. Step only as far as you can control keeping the body upright and the right knee well aligned. Photos 10a, 10b, and 10c.

10a   10b   10c

Part Two: Shift to the centre, a bit to the left, and coil into the left leg. Curl the left hand around the left knee then up behind the back in a hook hand. Shift slightly back, coiling into the right leg and brush the right hand by the right knee. Then shift back towards the centre and tuck the right

10d   10e   10f

hand in to the jaw. The hands arrive at the midpoints at about the same time – the left hook behind the small of the back and the right palm at the jaw. Photos 10d, 10e, and 10f.

Part Three: Continue to *nichan* both arms and extend them out on either side, the left hook still turned upside down. Then settle and *shunchan* to drop the right wrist while you *shunchan* the left hook to hang normally. In the final position the stance is angled northeast, the body is facing east, the right arm is aligned to the east, on the stance line of the right leg. The left arm is extended along the scapular line. Press into the rear calf to send power to the front hand. The rear knee will finish the push still bent, but with an expanding energy into the rear heel. Photos 10g and 10h.

Direction of Movements: If you started facing south you are still travelling east, but the stance is angled across.

Possible Applications: In the first repetition of this movement, seek out how to send power to the leading arm. Do the movement slowly and carefully, paying attention to the coiling power in the legs and how that connects to the coiling of the arms. If you do not take the time to do this, then you won't be able to apply this technique effectively. Find the power in the left arm behind the body, do not simply place it there. Good power in the assisting hand is the key to having good power in the leading hand. The power transfers from one to the other, though the body in a direct connection. If the assisting hand is weak or empty, there can be no power in the leading hand.

Internal Connections: In the final settling the left arm is giving power to the right push. Let the power come from the legs, roll the hook upright using the left shoulder to send power to the right hand. You will feel a rush from the left hand through the body directly to the right hand. Bring power from the legs by pushing back into the rear calf and not allowing the lead knee to go past the ankle. This is a readjustment of the whole body around fixed points that are connected to the opponent – the hands. Change the structural lines within the stance, do not move spatially.

About the Name: This may be a simple descriptive name, as the hands brush away by the knees. In Chinese wrestling, though, the same word *lou* is a leg and foot technique. It is a raking action with the leg, stepping in close to the opponent's front foot, pressuring thigh to thigh or knee to knee, then raking back with the heel, catching the opponent just behind the ankle. It also includes stepping on the opponent's lower leg, using the inner side of the foot to pressure him down. As a farming action, this type of raking with the legs is common, and Chen Taijiquan comes from a farming village. This may not be the meaning here, but we should not focus just on the brushing action of the hands and ignore the possibility of a tripping action with the legs.

The final move is done in a bow counter stance (*aobu*). In Chinese *aobu* is a straightforward name, but unfortunately there is no good translation for it, so you will see 'reverse bow stance,' 'counter stance,' and 'twist stance.' A standard bow stance is smooth – the same hand and foot are in front (i.e. right with right). A bow counter stance is one in which the opposite hand and foot are in front (i.e. right with left).

In both bow/smooth stance and bow/counter stance, the hips face the direction of attack and the feet can point in that way, or the front foot may be turned in slightly. In some styles, the rear foot may be turned out as much as forty-five degrees, but in this branch, the power pushes into the rear calf such that the heel is pushed back. It is important that the front knee does not pass the supporting ankle. The stance uses the power from the rear leg, not a weight shift forward, to drive power to the front arm.

<u>Additional Comments</u>: Here is a photo of the first brushing past the knee. You should sit down into the horse stance enough to easily reach the knee without leaning, going back and forth to brush both knees.

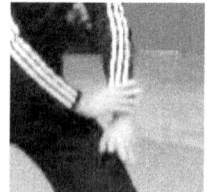

Another way to do this movement is to press the hands down, palms facing down, then separate them to brush in front of the knees. Then raise the right arm quite straight and bring it to the front over the top, and hook the left hand as it continues to the rear, staying low. There is less weight shift in this method, and the strike is directly downwards, as if breaking the collarbone of the opponent.

Chen Xin's illustration, which seems like an over complication, can be seen as a clear diagram of the move as how we still do it.

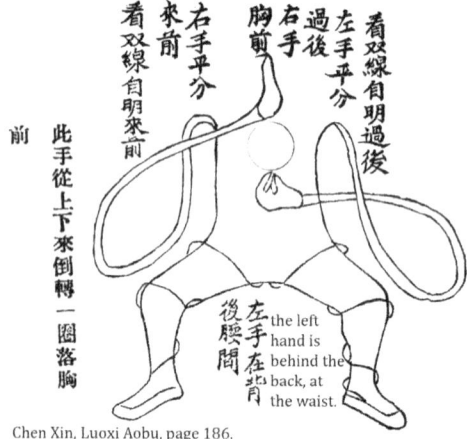

Chen Xin, Luoxi Aobu, page 186.

Yilu: The First Form

The *nichan* of the arms sets up the power of the final *shunchan*. The final settling releases the power built up in the *nichan*. In the setup, the arms *nichan* more than usual for Taijiquan. The elbows must be controlled and the arms must stay settled in the shoulder sockets. If the elbows lift, then all power is lost and the entire shoulder structure will lift. The final settling can be done as a short *fajin*, but only once you have become very comfortable with this action. Even if you can do the *fajin*, leave it for later sections of the form.

> My days in 1990 were basically train, eat, make notes. Everyone should do that at some point in their life. Longhua park had a teahouse that I would go to immediately after training, to make notes while my ideas were still fresh. I, and what seemed to be every retired gentleman in the area, spent many pleasant hours in the teahouse where one yuan (about twenty cents) bought you a thermos of hot water and a glass full of green tea leaves. You could stay all day as far as the employees were concerned, and they were happy to refill the thermos. The expense kept out the riffraff. There was no air conditioning, but the open air architecture made it cooler than most places. The old men would read the newspaper and play cards or Go. The teahouse was later moved outside the park and has a fence around it and a sign – 'old style teahouse.' Of course you can't go in.

The teahouse was also a favourite hangout of sifu on the weekend, and sometimes we would continue our practice outside it while he went inside and watched us as he sipped tea.

11. **Initial Gathering** chū shōu 初收

<u>Overall Movement</u>: Catch and pull back and forth, then bring the hands over and present in a high empty stance.

<u>Footwork</u>: Shift with the infinity symbol (∞) within the stance, then step the left foot forward into a high empty stance.

<u>Breakdown of Movement</u>:

Part One: Turn the body slightly left to bring the right hand across. Bring the left hook hand to sit in the right palm. Shift and turn to the right, bringing the hands together across to the right, the left hook staying on the inside. Draw the hands across at about chest height. When you get to the right, open both hands to reach out and draw small clockwise circles with the middle fingers, keeping power in the palms without over flexing the wrists. Photos 11a, 11b, 11c, and 11d.

Part Two: Sit back to the left leg and pull down and across to the left, palms out. Photo 11e.

Part Three: Draw small counter-clockwise circles with the middle fingers, then sit back to the right leg and pull across at chest height to the right. Photos 11f and 11g.

Part Four: Draw small clockwise circles with the middle fingers, then start to draw down and across, turning the action into a draw down. Photo 11h.

Yilu: The First Form

Part Five: Step the right foot in by the left foot and draw the hands down in front of the right knee, then step to the forward right. Step the left foot forward into an empty stance, bringing the hands up and over. Finish with the hands in front of the body, right hand near the left elbow with the palm up, left hand extended with the palm down. The distance between the hands is about the distance between the hand and elbow of an opponent. Photos 11i, 11j, and 11k.

Direction of Movements: The stance when shifting back and forth is angled across, and you step to finish facing east.

Possible Applications: This is an extended *cai* back and forth, coiling to release from a grab and gain control of the opponent, stepping in finally to increase control and pressure. Keep the movement gentle so that you do not lose contact with the opponent while weakening his grip. This movement follows along the line of attack, so works best from a grabbed situation.

If your opponent pushes or grabs your chest, coiling the arms in as you shift will serve to evade the attack and gain control of his arms. If he grabs your wrists, the movement serves to release his grip and gain control of his wrists or elbows. If you control his elbows by squeezing them in, then you can sit back, draw him further in, then push him away. Your left knee or foot is ready for a strike if you can't, or don't want to, push him away. If you do decide to kick, if you do not let go then you can injure his knee. If you let go then you can push him away with your foot.

Internal Connections: In part one, the hands are moving in towards the body while the power is extending away from the body. This is done by closing in the chest and opening the upper back, expanding into the arms. In the rest of the move, concentrate on the circles of the middle fingers. These circles are the way to change direction without losing power or losing the infinity circles (*yin-yang* fish movement) of the legs and body. The circles must be connected deeply through the body – they are not just finger circles. The middle finger draws a circle every time that there is a full change of direction, but this is the culmination of the coiling in the body. The more connected the body becomes, the smaller can all the circles become. This action is used throughout the form any time there is a drastic change of direction.

About the Name: 'Gathering' refers to the action of gathering yourself for attack, like a tiger gathers into its haunches. 'Initial' means that this is the first time you do a gathering action in the form. Up until now you have been advancing. This action is repeated later on. In other branches of Chen style, the gathering refers also to the withdrawing action of the foot into the empty stance, but we step forward into it. The withdrawing, gathering our forces, nature of the move is still there, though.

Additional Comments: Be sure to keep the hands attached to each other through your upper back from part two on.

There was usually at least one apprentice, both martial arts and painting arts, around doing odd jobs such as chopping things up, cleaning things, and running errands. They were also great just to hang around and keep me company. Very seldom training or getting taught, but always busy with some job. I wish we had apprentices like they did in China in those days. Those little stools are one reason our knees stayed flexible. The trick to sitting on them is to hold it in one hand and sit while placing it behind you, all in one action.

Cai Yuhua's step-mother preparing yarn for knitting, one of his apprentices working on the wood for a scroll hanging, and one of the kittens supervising.

Yilu: The First Form

12. **Left And Right Diagonal Stepping** (2nd and 3rd repetitions of Brush Knee Counter Stance, alternate version)   zuǒ yòu xié xíng
左右斜行

Overall Movement: Step and repeat an action similar to Brush Knee Counter Stance on both sides, but more angled. The stance is square with the limbs aligned to the four diagonal directions.

Footwork: Settle more to the right leg then step the left to the opposite corner of a box, then step the right leg to the next opposite corner.

Breakdown of Movement:

Part One: Keep sitting on the right leg and open the arms – the right up and back a bit, doing *shunchan*, the left down and forward a bit, doing *nichan*. Breathe in, relax, and keep the hands relaxed. Photo 12a.

Part Two: Turn the upper body a bit to the right and coil the forearms, *shunchan* the left arm and *nichan* the right arm. Step the left foot forward towards a bow stance to the northeast. Continue to coil the hands until the left palm is up and the third finger of the right hand is on the left wrist. Coiling the right hand until the palm faces down will build up the *peng* energy, the power will then go into the thumb side to assist with the *ji*. Press into *ji*, looking at the third finger of the right hand. Shift forward towards a bow stance, but do not complete the stance or push the rear heel back. Photos 12b and 12c.

Part Three: Coil the left hand over to face down and the right to face up, start to *lü*, shifting back. Then change the left hand to brush knee and tuck the right hand into the jaw, shifting forward again. Draw the right hand across and extend the left hand in a hook to the rear. At first, watch the third finger of the left hand, then watch the right hand. Open the arms to an open angled position and settle into the counter stance, the feet will be at the diagonal corners of a square, and the hands at the other diagonal corners. Photos 12d, 12e, 12f, 12g, 12h, and 12i.

Shadowboxing in Shanghai

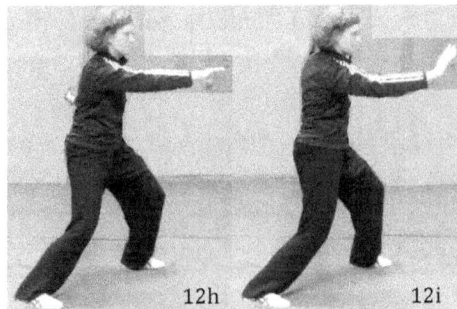

Part Four: Pull back the hands, coiling the left to an outer expanding (*peng*) energy and the right to a regular expanding (*peng*) energy. Step the right foot to the southeast. Start the same movement on the other side, *ji* with the left finger on the right wrist. Photos 12j, 12k, 12l, 12m, and 12n.

Part Five: Coil the palms over in the same movement on the other side, to pull, then brush knee, then into an angled open position with the left hand forward. Photos 12o, 12p, and 12q.

Yilu: The First Form

Direction of Movements: The main line of action is to the east. In the right posture, the right foot is behind in the southwest, the left foot is ahead in the northeast, the right hand is ahead in the southeast, and the left hand is behind in the north. If you draw a straight line between the feet, a ninety-degree line joins the body's midline with the right hand. The reverse is done for the left posture.

Possible Applications: Catch and put pressure on the opponent. Following Initial Gathering as it does, the opponent may be lured into thinking you are retreating, so you can charge in with a bit more confidence. Step in to control, strike, or throw. The final push is the same application as Brush Knee Counter Stance, but is more stable to the corners.

Internal Connections: This move involves a continuous internal adjustment of the lines of force so that *ji*, *lü* and *peng* can be properly executed. Unlike the previous Brush Knee Counter Stance, the final push in this move has the hands and feet at opposing corners. For this to be effective there needs to be proper internal alignment, which the earlier parts of this move help find.

The third finger is on the wrist of the other hand in each assisted press (*ji*). The Jue Yin channel of the arm ends at the tip of the middle finger. The Jue Yin channels are the deepest of the regular channels, acting as an anchor for the channel system. The acupoints on the inside of the wrist have an effect on the chest and on the Heart and Lungs. Touching the wrist with the third finger helps the Jue Yin stabilize the Heart and Lungs, keeping the breathing and heart rate smooth.

About the Name: Both steps are taken diagonally, the feet should step to the corners as if in a box. The body turns with the actions, but on the final posture it is facing straight, in a reverse stance. The arms in the final posture are also on opposite corners of the box, so the final strike is angled.

Additional Comments: Do not let the feet squirm around. Go back and forth in a horse stance, do not press (*ji*) into a full bow stance.

The feet should never squirm during the form. Step cleanly to where you want to go. On occasions that call for a clear pivot, the pivoting foot will press back into the heel to make a clear *yin-yang* fish pattern in the dirt.

One day when sifu was in a good mood about my ability, he said that he liked the fact that I placed my feet well and did not squirm. It is nice once in a while to get positive feedback from your teacher, especially in China where 'not so bad' is considered wild praise.

13. Brush Knee Counter Stance (for the 4th time, alternate action)

lōu xī ào bù   搂膝拗步

<u>Overall Movement</u>: Step forward and bring the right arm over the top, first controlling with the left arm.

<u>Footwork</u>: Lift the right knee, then land and step the left foot forward into a horse stance then press into a bow stance.

When stepping into a horse stance, sometime a digging step is used instead of the circular step. Land the foot on the inside of the heel and keep pushing into so that it slides a bit more in the same direction. If you want to take a slightly wider stance, you may use this digging step. Do not overdo the distance, as an overly long stance inhibits your next step.

<u>Breakdown of Movement</u>:

Part One: Coil the arms, open the right hook, first drawing it in and *nichan*, which turns into *shunchan*. *Shunchan* the left arm and bring it towards the right. The hands are then ready to *lü* together. Hook the right foot in as you catch with the hands. Photos 13a and 13b.

Part Two: Lift the right foot, coiling it to step forward, and pull in the hands. Land the right foot turned out, and continue to bring the left hand around to the right until the forearms are crossed near the right thigh, left palm facing down, right palm facing up. Photos 13c and 13d.

Part Three: Step the left foot forward into a horse stance. Turn both palms down and brush past the knees on each side. Curl the left hand into a hook and bring it behind the back (not touching), with the fingers pointing up. Bring the right arm quite straight over the top then down into a push (palm faces almost down as it comes around, wrist leading). Press into a

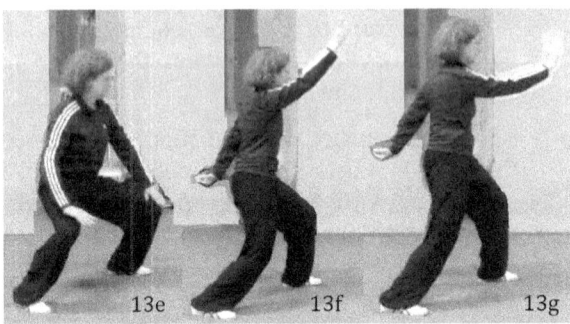

Yilu: The First Form

bow stance. The push is directly east, the feet are aligned more northeast, the body is aligned directly east. Do not extend the shoulders into the push. The right fingertips are in line with the nose. Photos 13e, 13f, and 13g.

Possible Applications: Clear the opponent's attack, step in and drop him straight down. This time the right arm comes directly over the top, to take him directly down. This depends on the left hand and left leg getting control of him and stretching him out.

Internal Connections: Develop a strong twisting energy between the left and right hands. Be sure to coil and rotate the arms to the fullest extent in the final position. The more twist in the left arm, the more power is built up for the following elbow coil.

To find the internal connection of the final posture you may stand in counter stance in a hallway that is exactly the size of your stance, bracing the feet on the walls, the right palm and left foot on the forward wall, the left palm and right foot on the rear wall. Press the right calf back without moving forward into the left leg, and concentrate on the feeling of expansion of the whole body, connecting through to both hands on the walls.

About the Name: Descriptive of the actions, brushing the knees and finishing in a counter stance. This movement can also be done the same as move 10, with alternating knee brushes, then a twisting and extension of the arms.

Additional Comments: Hook all five fingers of the left hand together, the fingertips touching. Sink the hip joints.

Here is a photo of the final posture from the front.

We talk a lot about the 'hips' in Taijiquan. Usually this means not the pelvis, but the hip joints. I tend to say 'hip joints,' while some translate *kua* as 'inguinal crease.' The best thing is perhaps to think of the *kua* as the area of the body that extends from the inguinal ligaments, through the inside of the pelvis, to the crest of the hip bone. This makes you think more of the link from the lower back to the thighs, and to think deep inside the body.

When we say 'hips' meaning the pelvic crest, the term is used when referring to not sticking out the hip when standing on one leg. The term 'hips' is also used when saying that the pelvis is facing a certain direction.

14. **Gather In Again** zài shōu 再收

<u>Overall Movement</u>: Step back and control with the elbows.

<u>Footwork</u>: Sit back to the right leg, step back the left foot, sit back to the left leg, then step back the right foot and settle into a sixty-forty stance.

In any stance where the weight is on the rear leg, the front knee must not pass the front heel. This is well balanced and allows you to advance with a following step (the rear foot comes in so the lead foot can step forward), which is more lively and safer than advancing with a step forward (the rear foot steps, going past the lead foot).

<u>Breakdown of Movement</u>:

Part One: First shift slightly forward and coil the right hand to turn the palm diagonally up. Sit back onto the right leg, turn right, and bring the left elbow over to come down on the right palm. Place the back of the left wrist on the body as you start the movement, and keep it tight to the body as you turn. This keeps the movement compact and strong. Photo 14a.

Part Two: Step the left foot back and sit back to the left leg. Bring the right elbow over and turn the left palm up. Keep the right hand tight to the body so that the right wrist ends up on top of the left palm. Photos 14b and 14c.

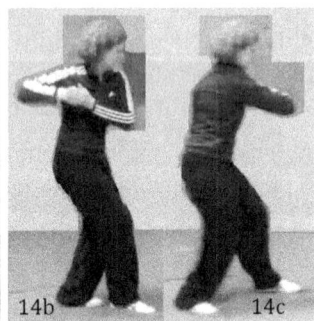

Part Three: Drop back with a right leg stamp into a high empty stance, lift the hands and come down with a double splitting palm. The left hand comes up inside the right, both palms turned in, then both turn down and drop down. Turn the left foot straight as you extend the left hand forward. Photos 14d and 14e.

<u>Direction of Movements</u>: The main line of action is directed towards the east, but you are stepping back to the west.

<u>Possible Applications</u>: The left elbow can do an arm break or control. Then grab the opponent's wrist or arm with the left hand and keep it pressed against the right arm as you roll his right elbow over to break or control.

Yilu: The First Form

I was lucky one day to have my camera when sifu was playing with applications.

Internal Connections: This move uses the close connection of the elbows to the body – keep the movement close throughout. This trains the application of short (or close) power – the expression of the power is not at the hands, but is instead at the elbows.

About the Name: This action is different from the Initial Gathering, but the final action has a similar control, so it has a similar name. In other Chen branches the two movements are often done the same.

Additional Comments: Roll with the back, keep the arms quite tight to the body and use the power of the body.

This movement may be done with different timing, striking with the right elbow and stomping with the right foot at the same time. This means there is a double step for the overall action. The left foot slides in and back, then the right foot slides in and back to a stamp. With this timing, the stance remains more forward with the elbow strike. After the stamp, settle into the high empty stance and double split.

Here is the move from the front.

Nothing like orange Fanta and steamed meat buns for breakfast, especially when you are teaching and your students are working hard and getting dizzy from hunger. To get to the park on time I often didn't eat before leaving on my bike, so got pretty hungry part way through practice. Someone always brought sifu buns and a drink, part of taking care of your sifu. When he was eating he tended to not smoke, so I preferred the tasty smell of the buns.

In 1990, I arrived in early June and stayed for six months, so was there in the autumn. We trained in the same place every day, but one day I arrived to find no one there. I thought this odd, but never had too much idea what was going on, so just started training. Eventually someone ran over to tell that they'd switched to the winter training grounds that got more sunshine. They had been wondering where I was, and finally realised that they never told me about the switch.

I've liked to switch training areas by the season ever since. It makes a lot of sense to seek the shade in the summer and the sun in the winter. It is also fun to not mention it to my students. One of the tests to see if you are 'worth teaching' is the ability to find your teacher.

Our regular training grounds, lots of space for the various groups.

15. Diagonal Stepping To Counter Stance xié xíng ào bù 斜行拗步

Overall Movement: Coil the body in and step forward.

Footwork: Turn into resting stance (*xiebu*) then step into horse stance, turning again into resting stance.

Breakdown of Movement:

Part One: Turn the left foot and turn left into a resting stance – a high crossed stance, the right knee tucked in behind the left knee, but not fully sitting down. Extend the right palm to cross over the left forearm, towards the west, *shunchan* to palm up. *Nichan* the left hand to turn the palm down and out with an outer *peng* energy.

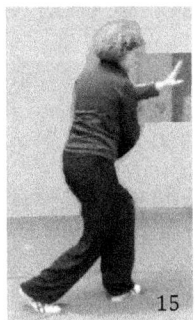

Part Two: Step the right foot forward to half horse stance, block the knees with both hands, then step the left foot forward to a resting stance. Reach the left hand over the top and coil the right hand under to beside the left leg. Photo 15.

Possible Applications: Step forward into your defensive block, getting in close to the opponent to prepare for the counter attack.

About the Name: This move seems to be a transitional move, and does not go completely into a counter stance. The power is counter stance. So, although it shares the name, is not considered a repetition of move 10.

Additional Notes: Part one can also be done with a full circular walk using *koubu* and *baibu* before part two.

I do the moves the way I learned them, so go straight from the resting stance into the next move. The described version is an optional way to do the move.

As with any traditional name list, some moves don't have a name and some moves have a name but aren't really there. This move is kind of part of the following move. I do not do this move as a counter stance, just a coiling into a resting stance.

16. **Cast The Frame**   pāo jià zǐ   抛架子

Overall Movement: Step forward three times with a lowering controlling action coupled with a rising action and a strike behind.

Footwork: Step forward into bow stance three times, first bringing the lead foot back to tuck in behind the supporting knee, then stepping it forward.

Breakdown of Movement:

Part One: Step the right foot forward to a half horse stance, then shift to a bow stance. Open the right arm up and the left down. Reach the left arm over to slap and control. Turn the hips straight (using the term hips as simply the direction in which the pelvis is facing), and press power from the rear left heel, don't rise the body. *Nichan* the left hand to the rear, rotated palm back, pressing back beside or slightly past the left leg. Press into the left palm, enough to bend the wrist slightly. Extend the right arm away and up (*shunchan*), in line with the right leg at head height. Photo 16a.

Part Two: Bring the right foot back halfway, then turn it out and stamp, tucking the left foot behind the right knee. Cross the arms. Then step the left foot into a half horse stance. Coil the right hand to reach forward and bring the left hand through low, crossing the arms. Shift forward to bow stance and turn right, straightening the hips Raise the left arm, pressing out and up with *shunchan*, and push the right arm back with *nichan*. Photos 16b and 16c.

Part Three: Bring the left foot back halfway, turn out and stamp, tucking the right foot behind the left knee. Cross the arms as before. Step the right foot forward to half horse stance, then shift to bow stance and do the same action with the arms again. Photos 16d and 16e.

Yilu: The First Form

Part Four: Sit back to the left leg and lift the right knee (this will be slightly diagonal, since the bow stance was not directly aligned west to east). Bring the left forearm to cross, coil the right hand over to face down, then open the left up and the right down in line with the direction of the stance. The left hand finishes about head height and the right hand finishes below the right knee. Do not look down at the right hand, but look straight out in that direction. Photos 16f and 16g.

Possible Applications: Step in to throw, controlling the opponent with the hand that is pulling back. The type of throw is similar to Tuck In The Robe Casually, but more angled upward, so it is intended as a throw away rather than a takedown.

You may also focus on the rear hand, as if you were grabbed from behind. Hold your place and strike strongly back to the assailant's groin with the rear hand using the forward arm to help break his grip.

Internal Connections: To find the internal connection of the posture in parts one, two, and three, you may stand in smooth stance in a hallway that is exactly the size of your stance, bracing the feet on the walls, the right palm and right foot on the forward wall, the left palm and left foot on the rear wall. Press the left calf back without moving forward into the right leg, and concentrate on the feeling of expansion of the whole body, connecting through to both hands on the walls.

About the Name: If done with a *fajin*, you can see that the movement is like casting a fishing net that is in a large wooden frame. The word *pao* is used for casting a net or throwing a ball, with a feeling of throwing for distance. The posture has the feeling of casting out a fishing frame. A Chinese fishing frame is a large light wooden square frame that is held at the sides in open arms and thrown with a turn of the body. The big posture at the end also looks like casting a frame.

There are two different name lists for this form. The name list I am using here is the 108 list, which sifu gave me in 1990. The other name list is 106 movements, which sifu gave to my martial elder brother Cai Yuhua in 1982. The form remains the same, though. The 1982 list at this point is: Gather In Again, Counter Stance, Punch. The 1990 list is Gather In Again, Diagonal Stepping To Counter Stance, Cast The Frame, Front Hall Counter Stance, Punch. One possibility is that the original sequence was Gather In Again, Front Hall Counter Stance, Punch, as written in the work by Chen Xin.

The position during Front Counter Stance shown in that book is the same as the three moving forward actions during Cast The Frame, except that the rear hand is a fist instead of the flat of the palm. This may have been confusing to practitioners because it is called Front Hall Counter Stance but is a smooth bow stance, not a counter stance. So maybe at some point someone started calling the stepping move Cast The Frame, and somehow ended up with the new name and old name in twice. The transitional move that comes in between the Cast The Frame and the Punch thus became Front Hall Counter Stance, although it is not a counter stance either. This is all guesswork on my part.

Additional Comments: There are a few variations on this technique. The steps forward in parts one, two, and three can also involve low kicks when landing the foot forward. Part four may be done as a low half horse stance weighted to the left leg instead of a knee lift.

When the casting action is done with a *fajin*, the power goes to the thumb side of the forward wrist and the palm of the rear hand.

Here are photos from the front.

Cai Yuhua and a friend showed me their Xingyi quite early on in our friendship. It was too different from the Hebei Xingyi I had learned at college, so I didn't study it. Only years later did I realise it was Jiang Rongqiao's so would have fitted in well with the Bagua that we did. I missed out there, it would have been cool to do. I don't really mind. Sticking with Hebei Xingyi meant that I was not confused when I started training with Di Guoyong in Beijing in later years. But still, I should have been more open to differences and oddities.

One reason for my reluctance to take up their Xingyiquan was that his friend got so excited showing the Xingyi sabre that he leapt up, swinging the sabre, and cut his hand open on the ceiling fan. Spending the rest of the day wandering around with the guy and the bloody rag around his hand kind of turned me off the style.

When I saw more of it later, training again in Shanghai, I realised how special all of Jiang Rongqiao's kungfu was.

Yilu: The First Form

17. **Front Hall Counter Stance** (for the 5th time, alternate version)
    qián táng ào bù   前堂拗步

Overall Movement: Land and settle into a Brush Knee Counter Stance type position in an aligned stance, and weighted to the rear leg, body facing south.

Footwork: Turn the right foot to do a coiling kick before landing with a stamp. Step the left foot to the east and coil to settle to horse stance.

Breakdown of Movement:

Part One: Coil the right foot out, turn quickly, and stamp. Turn to the right and bring the left hand across quickly as you stamp the right foot. Both arms stay in the same positions relative to the body throughout, so sweep around with the turning of the leg and body. Photos of James, to keep things interesting, 17a and 17b.

Part Two: Land the left foot to the east and shift towards the left leg. Turn left and bring the arms to the left. Turn the left palm down and sweep the arm left as you shift to the left. Block past the left knee then hook and lift the hook upside down and extend the arm to the rear left. Coil the right hand by the face. Photos 17c, 17d, and 17e.

Part Three: Turn left. Keep power in the left forearm and roll the hook upright to send power through the upper back to the right hand in the final stance. Extend and uncoil the right arm to the right. The final position has the arms aligned with the legs. Photo 17f.

Possible Applications: First lift the right knee to avoid a kick or low strike. Catch with the right leg and stamp on the opponent's foot if you can. Extend the right arm to control, blocking or grabbing at the right side. Then control and move in to throw. If you are avoiding a kick you can get the arm under the attacking leg then envelop and lever the leg for the throw.

Internal Connections: This trains the same type of power as the previous Brush Knee Counter Stances (moves 10,12, and 13), but applying it to an aligned stance. The power comes from the rear leg to the front, directly through the body.

About the Name: The Front Hall commonly refers to the torso or chest in martial arts terminology. The action is the same as Brush Knee Counter Stance, but to the other side, with the torso (front hall) facing straight on.

> Within the first section of the form, you practise the same strike or throw on the front leg, opposite leg, right arm and left arm during Dantian Transforms, Brush Knee Counter Stance, Left and Right Diagonal Stepping, and Front Hall Counter Stance – moves that are variations of Single Whip. This form is quite well balanced in terms of applying power in different directions with both sides, and in terms of the weight distribution of the legs. As with all Taijiquan, it is still basically a right handed form, assuming that most people fight from a basic stance of the left hand and foot forward, and prefer to come in with a strong right punch.

Yilu: The First Form

18. **Hide The Hand And Punch**   yán shǒu hóng chuí   掩手肱捶

<u>Overall Movement</u>: Step forward to punch directly forward.

<u>Footwork</u>: Stamp the right foot, lifting the left foot beside the right ankle. Then step the left foot forward as you prepare to punch, and complete the punch with a bow stance.

<u>Breakdown of Movement</u>:

Part One: Stamp the right foot, bringing the left foot up beside the right ankle with the foot flat. Bring the hands quickly (a small inwards *fajin*) towards each other, palms facing each other, as if covering an attack. Land the left foot forward to the southeast, crossing the forearms, palms facing each other, left on top. Photos 18a and 18b.

Part Two: Sweep the left palm across to the front, palm facing left, then bring it in to the waist. Sweep the right palm across to the front, *nichan* to turn the palm over as much as possible. Extend the left palm out to the front in a character eight shape, palm up, and *shunchan* the right hand and clench to fist while bringing it in to the waist. The right elbow is at the waist, the fist to the front on the midline. Photos 18c, 18d, 18e, and 18f.

Part Three: Shift to a high counter stance, but keeping the weight a bit back, almost a crouching stance. Snap the hips into the punch, extend the right shoulder, and turn the upper body to face almost east while punching south. Coil the left palm over to face down, slide the right fist along under the left elbow, then punch to the front and slightly to the left. Slide the left palm around the belly to the side. Photo 18g.

<u>Direction of Movements</u>: You are punching to the south.

Possible Applications: If the opponent punches or pushes to your chest from the front, bring your left foot in to give a smaller target and gather yourself, trapping his arm or arms with both hands. Then advance the left foot to get close enough to hit, controlling him with your left hand. Backfist to his head with the right hand or fist. Then, keeping control with the left hand, punch to his solar plexus if you can get to the midline, or to his ribs if you are on the outside. If the power is properly transferred, you may punch with the fist or any part of the arm, depending on the distance and target.

About the Name: *Yanshou* means to screen or hide the hand. It can also mean to screen or hide <u>with</u> the hand. It is normally understood as an action that covers the punching hand, to conceal it, but may also mean to cover the opponent's attack with one hand then punch with the other hand.

Using *chui* instead of *quan* generally means that the backfist or heel of the fist is used instead of the knuckles. *Hong* means the arm. *Hongchui* means to punch using the forearm, and punches that are more with the whole fist than with the knuckles. The use of *hongchui* for the punch emphasizes that the punch throws the arm out differently than a regular straight punch. In our style it tends to be a more direct punch than in most Chen styles, which curl a bit more. The character 肱 is *gong* in the dictionary, but martial artists usually use the alternate pronunciation of *hong*.

This move occurs in all Chen styles, with slight differences in the name and performance. Sometimes it uses 'play' with the hand (演手 *yanshou*), and sometimes uses 'arm/fist' punch (肱拳 *hongquan*). The word 'play' can be understood essentially the same as the covering action. Perhaps *hong* <u>*quan*</u> is used instead of *hong* <u>*chui*</u> to suggest that it is really a punch, to not get carried away with the idea of the arm. It is possible that the differences are due simply to oral transmission, as they all sound similar, and we shouldn't fuss too much about them.

Additional Comments: When you sweep the right fist out the first time you may do a small *fajin*. Before the punch you may slide the right fist along on top of the forearm instead of underneath.

When you punch, keep the fist relaxed throughout, tighten when you hit, then relax immediately. Focus your power on the fist (or the forearm if that is where you are thinking of connecting) in order to shoot the energy to there and beyond to the opponent. Do not shake the body or head. Aside from the possibility of hurting yourself, shaking dissipates energy that could be transferring to the punch. Keep the *fajin* crisp and clean with a clear directional application, funneling the power from the body core to the focused point of contact. The higher the punch, the more turned the shoulders, you can punch anywhere from groin to shoulder height. Keep the whole body relaxed until the actual *fajin*, then you need to protect your body from the acceleration, so there is a brief instant of tightening. Although there is a hip snap, the power comes from the centre of the body.

Yilu: The First Form

The left hand can either pull back as a fist at the side, or slap into the body with a palm. Note also in the photos that the punch is well extended, not drawn back.

> When punching with a *fajin*, snap the hip, then release, so the power flows from the rear heel to the fist, then back to the heel. The hip snap (*kou kua*) is very sharp. This is a release, not a recoil that draws the shoulder and hand back. Sifu told me to snap the hip and not recoil. I could see that most of our group did a recoil, but I always try to do what I'm told.

> This is the first standard *fajin* movement in the form. A punch is the easiest *fajin* to understand. If you are doing the infinity symbol within all your motions, when there is a break in this action the power will continue to shoot out in a straight line, following the last direction of the coiling (like braking a bike while speeding around a corner will shoot you into the outer ditch).
>
> You could *fajin* at any time, but the first part of the form is focused on building and storing of energy. The actions themselves do not change, at least up to the instant of releasing. The coiling and settling prepares you to *fajin* at any time. *Fajin* means to release power or energy, so should not be overdone.
>
> It is common knowledge in China that the Chen practitioners who concentrated on *fajin* were not as healthy and perhaps died younger than the people who concentrated on the building and storing of energy. That is one reason why there are standard places throughout the form that you do a *fajin*, to ensure the right balance of storing and releasing.
>
> My branch uses fairly light *fajin*, and does not do a *fasheng* (noise) with them. There is, of course, an exhalation to *fajin*, but the throat remains relaxed, so does not make much of a sound.
>
> In our style, we often do the *fajin* near the end of the movement, more of a one inch power than many Chen stylists that you see. It seems to be a small *fajin*, but it hits solidly. If you are throwing someone, so are already in contact, and add a *fajin*, they go flying or drop hard, depending on your direction. The *fajin* is part of the entire movement, not something separate, so it is not a big effort thrown at the beginning of a move.

The Shanghai Climate

Although its name suggests it is 'Above the Sea,' Shanghai is actually on the Huangpu River, not the ocean, in a flatland below sea level, crisscrossed with creeks and canals. It should be translated as 'Upriver of the Sea,' and the Huangpu is a flat, tidal, river. The humidity index is thus always between seventy-five and eighty-five percent. All year. Cold or hot. The saying 'it isn't the heat, it is the humidity' applies equally for cold, in terms of describing unpleasantness.

If you want to visit Shanghai, it is best to avoid winter, spring, and summer. Autumn is a bit dodgy, but it is your best bet.

The winter is humid and windy, intensifying the cold, which in January and February can go down to 2 degrees at night, and up to only 8 degrees during the day. Zero centigrade with 75 percent humidity and a dusting of snow is about as bone chilling as it gets. When I went down from Beijing, Shanghai should not have felt cold in the winter, but because it is just south of the Yangzi river, there was no heating in the buildings (a government regulation, perhaps to save coal?). Warming up for training in the park was ok, because there was always the bike ride to get there. But inside, sometimes in the winter the whole family would just sit on the big wooden bed and play cards, wrapped up in all the bedding. My training notes say "can be cold, long underwear, gloves, but may be hot."

Spring is damp, which is an understatement. When I was there in the spring, the family would spread out all the bedding and all shoes in the sun on absolutely every sunny day. 'Sunny' meant that it wasn't raining, because you couldn't actually see the sun in Shanghai in the 1980s and 90s. You could safely look directly at a hazy ball through the pollution. In April, there were flowers and blossoming trees, so when it wasn't raining it was really lovely, and lead me into a false sense of weather security.

Mid-June to early July is called the plum rain season, which sounds pretty, but means that if you didn't air things as much as possible, the humidity rots them. The temperature is in the mid-twenties, which should be nice, but with the rain, isn't that great.

Summer is unbearable. I didn't know how draining heat could be when I lived in Beijing. Beijing gets hot in the summer, but usually cools off enough at night to sleep. When you don't sleep for weeks, it really does something to your mind. In Shanghai you can't sleep on a normal mattress, even a hard one, because the little bit you sink into the mattress makes you think you're going to die from the heat. You sleep on a plank with a woven bamboo mat, but you don't really sleep, you lie there wishing you were dead so that you didn't have to try to sleep any more. People in the city would take a mat out to the street to try to catch a stray bit of breeze.

The temperature in the summer, with humidex (to reiterate, the average humidity is near eighty percent, year round!) is beyond hot. It is easily 35 degrees for days on end in July and August, no matter what the temperature chart says. And it can dump down rain, over 200 millimetres per month in June and August, and only a bit less in July. In the 1980s and 90s, to make sure everyone got to work, the temperature was reported without humidex, and stopped at 36 degrees. At 37 degrees the factories had to shut down by law, so it had to be well above that to be reported as over 36.

Late August to mid-September is typhoon season, which brings heavy rain and winds. Best avoided. My training notes say, "humid, rain off and on for extended periods. Do not come in August. September good weather when not raining. Late September rains less than early."

So you have October and November to visit. October can be lovely, with temperatures in the low-twenties and blue skies. November starts to drop a bit, so morning can be a chilly 9 degrees, rising only to maybe 19. My training notes say, "October warm, no rain. November need light gloves, sweater, feels colder than it is (humidity)." But it can bucket down rain, you never know.

All this being said, I never went to Shanghai to enjoy the weather, I went for the training. I had to go when I had the chance, and so got to experience all the nasty variations on humidity.

19. **Temple Guard Pounds With The Pestle** (for the third time)

jǐn gāng dǎo duì   金刚捣碓

<u>Overall Movement</u>: Repeat Pound With The Pestle (moves 4 and 8), but dropping down without the double coiling.

<u>Footwork</u>: Drop back to pouncing stance, come through to high empty stance, lift the leg and stamp.

<u>Breakdown of Movement</u>:

Part One: Turn the upper body slightly left, turning the right fist over to face up. Turn right and draw the left foot in to a high empty stance. Place both fists to the right side of the body, quite high, fists obliquely facing in. Photo 19a.

Part Two: Tuck the left fist in to do an elbow strike (tuck the wrist in, flexing and *nichan*. *Nichan* the right forearm. Step the left foot forward and lower to a low pouncing stance, opening the hands to reach back a bit, pulling down as you step out. Photos 19b and c.

Part Three: Shift forward and bring the right foot ahead to a high empty stance, foot flat, touching the left hand to the right forearm as before in move 4. Photo 19d.

Part Four: Lift the right hand and foot. Do one flowering action instead of the triple coiling action. Land the right foot with a stamp, lifting the left foot to the right ankle and dropping the right fist directly to the left palm at the *dantian*. Photos 19e, 19f, and 19g.

<u>Direction of Movements</u>: You are facing south.

<u>Internal Connections</u>: As the right hand and right leg are lifted, settle the chest and back to keep the *yin-yang,* up-down, left-right balance.

20. Three Basins Lower To The Ground   sān pán luò dì   三盘落地

<u>Overall Movement</u>: Drop down and open the arms down to the knees.

<u>Footwork</u>: Drop to a slightly turned horse stance. This is one case where you may use the digging step. Touch the left foot's inside heel down lightly and push from the right leg to widen the step slightly.

<u>Breakdown of Movement</u>:

Drop the left foot out to the side to land directly into a horse stance. Open the arms, so the left hand strikes with a backhand just over the left knee and the right fist strikes with a backfist just over the right knee. Photo 20.

<u>Possible Applications</u>: Following from your right knee strike to the groin and/or foot stamp of the preceding move, step into the opponent with your left foot and take him down to the left.

<u>Internal Connections</u>: Connect the power through the arms. The main force is in the left hand, the right fist assists.

<u>About the Name</u>: The three basins of the body are the shoulder girdle, the hip girdle, and the lower legs. They are all lowered towards the ground, moving as one unit. *Luo* means land, or lower, not in the sense that the three basins actually touch the ground – you are just in a horse stance.

<u>Additional Comments</u>: Here is the posture from the side.

In the horse stance, close the knees and open the hip joints to round the crotch. The thighs are parallel to the ground, the shins vertical, the back flat, the upper back open, and the shoulders relaxed. The feet point forward, not out. It is important to settle into the hip joints, the roots of the thighs, to keep upright.

21. **Seven Inch Shoulder/Body Strike**   qī cùn kào   七寸靠

Overall Movement: Circle and drop to a pouncing stance, then shift forward to strike with the body and shoulder.

Footwork: Rise, then drop to a pouncing stance, then shift forward to the right leg.

Breakdown of Movement:

Part One: Rise in the stance and circle the arms up to each side, then down in front of the chest. Turn right during the upward circle so that forearms cross to the east. Turn back to face forward as the arms lower. The palms face in, the right on the inside. Photos 21a and 21b.

Part Two: Drop on the left leg to a pouncing stance and lower the whole body to touch the right shoulder to the ground. Keep the back flat. Photos of Cai Yuhua 21c and 21d.

Part Three: Shift forward to the right leg and move forward, keeping the shoulders down. Put power to the right side, especially the upper back and shoulder. Photo of Cai Yuhua 21e.

Possible Applications: In part one, rise and trap the opponent with the upper arms, driving him down to the ground in front of you.

The actual *kao* action is a strike with the right side, shoulder, or elbow, but is mostly thought of as a shoulder strike or throw. You need to move in tight to the opponent for this to work.

If you are low down and the opponent pushes down on your head or shoulders from the right side, put yourself into a stronger position by setting your torso on your right thigh, your leg reinforcing your body. If he is close enough to push you down, then your right leg is practically already inside his stance, close enough to move forward into him.

Yilu: The First Form

Internal Connections: Part one first opens and then contains the chest. Properly done, it creates the right internal alignment for the *fajin* in the next move as well as the *kao*.

About the Name: The upper body is supposed to pass seven inches from the ground as you come through. *Kao* is a strike with the body, anywhere from the lower ribs to the shoulder edge. It helps to think of the non-martial use of the word *kao*, which is to lean up against a wall. You can see that this is done by the ribs under the shoulder when you settle comfortably into the wall, although the shoulder also touches the wall. In the same way, the strike makes more contact with the body than the shoulder itself.

Additional Comments: If you can drop down and stay down as you come across easily, you may slide the elbows along the ground as you come across. You are supposed to at least touch your elbows to the ground, but the important thing is getting the hips down, the rest follows.

Cai Yuhua could sit right down and keep his chest on the ground as he came through. Not many people will have the flexibility in the hips and through the back and legs to do this. He may be made of rubber, though it may be the years and years of training.

If you cannot yet or are no longer able to do a drop stance, sit down well into the left leg. Lean the body appropriately to your stance height to find a solid line for the *kao*. Do not lean down to place your torso on your right leg if you are not in the full drop stance. The important factor is the alignment into the *kao*. The power comes through the body from the left leg.

Photos of alternate performance, setting to half horse stance and moving directly into an aligned *kao*.

22. **Ambush The Tiger**   fú hǔ shì   伏虎式

<u>Overall Movement</u>: Coil back and explode into both arms.

<u>Footwork</u>: Shift smoothly around and into an angled horse stance. The weight is a bit to the right leg, and both feet are turned a bit to the right.

<u>Breakdown of Movement</u>:

Part One: Continue to move forward, coming up and keeping the arms crossed. Turn the waist to the left, coiling the right forearm to keep it on the inside of the left. Keep the right wrist on the left hand throughout the circle. Photos 22a and 22b.

Part Two: Drive into the left heel, snap the hip, and shift to an angled horse stance to *fajin* into both fists. Punch the left fist to the left at chest height, the right fist by the right temple. Both fist centres are angled downwards. Keep the back straight. Photo 22c.

<u>Possible Applications</u>: Release a grab of the right arm, then maintain control of the hand that the opponent grabbed with, taking it out to the right. This allows you to punch with the left hand.

From a grab around your body from the rear, open out both arms to release the grip. This will only work if you explode suddenly, using your whole body power. If you turn slightly you may hit the opponent with your right elbow.

<u>About the Name</u>: This type of punch, with one fist up and the other down, is called Ambush The Tiger, or Hit The Tiger, in most kungfu styles. It brings to mind the stories of tiger fighters, and has a brave look. Although both hands move away from the body, the posture gives the feeling of the one arm holding the tiger while the other fist pounds away at it. This posture can also be thought of as taming your own tiger, or your vicious heart.

<u>Additional Comments</u>: If practising in dirt, the snap into the back heel for the punch will draw a *yin-yang* fish symbol in the dirt.

All *fajin* movements, not just this one, should be done calmly. You need to remain stable and centered in your heart in order to be stable and centered in your body. This posture, which opens up and out directly from the heart is the *fajin* that most clearly shows and works on this.

In China of the 1960s and 70s, you had it made if you were of a worker-peasant family, as was Cai Yuhua. This was partly why he had the audacity to let me stay at his house, which was illegal. (The other reason was that all Shanghainese hate government authority, so no neighbour would report.) His pedigree meant that he couldn't put a foot wrong. His father was a farmer, his step-mother had been a factory worker and was now a market-farmer. They still lived in the farmhouse (the actual land much reduced and separate from the house), and he worked in a factory not far from home. As a child of the revolution, born in 1949, his life was made easier by this worker/peasant background. He had spent a lot of time during the Cultural Revolution doing not much at all, since he was unassailable. He did not need to be 'sent to the countryside' or to 'prove his redness.' Factory workers spent a lot of time playing cards rather than taking part in political movements. His generation was one of the most politically cynical age cohorts that I know.

Throughout the 1980s he competed in Shanghai municipal wushu competitions and was a member of the Shanghai team for national amateur wushu meets. He won five gold medals with this Yilu, and was named one of the best martial artists of Shanghai six times (and Shanghai has a long history of martial arts excellence).

Because he won, he brought glory to his factory and the city, so would be given leave to prepare for competitions, and a full three months leave before each national competition. He'd spend that time training Taijiquan and Baguazhang for a couple of hours in the morning, then painting the rest of the day. His martial arts and painting were his way out from a hard life. He commented once, though, that after achieving prosperity he seemed to have less free time.

23. **Dislocate Bones And Separate Tendons** cuò gǔ fēn jīn 锉骨分筋

<u>Overall Movement</u>: Settle in the horse stance and open and coil to either side of the body three times.

<u>Footwork</u>: Stay in the horse stance, keep upright, roll in the waist, shifting weight only slightly. Be sure to maintain the figure eight coiling in the legs when shifting.

<u>Breakdown of Movement</u>:

Part One: Draw the right forearm across to the left and tuck the left fist in to the waist. Tuck the right fist in and take the right elbow out to hit to the right. Turn right and extend the right elbow. Then snake the right fist out to the right. Then snake the left fist out to the left, arm rolled under. Then roll the right fist in, then roll the left fist in. Then draw the left forearm across to the right and allow the left forearm to come to meet it naturally, so they end up pulling across to the right with the left forearm cutting. Photos 23a, 23b, 23c, 23d, and 23e.

Part Two: Tuck in the left elbow and turn to the left, to hit out with the left elbow. Snake out the left fist, then the right fist, both rolled under. Roll over the left fist then the right fist. Draw the right forearm across to the left, bringing the left fist to meet it. Draw across to the right. Photos 23f, 23g, 23h, 23i, and 23j.

Yilu: The First Form

Part Three: Tuck in the right elbow and turn to the right, to hit out with the right elbow. Snake out the right fist, then the left fist, both rolled under. Roll over the right fist then the left fist. Draw the left forearm across to the right, bringing the right fist to meet it. Draw across to the left. Photos 23k, 23l, 23m, 23n, and 23o.

Possible Applications: This is excellent training in dissolving controls. Once you have dissolved a grab, catch the opponent's arm and break his elbow with your forearm.

Internal Connections: The name refers to one of the three internal harmonies: harmonizing bones and tendons. Bones implies the frame, skeleton, or structure of the body. Tendons include tendons, ligaments, and connective tissue. Coordinating these allows the movements to be effective without relying on muscular strength. You are also working on deep suppleness of the tendons of your upper body during this movement.

About the Name: In this context *cuo* means to dislocate, and *fen* means divide, separate, or differentiate. So the intent is to twist the opponent to dislocate his joints, separating the ligaments of the joints, controlling him through pain.

Sometimes while doing this, one wonders whose tendons and bones are being dislocated and separated. Indeed, there is a phrase that describes a goal of the internal arts: 脱骨 *tuo gu*, that means to release the muscles from the bones such that the muscles slide freely with no obstructions. This is a goal in internal styles, that the *qi* and muscles move freely, as if released from the skeleton. The sort of twisting, twining action in this move helps to achieve this goal. The sound (*cuo* vs *tuo*) is quite similar, so there is a possibility that some of this meaning is intended.

Additional Comments: First hit with the elbow, fist centre facing up. Turn the body towards the elbow strike. Then roll the fists out at almost the same time, the opposite fist slightly first, when it can easily go out because the shoulder is rolled under when the body is turned away. Turn to the opposite fist, then to the fist that did the elbow strike.

An option during the forearm draw is bringing the other fist in to the waist instead of assisting with the forearm draw. It is less practical, but looks cool.

> This is a good time to discuss bones, muscles, and tendons. We train our Taijiquan to develop the body to move as a whole. The classic Western understanding of bones and muscles that operate separately and mechanically is not useful to us. More useful is an understanding of myofascial meridians that connect the bones, muscles, tendons, ligaments, and connective tissue throughout the body in a web from the ground to the head. The term myofascial refers to a unit comprised of muscle plus connective tissue. Instead of thinking of separate muscles, think of them as a unit: the connective tissue connects a chain of muscles together. If the muscles are viewed as floating in bags of connective tissue, all movements and all structures are possible through the interaction of the contracting muscle with the connecting tissue. Each muscle may exist alone, but the fascia permeates the entire body and connects the muscles like a net.

Bones, cartilage, ligaments, and tendons are built of varying degrees of the same substance – collagen. They transform and change shape and structure when stressed. Stressed the wrong way, in time the body can become deformed – the legs bowed, the back bowed, the shoulders hunched, etc. This is because when collagen is pulled continually out of alignment by poor posture and bad habits, it will eventually stay there. Correction is possible, if we work both the muscles and the fascia the right way in our Taijiquan. Training can rebuild the supporting structure and reopen the tissue. One of the goals of training is to reshape the body back to its natural, balanced, childlike state. The Chinese word *song*, which is normally translated as 'relax,' is more related to this process of opening and release than to 'relaxing.'

Muscles themselves do not attach to bones – they pull on fascia, which pull on the periosteum, which in turn pulls on the bone. We should look at our muscles as a long bag of muscle that touches down at some points along the line that goes through the whole body. This is how we work in training; we never try to isolate a muscle, even if we could.

> "There is only one muscle; it just hangs around in 600 or more fascial pockets."
>
> (Thomas W. Myers, *Anatomy Trains: Myofascial Meridians for Manual and Movement Therapists*, Churchill Livingstone, 2001, page 40. Get this book for details and drawings about this concept. Also, go to the website www.anatomytrains.com.)

The muscles and connective tissue are the lines of pull that are visible in the body (if you were to cut the body open and look at what is attached to the skeleton, you would see them). These myofascial meridians do not follow the exact lines of the Chinese *qi* meridians, which are an energetic connection, not visible. But the body is a relatively limited space – there cannot but be some overlap. Both can be described as an endless web. Unimpeded movement, sought in the Chinese internal martial arts, involves unblocked *qi* meridians and aligned myofascial meridians. Training Taijiquan unblocks both myofascial lines and *qi* lines.

The Chinese words *shun* (smooth, aligned) and *tong* (connected, communicating) refer to a combination of *qi* and myofascial clearness and alignment. The word *fangsong* (relax) is better translated as 'release.' *Fang* means to let go, release, set free. *Song* is to loosen, unfasten. Together, they should be seen as releasing unwanted tension to allow the mind and body to move freely – to release stress in the mind, release tension in the body in order to expand, settle, and move easily. If you relax too much, caving in, you prevent yourself from letting Taijiquan change your body using the fascial reshaping.

24. **Bend And Hit With The Back**   bèi zhé kào   背折靠

Overall Movement: Coil the body to strike with the torso, shoulder, and elbow.

Footwork: Shift, then set into a very turned stance with the left foot, knee, body, and both elbows all on one line.

Breakdown of Movement:

Part One: After drawing the left forearm across, shift to the left and draw the right hand up, around, and down to the left knee. Bring the left hand diagonally across the body from the right shoulder to the left hip. Photos 24a and 24b.

Part Two: Curl the left wrist down and fingers up, then curl the wrist around to the front to place the fist on the hip. Draw the right elbow up. Shift to the right leg and turn the left hip and foot in. Align the left foot, left knee, left elbow, and right elbow. The right forearm is *nichan* to put pressure outward. The right forearm is relaxed, so that power is not drawn away from the elbow and body strike. This means that the elbow is not bent acutely. The forearm completes its action horizontal to the ground, not tucked in to the upper arm. Turn the hip into the hit, turning the left heel. Look down past the left foot. Photos 24c, 24d, and 24e.

Direction of Movements: The overall feeling is of facing south, but the alignment of the left foot to right elbow is east to west.

Possible Applications: Strike with the back, shoulder, or elbow. You must be very close for this to work. If the opponent grabs your body or around your neck from the back then he will be close enough for you to strike without stepping into him. You may start out by trying to hit him with your elbow. Then, if he blocks that by grabbing your elbow, he leaves himself open to your strike with your upper back/ shoulder/ high rib area.

Internal Connections: As you roll the right hand into a fist, start with the little finger, flexing the wrist in that direction. Continue to flex the wrist to make a small circle before drawing across and up. This sends the power up to the right back, setting up for the back, shoulder, or elbow strike.

In Part Two, the coiling and alignment of the left leg and right arm guides the flow of *qi* into the upper right area of the back and up to the right elbow. Put pressure into the outer back edge of the left calf to direct force up to the right back and elbow. The elbows are aligned so that the power is connected between them, drawing a line through your upper body and binding the whole body together as a unit in the final posture.

About the Name: *Bei* is often translated as upper back, and people sometimes think is means just between the shoulder blades. It actually includes almost the entire back, the shoulders, in between the shoulders, and the lower ribs down to, but not including, the waist. You can strike very strongly with the side of the body just behind and under the armpit, if you bend your body and form a strong flat surface.

Additional Comments: Make sure the left fist is formed before the strike so that the fist can travel forward a bit and you can use the left elbow to strike as well with the body turn. Keep the wrist straight and the fist set into the ribs.

This can also be done with a hip turn into the strike then a relaxation. In this case, the final position is an open *hengdangbu* stance with the left foot straight instead of turned in.

Here is a photo of the final posture from the side.

Do not forget that the final posture is the photo op of a move. If the action is done properly, the technique has already been completed, the opponent is long gone. In Aikido this is the fun part of looking at your partner on the floor and being in balance, looking good. It is how you get to the final posture that is important – the action opens your channels; the action is the practical application. Find the posture by moving into it and out of it, not by fixing yourself in place. It is more helpful to practise slowly, feeling the changes on the cellular level, than to hold stances for long periods of time.

> Chen Xin wrote (page 176), "When practising your form, when your heart/mind is free of all attachments you have the most clarity. In this way your chest contains everything, but all outside interference is emptiness."

This is the same advice given me by my martial eldest brother, Cheng Jiefeng, in different words and different context. We lived and trained in what were still the outskirts of Shanghai in the 1990s. Any time I rode my bike downtown I would take days to recover from the noise and craziness. The extraordinarily loud and harsh truck horns (why use brakes when you have a perfectly good horn?) made me jump out of my skin. Fist fights would break out at traffic lights. Cyclists and drivers did not shoulder check, ever. One day I mentioned I had a sore throat and headache because of a recent trip into town, Cheng said, simply, "Don't let it in."

At first this seemed impossible, even dangerous, considering how alert you needed to be to survive in traffic, but it was the best advice, which I have applied ever since. It is actually quite a deep *qigong* skill; to be aware of what is going on (so as not to get hit in traffic) but not let it disturb you. I think this ability has been more useful in self-defense against external aggression than any defense-against-people aggression involved in the martial arts.

When I trained with them in the 1990s, Cheng Jiefeng and Cai Yuhua did the best Chen Taijiquan I have ever seen. Cheng Jiefeng's was an ideal mix of softness and heaviness. Cai Yuhua's was a just as ideal mix of twisty and athletic. Both were too good for me to emulate, but that didn't stop me trying. My own developed in between the two; soft and heavy, but twisty as well. It was athletic, but nowadays hopefully has some other redeeming feature.

Yilu: The First Form

25. **Three Urgent Hits**   jí sān chuí   三疾捶

<u>Overall Movement</u>: Strike with the right fist, left palm, and right fist.

<u>Footwork</u>: Shift left, step the left foot over and step the right foot forward.

<u>Breakdown of Movement</u>:

Part One: Shift a bit to the left. Bring the right elbow up as if someone were pushing on it, forcing it into your head – go along with that line of action. Bring the right fist in to the chest with the fist heart facing up. Start to slide the right fist along the body along to the right (west) with the little finger side on top. Photos 25a and 25b.

Part Two: Stay on the left leg, turn the upper body to the right, snake the right arm out to the west with the little finger side on top. Set to almost a horse stance. Low punch the right fist to the west with the fist eye down, almost twisted over to the top. Turn the body so the punch is almost behind. Place the left palm on the *dantian*. Do not *fajin*. Photo 25c.

Part Three: Roll the body back from its twist. Bring the left hand over the right forearm to control or slap down. Bring the right arm back in front of the body, close in, turning the body well to the left to bring the arm through before the backfist. Step the left foot through, turned out to kick (you may also stamp after the kick). Step the right foot forward to horse stance and do a right high backfist, with the left fist guarding the groin. The right index finger is extended to the second joint with the thumb supporting it. This is a light, flicking *fajin*. Photos 25d, 25e, 25f, 25g, 25h, and 25i.

Direction of Movements: The strikes move to the west.

Possible Applications: Get out of a grab to your elbow, or pressure into your upper back/shoulder, which will come if your previous attack is not successful. Go along with the line that the opponent is pushing, to draw him further towards you, weakening his ability to push. Bring your right fist in onto your body so that he cannot control it even if he is holding onto it. Then drive the right fist in to his body. Then use your left hand to scrape off any further attempt to control your right fist. Follow through with a flick to the temple or eye. The right hand should stay on the body as much as possible throughout, to practice the ability to send out a strike from a caught position.

Internal Connections: Keep the right fist pressed to the body both on the way down and on the way up. Press the left hand onto the right arm and slide it down, creating a pressure between the right fist and the left hand, until the last instant. This stimulates points all along the arm. The backfist pops out from a release of this pressure.

About the Name: These strikes are a result of being caught in a disadvantageous position. That is why they are 'urgent.' The first strike slides along the line of power from someone grabbing and pushing the elbow. The left hand slides along the right arm to release it, then the right hand can manage a stronger strike.

Additional Comments: From here to move 27 the shifting and stepping is constant. Do not focus so much on the intricate hand movements that you forget to pay attention to the legs. In any stance where the weight is on the rear leg, the leading leg must not pass the heel. When stepping, always lift from the hip. When moving within a stance, always coil in the legs, drawing an infinity symbol (∞) around the edges of the feet. When pushing or punching forward, force comes from the pressure put into the rear calf, which turns the heel and settles the hip.

Yilu: The First Form

26. Punch Into The Dens   wō lǐ pào   窝里炮

<u>Overall Movement</u>: Draw back and advance to a double punch to the ears or armpits.

<u>Footwork</u>: Stay in place or bring the left foot in beside the right.

<u>Breakdown of Movement</u>:

Part One: Bring the right fist in to the left palm at the waist, dropping back to swallow the hands in to the body, right fist nestled in left palm. Photo 26a.

Part Two: Open the hands and raise them, *nichan* both and extend to the front, clenching to fists in the strike the ears position. Photo 26b.

<u>Direction of Movements</u>: You are still moving west.

<u>Possible Applications</u>: Cover an attack then double strike to the ears. The strike is quicker if it travels inside the attacker's arms, so keep the line of attack ellipsoid, not circular. It can, obviously, also be a strike into the armpits of the opponent, should he have raised his arms to deal with your previous attack.

<u>Internal Connections</u>: The power for this strike is generated by a closing movement in the chest and upper back. When doing opening and closing actions within the torso, be careful not to overdo the rounding of the upper back. Do the movement from inside the body, so the 'chest' and 'back' are reacting to that, rather than doing the action with the 'chest' or 'back.' This results in a crisp *fajin*.

<u>About the Name</u>: Because of the shortcuts of the Chinese language, Punch Into The Dens is just one possible translation. *Wo* means a depression, and is used for armpit, groin, or ears – basically any depression in the body. If you take that meaning and consider the height of the punches, then the name can also mean it was a strike into the ears or armpits of the opponent.

Sometimes movement names refer to your body action rather than the applications. So, if you take the original meaning of *wo*, then it can mean to strike by sucking the body in, effectively making the whole torso into a depression. This is the action done for the strike.

Wo means 'den,' so punching 'within a den' also emphasizes how the elbows must stay tucked in. The line taken by the fists is quite tight for a double hit, as if fighting in restricted surroundings like a den.

Cai Yuhua had started training when he was nine, in the Shaolin style, and had a good reputation. He's a good fighter, and had a good group of people training with him. (He actually was asked during the 1980s to work towards the development of the new fighting rules of *Sanda*, as a fighter, coach, and referee.)

One day, one of his students brought along a friend, a big guy. He wanted to learn wushu, too. Trouble was, he was as dull and slow as he was big. But he was eager, so Cai sent him off to one side to lift up a big rock. It was so big he had to spread his legs and sort of sit and embrace it to get his arms around it. He was happy to be with his friend, and be training like the others, so he lifted that rock every day for hours. After he had been there a while, they got used to him lifting his rock in the corner and didn't really think about it. They practiced their forms and fighting and he lifted his rock. Afterwards they would all go together for tea or something and he was one of the club.

One day, after a few months of this, a challenger came looking for Cai. He'd heard, as fighters do, that Cai was good. Cai didn't like fighting that much, and thought the guy looked like a jerk. He just didn't want to bother. He thought he could scare the guy away with his big student (he was really big). So he said, go fight my student in the corner, if you can beat him maybe I'll fight you. The guy was game, went over and challenged the student. "What do I do?" He'd never fought before, just lifted a rock. "Just grab him like you've practiced" So he did. He just picked up the guy and held on. They were so busy laughing they didn't notice the guy turning blue. They had to take him to the hospital to resuscitate him.

I don't know if the moral is that you should never underestimate anyone, or that if you learn one technique and learn it well, you're better off than someone who's learned a hundred.

Yilu: The First Form

27. Green Dragon Shoots Out Of The Water   qīng lóng chū shuǐ
青龙出水

<u>Overall Movement</u>: Bring the hands back to the *dantian* then strike with the right, left, and then a right backfist.

<u>Footwork</u>: If you did not bring the left foot in during the last strike, do so now, and then step the right foot forward.

<u>Breakdown of Movement</u>:

Part One: *Shunchan* the arms and bring the hands back to the *dantian*, right fist settling into the left palm. Bring the left foot up to stamp as the hands hit, and lift the right foot by the left ankle. Photo 27a.

27a 27b

Part Two: Step the right foot forward to a horse stance and punch the right fist forward (west), doing a slicing strike (*nichan*) to hit with the heel of the fist, fist centre down. Bring the left hand back to the *dantian*, striking the body. Photo 27b.

Part Three: Turn the upper body right, reach the left hand out over the right arm, keeping the elbow down and the action fairly tight. Bring the right fist up inside the left arm then hit forward with a backfist (*shunchan*) (to the right, on line with the stance). Photos 27c and 27d.

27c   27d

<u>Direction of Movements</u>: You are still travelling and striking to the west.

<u>Possible Applications</u>: Advancing multiple control and attack, alternating low and high strikes. Move in during the controlling action and strike when you are close enough. If, on the first low strike, the opponent tries to trap your right arm, cover his hand with your left hand to release his grip and enable you to punch again with the right fist.

<u>Internal Connections</u>: The movements of the upper body need to be smooth and relentless. Any tension in the chest, shoulders, arms or hands will block and disrupt the flow of the movement, resulting in jerky movements 'unbecoming of a dragon' (that is James' phrase, he has such a nice way with words). Be aware of the *nichan* and *shunchan* feeding off each other to transform from one punch to the other.

About the Name: This multiple punch, or just the last low punch to the side in horse stance, is traditionally called Green Dragon Shoots Out Of The Water in many styles. It should be done with the feeling of a dragon, fierce and unstoppable. The colour *qing* means a natural colour, so is variously translated as green, blue or black.

Additional Comments: The last two hits are done in quick succession, breathe out, in, and out, and do three slaps on the body in quick and even rhythm. When you hit with the right fist, slap the left palm on the belly. When you block over with the left palm, slap the right back of wrist on the right ribs. When you hit with the right backfist, slap the left hand on the right ribs.

Practise slowly to get the circles correct, then do with *fajin*. The *fajin* makes it feel even more like a dragon, arriving with a rush of sound and fury. As always, the slow movement is to find and develop the lines of power, balance, and elasticity through the body, so that fast movement is unimpeded. As a martial art, slowness, in and of itself, is not the goal of Taijiquan, but is a necessary process.

> *Yin* and *yang* need to remain balanced throughout the body, always, in every single move and action, never one without the other. *Yin* and *yang* need to interact with each other – not mutually opposing, but mutually co-existing and assisting. *Yin* and *yang* each wax and wane, constantly transforming, and constantly flowing from a bit more emphasis on one, then the other. With the proper understanding of *yin* and *yang* in the body, then hard and soft, open and closed, empty and substantial, light and settled, fast and slow, left and right, above and below, inner and outer linkages, moving forward and moving backward, etc. each assist each other, constantly changing in a balanced way.
>
> The moves do this for you, that is what they are there for. You cannot think of all this all the time. The most you can do is watch it happen, notice when it doesn't, and try to correct that place next time.

> One of my teachers made an odd remark once, when talking about animal metaphors. He said that it was hard to think of copying a lion because most people hadn't really seen one, but that everyone knew what dragons looked like.
>
> That is perhaps why lion actions in the Chinese martial arts often copy the ball playing actions of the traditional lion dance that is performed on festive occasions. And since 'everyone knows what dragons look like,' dragons are always a handy metaphor to use. This says something about Chinese culture, though I don't know quite what.

Yilu: The First Form

28. **Cast Away And Hit**   piē shēn chuí   撇身捶

<u>Overall Movement</u>: Turn and open to either side with the fists.

<u>Footwork</u>: Turn from a horse stance facing south to a bow stance facing east. Snap the hips and heels back.

<u>Breakdown of Movement</u>:

Part One: Draw the right fist in towards the body, coiling the fist centre up. Clench and extend the left hand to the right elbow, turning the fist centre down. Cross the arms with a clear action of scraping off, quite close together. Photo 28a.

Part Two: Draw the forearms past each other, simultaneously turning the right fist centre down and the left fist centre up. Turn to face east, shifting to a bow stance. Strike with the left fist to the east, at head height. Simultaneously strike with the right fist to the west, behind the body, at chest height. Photo 28b.

<u>Possible Applications</u>: Clear a grab of either arm and strike. The power goes through the body, so it can be a strike with both or either arms. It may also be an escape from a hug, with expanding force in all directions.

<u>Internal Connections</u>: The *qi* should settle firmly into the *dantian* in Part One so that the expansion in Part Two can be evenly guided through the limbs. Left and right as well as upper and lower body needs to remain balanced during the strike.

<u>About the Name</u>: This is a strong action that is meant to cast off any grab of the opponent.

Another traditional name for a similar move is 庇身捶 *bishenchui*, which means to protect the body, with the same idea that the arms protect the body in all directions.

<u>Additional Comments</u>: In the final posture the arms are quite extended, on line with the legs, to east and west. The torso faces almost east.

This is one of the moves in our style that appear unusual and awkward until you understand within your body how to use the body to gather and release energy through the coiling of the whole body. To be able to perform a *fajin* while turning from a horse stance to a bow stance, you have to have mastered the coiling in the legs, the push into the rear calf, the adjustment of the hips, the attachment through the torso, closing and opening of the chest, the rolling of the shoulders, and the coiling of the arms. The coiling looks a little extreme to practitioners of more sedate Chen styles, and has to be well done indeed to not break Taijiquan rules.

> The sequence of moves from 25 through 28 shows the natural springiness of your body.
>
> Each person has a different speed and degree of oscillation within them. The oscillation gives a natural rebound, like different balls bounce, bounce, and gradually settle down. This sequence of moves, which feeds on the oscillations to continue and grow, is natural at varying speeds. If you catch the oscillation before it settles down, you can connect the series very quickly and easily (like giving a little push to a bouncing ball to bring it back up). This is used throughout the form to link moves from within the body. If you let each *fajin* die down, you start again at the beginning on each one. Which method to use is a matter partly of personal preference and partly of skill level.
>
> Also, you do not have to do the whole series of moves 25 through 28 with *fajin*, you may do fast, slow, fast, slow, whatever feels right at the time.

> When thinking of the possible applications of the movements during the form, the tradition is to think of four or five types of application.
>
> One, striking: with hands, arms, or body.
>
> Two, leg techniques: kicks include straight swings (*ti*), swings (*bai*), hooks (*gou*), snaps (*tan*), sweeps (*sao*), and entrapments (*gua*), among others.
>
> Three, throws: take down or throw with any part of the body, using leverage.
>
> Four, joint locks: control or take down with any part of the body, using pain to joints.
>
> Five: pressure points, usually with fine control using fingers, but not necessarily (sometimes included within type four).
>
> These groupings are not mutually exclusive. That is, a throw can, and usually does, combine arm strikes, body and leg techniques. Do not let yourself get trapped by the name of the movement into thinking that is 'what it is' or 'what it does.' Almost all movements have at least three types of applications, and usually have a variety of each of them. In Taijiquan, there is an emphasis on dissolving oncoming attacks, and in connecting your defense and your attack closely. But I still think that the essential categories stand.
>
> It is also important to remember that the hips, knees, shoulders, and elbows can be used, either as a setup for the final technique, or as a close range finish of a technique. Most moves have this hidden within them.

29. **Double Push**   shuāng tuī shǒu   双推手

Overall Movement: Step forward and push with both hands.

Footwork: Step the right foot forward to a bow stance.

Breakdown of Movement:

Part One: Turn right, roll the right shoulder over to extend the fist further to the west. Allow the left shoulder to roll over as well, but the right is the main side. Look at the right hand. Turn completely to a bow stance facing west. This transitional position is almost the same as the previous posture except that the rear arm is a bit more rolled over.

Part Two: Uncoil the shoulders, pivot on the left heel, and bring the arms through. Step the right foot forward to the east. Coil the hands in a high opening block that ends with them tucked in front of the chest. Settle into the right hip, and then push into a bow stance, pushing the hands to the east. Photos 29a, 29b, and 29c.

Direction of Movements: Push to the east.

Possible Applications: Release from a grab, uproot and push the opponent away.

Internal Connections: Find a strong line from the rear heel to the hands through the middle of your body, expanding into the rear calf and the hands, rather than just shifting forward.

About the Name: This name is straightforward, it is a double push. You need to move in and gain control of the opponent for this to work. You put him into an uncomfortable, unbalanced position by drawing him back and forth (perhaps levering his elbows) before stepping in for the final push.

Additional Comments: Twist the arms fairly directly into the block/push in part two, using the waist to twist the arms.

> There are many different types of names.
>
> Straightforward naming of the action or posture (Double Push, Brush Knee Counter Stance, Double Chop).
>
> Names that use common martial terminology that outsiders might not understand (Three Basins Lower To The Ground, Swaying Lotus).
>
> Descriptive names using the actions of animals (White Goose Flashes Its Wings, Wild Horse Tosses Its Mane, Wild Monkey Presents Fruit).
>
> Names that call on a common cultural heritage to suggest the feeling of the posture (Temple Guard Pounds With The Pestle, Ambush The Tiger, Needle At Sea Bottom).
>
> Names that give clues to the posture from a more common action (High Pat On Horse, Brace The Roofbeam, Throw The Shuttle).
>
> Names that tell the application (Hit To The Groin, Sweep The Shin And Double Strike).
>
> In all cases, they are intended to help you remember, so are succinct. A name is two, three, or four characters long.

One weekend in the mid 1980s we went with a friend to a small park to meet some masters in his nearby park. He lived in one of the traditional downtown *shikumen* houses, which was very cool for me to visit. Then they decided we'd go further downtown to People's Park to meet some more masters. In those years the parks were still full of people practising wushu early in the morning. Later, ballroom dancing became a popular park activity. Still later, exercises done to loud music came along.

One Xingyi master explained to us how Xingyiquan's chicken should be done with the rooster's crowing – at full volume, complete with head bobs. Everyone seemed to find this quite normal.

Because it was Sunday, training didn't stop at seven. I learned that in some respects there was more freedom in China than Canada. Our friend had on his pyjamas, because he'd planned on just going down to his local park. I think in Canada he might have been arrested in pj's at noon on a downtown bus. I'm not too sure about the rooster man crowing in the park, either.

30. See The Fist Under The Elbow   zhǒu dǐ kàn quán   肘底看拳

Overall Movement: Grab and move forward to empty stance with the hands in an on guard position, the right fist under the left elbow.

Footwork: Pivot the right foot out then step the left foot through to a high empty stance.

Breakdown of Movement:

Part One: Sit back and pull back (*lü*) to full extent, then roll the right arm under (*nichan*) to roll the palm up in front (east). Photo 30a.

Part Two: Turn the right foot out, pivoting on the heel. Coil the right hand around, palm up. Bring the left hand across so that the two perform a *cai*. Photo 30b.

Part Three: Step the left foot forward to a high empty stance or 70/30 stance to the east. Drop the right elbow and continue to roll the hand into fist. Reverse the direction of the coil so that it coils over similar to during Pound the Pestle. Bring the left palm down in front, upright, with the palm facing obliquely inward. The left hand also coils around a bit to place it upright. In the final posture the right fist is under the left elbow. Photo 30c.

Direction of Movements: You are facing east.

Possible Applications: Grab and pull, roll over with a control. The final posture is the completion of the control. You are holding the opponent's elbow and hand, so twist it over, finishing with the left hand pressing above his elbow, rolling it over, and your right hand holding his hand, bending the wrist sharply.

   The movement can also be done as a simple brush aside and punch to the ribs, but you have to be really close to your opponent for that to work. The final posture can also be an on guard and preparation to hit forward.

Internal Connections: The internal feeling is the same as the Gathering In.

About the Name: This is kind of an amusing name. The fist is under the elbow, but it is hidden so you can't see it.

Additional Comments: This may also be done with the right fist on the left forearm, the back of the fingers lightly touching, ready to punch out over top of the left forearm.

Here is the final posture from a slightly different angle.

How to cook Shanghai spareribs. Get a nice rack of spareribs, cut between the ribs so they are all separate. Braise them in the wok, high temperature, to brown the meat. Give it a quick shot of soy sauce, so it goes 'sssstt,' which seals the flavour on the outside and browns the meat. Then add water and simmer for at least two hours. Bring the heat up again and add sugar and cook at high until it caramelizes. Give it a quick shot of Chinese dark vinegar at the end, keeping it on high so the vinegar evaporates – this takes away some of the sweetness.

I think the Shanghai style of cooking is due to the type of fuel available. It is not possible to do a quick Cantonese stir fry on a roaring flame. Shanghai food is *'shao,'* not *'chao.' Shao* involves a bit of a quick fry at the beginning to sear in the flavour, then a little water and covered simmer. With the coal briquettes, twigs and grass, you couldn't develop that much heat. This type of cooking is well suited to electric stoves, which never get hot enough for Cantonese stir fry, so my home cooking style is definitely Shanghai based. I also like the little bit of sweet added to the salty, well suited to Canadians' love for maple syrup.

Western innovations: braise the meat in the wok, then use a slow cooker for the two hours simmering, which keeps the juices in better, and needs less watching. Then let it set a bit to take some of the fat off the top, and then add the sugar (or better yet, maple syrup). Take the meat out of the slow cooker and back into a hot wok for the final shot with the vinegar.

Yilu: The First Form

31. Backup Twisting The Arms   dào niǎn hóng   倒念肱

<u>Overall Movement</u>: Step back three times while rolling the arms, connecting the movement from the feet all the way through the body.

<u>Footwork</u>: Step back three times, pressing into the leading foot to send power into each arm for the technique on each roll.

<u>Breakdown of Movement</u>:

Part One: Turn the body right, bring the right hand into the waist, then open it to the rear, palm down, then up, arms forming a straight line east to west. Then tuck the right hand into the jaw. Tuck in by continuing to coil the arm so that the hand circles out and continues to roll, coming in to the ear by pressing out, so that it is already starting to press forward. Do not simply bend the elbow to bring the hand in. Photos 31a, 31b, and 31c.

Part Two: Turn the body left to face east, step the left foot back with a circular step. Push the right hand forward in front of the nose, fingers pointing up. Twist the arm into the push – start a bit turned out into the heel of the palm and then coil to a vertical palm. Both arms are doing a *nichan*. Bring the left hand into the waist, palm up, then back to shoulder height, gradually turning the palm down. The pulling back hand starts out palm up, gradually turning palm down at least as it passes by the hip. Reposition the right foot straight. Put pressure to the outside, the little finger edge of the forearm. Do not turn the head to look at the back hand, keep focused on the leading hand. Photos 31d and 31e.

Part Three: When both hands have arrived in their final positions with the palms vertical, you may start coiling into the next side repetition. Step the right foot back in a circular step. Both feet point forward (east), you do not need to reposition their direction. Bring the left hand in to the jaw then push forward. Coil it around, do not just bend the elbow to bring the hand in. The 'coiling out' goes to the extreme limit so that it becomes 'coiling in.' Coil the hand in towards the jaw before pushing forward, chopping in with the palm edge, do not release pressure. Coil the front hand forward as if to grab before starting to pull it back. Photos 31f, 31g, and 31h.

Part Four: Step the left foot back in a circular step, keeping both feet pointing forward, with no need to reposition the direction. Coil the right hand in then push forward, coil the left hand then pull back. On this last pull back, do not follow all the way through, but stop the hand at the waist. Photos 31i, 31j, 31k, 31l, and 31m.

Direction of Movements: The stepping moves backwards, westward.

Possible Applications: The first part of the form up to the first Travelling Hands concentrates on power flow. The coiling energy of this movement is quite intricate. You need to focus completely on finding the power flow from the feet to the hands, pressing from the feet, and opening and closing the body. You will repeat this movement again later in the form.

Yilu: The First Form

<u>Internal Connections</u>: The coiling must come through the whole body from the press of the foot into both arms equally. The waist turns first toward the rear hand, then straight, and then take the step. Sit back into the rear hit, then shift to a midpoint, then push up with the lead foot into the coiling. The heel raises, but because the foot is pushed into the ground, not because of a lifting action – think of pushing on the pedals of a bike – you push down just behind the ball of the foot.

When the power stretches across the upper back to the hands a circle is created so that you exert power in all directions. If you only exert power in one direction you are unstable. If you exert power in all directions you are stable.

It is important to be able to keep good power through the body whilst retreating, and to not become flustered. Practising this move will help you figure out how to draw someone into your power whilst seeming to retreat.

<u>About the Name</u>: The character 念 *nian* is probably written wrong, due to oral transmission. It should probably be 捻 *nian*, meaning to twist, pluck, or nip with the fingers, as it is in move 83. There is another *nian*, written 黏, which means to adhere to, which also makes sense to the move, keeping the arms stuck to the opponent. Some branches of Chen style use the character 卷 *juan* here, meaning rolling arms, and this name is descriptive of what you are doing.

The word in our list, 念 *nian*, just means to remember or think of. Martial artists were often nearly illiterate, so might just pick the character they knew for a certain sound. They probably knew what they meant, and didn't think that their choice of character would be passed on with the meaning perhaps forgotten.

Hong means the upper arms. Chen Xin and others write *hong* as 红, which means 'red,' and which is said to mean 'a silk thread,' so again suggests the coiling action, suggesting the silk reeling. Then again, 红 was maybe just an easier character to write. In addition, 肱 *hong* also means the upper leg in Chen village dialect, so the original meaning may be to retreat by rolling the legs. The retreating action is not directly to the rear, but the legs move in and out, curling and rolling back.

<u>Additional Comments</u>: The pushing-forward hand has the fingers pointing up. This keeps the elbow sunken and keeps balance for the throw.

Follow the line of the middle finger of the forward hand to see what line the power of the whole body is taking. The tip of the middle finger should draw a circle on each change of direction. The same should be happening with the rear hand.

I originally learned this with a circle step with no drag, and slightly open stance, sinking back into the heel with a push. Later I also learned it as a dragging circular step back with a *fajin* as the foot lands.

The actions are normally done with each hand coiling on its respective side. The rolling may also be done by bringing the rear hand around to meet the leading hand in front, then pressing apart at the same time, so that both palms face down right away. This is a good example of the feeling called 'the tiger's mouths talk to each other' that is in many moves – the thumb and forefinger webs are stretched and facing each other. When concentrating on double pressure, it is easier to get the control and timing this way.

Here are photos from the front and side.

Chen Xin's illustration shows the movement much as we do it. It seems strange to other schools of Chen style, who do not twist, push into the foot to lift the heel, or seek out the angled arms. He does it with a lean, as well. While we have a leaning sort of power, we tend to keep the back straight.

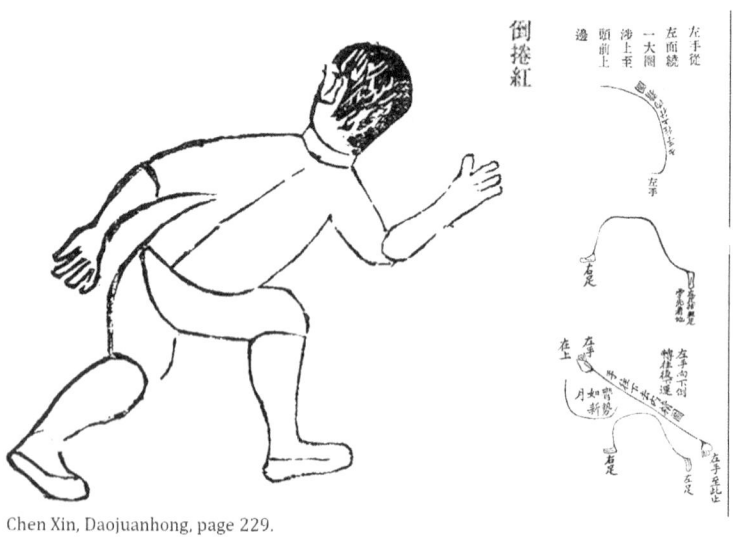

Chen Xin, Daojuanhong, page 229.

Yilu: The First Form

32. **White Goose Flashes Its Wings** (for the second time) bái é liàng chì 白鹅亮翅

<u>Overall Movement</u>: The same as move 9, starting out from a different posture.

<u>Breakdown of Movement</u>:

Part One: On the last push, don't follow through, but continue on to grasp and slice up. Shift a little forward as you circle the arm, then shift to the left as you slice up.

Part Two: Continue on the same as move 9. You may do the right backhand (photo 32h) as a *fajin*. Photos 32a, 32b, 32c, 32d, 32e, 32f, 32g, 32h, 32i, 32j, 32k, 32l, 32m, 32n, 32o, and 32p.

<u>Internal Connections</u>: When the crossed forearms come towards the chest, the body does a fairly extreme closing of the chest and opening of the upper back in order to bring the hands in and then out without losing power. This

trains the ability to press outwards with the hands and forearms while they are moving inwards. The push from the right foot drives this power.

Complete the push through the rear leg before stepping it or lifting it, so that the connection to the hands is not lost.

Possible Applications: The raised knee can be a simultaneous knee strike and palm strike or forearm press. But because the main angle of attack is in the other direction, it is more likely a strength and balance training. It also accentuates that you do not need the rear leg in contact with the ground to apply force to the opponent once you have moved the right foot in.

Coming down from the raised knee can be an elbow control with the right arm, or pulling the opponent off balance and striking down on his back with the point of the right elbow. The left foot can assist in putting the opponent off balance.

When the left hand curls in, it traps an opponent's attack to your head and the right snakes out along his arm to strike his face or neck. The right hand then immediately grabs his neck or hooks onto his trapezius, to pull down, with both hands. The left hand grabs his hand or wrist after defending. You may also trap his hand on your shoulder with your left hand, then coil your right elbow over his arm to do a wrist lock.

Step left and get the opponent off balance by pulling down, then step right to move in tight and then take the opponent over backwards, stepping in and controlling with the outside of the right arm, or if very close, with the left arm. In this case keep hold with the right hand and let go with the left. Place the left arm on the opponent's chest and over his right shoulder/neck. Circling the left hand up high will control his body with the arm (similar to Aikido's *iriminage*). This works better if you have pulled the opponent well down first.

If the opponent is not down yet, then he is pushed directly down at the solar plexus. when you step further forward into the *kaibu*.

Closing and opening controls the opponent's arms and opens his elbows to throw his arms over, crossed, throwing him off balance ready for the follow up, which is the knee attack and push.

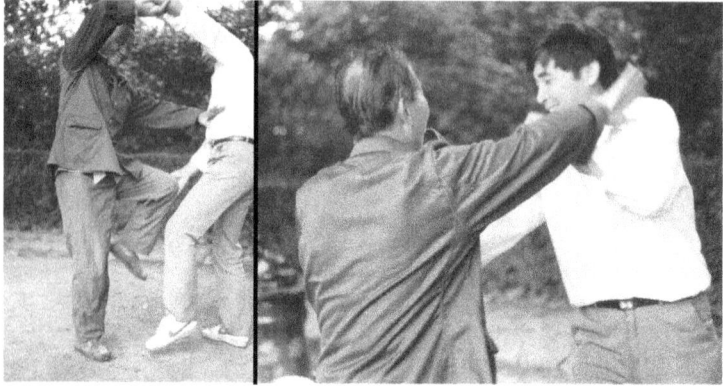

Yilu: The First Form

When this movement follows Wild Horse, lure the opponent in by seeming to withdraw further.

<u>Additional Comments</u>: If you *fajin* for the backhand slap, the timing with the leg action is slightly different than when you don't. You should be back upright as you *fajin*, getting some push from the legs, but not using the whole rise.

Despite the personal nature of how exactly the actions are done, you should never try to put your personality into the form. The process of finding the perfect actions and feeling is the process of taking away, not putting in. Any attempt on your part to 'do' something can only destroy the purity of Yilu. Only when you are no longer there as a person are you fully there in the moment of performance. Adding in twizzles in your body or mind takes you further from the root. Watch yourself throughout the form as an interested bystander.

If you think that you look cool or that the actions are cool, that is still impersonal. Having a personal way of doing the form is natural and unavoidable, and is why we try so hard to copy exactly what our teacher says. This is not the same as trying to express yourself through the form.

Getting it right will change you in ways that you cannot imagine, so you need to back off your 'self' and allow this to happen. And getting it right entails quite a lot. I have read a list of an astounding fifty things that can go wrong, and their corrections.

Cai Yuhua's step-mother would spend hours cleaning up the vegetables she sold, peeling off the outside bits of spring onions and making all the vegetables look good before taking them to the market. She said they sold quicker if they were clean. The vegetables grown in Shanghai's poor soil were so small that it took her forever. I guess hours spent at home were better than hours at the market with a few sad bundles of spring onions. I swear we ate the bean stalks after she had sold the beans, which is the most inedible vegetable known to humankind. All I could do was chew until I figured I wanted something else, then swallow it whole.

33. **Brush Knee Counter Stance** (for the sixth time, the second non-alternative style)　　lōu xī ào bù　　　　　　　　搂膝拗步

Overall Movement:

This is the same as move 10. See photos 10a through 10h. Photos 33a and 33b also show the completion into stance.

Possible Applications: This works well as a throw or a strike. Step in close to control the opponent's knee or any handy part with the left arm, then draw the right arm across his body to throw.

If the opponent is not quite taken down, keep the right hand on his chest and coil to return to push again. Keep the movement small, keep power in the forearms, readjust the power within the body to change the direction of power application in the arms.

It can also be a strike that works its way in gradually, and seemingly quite softly, so that the opponent is not expecting such a hard strike from no apparent wind-up. In this case, brush his arms aside to place the right hand near his heart, readjust without seeming to, and give a sudden shock to the heart area. This should not be done in just a sparring match, because if done properly, the speed of the strike, more than the strength, can stop the heart.

Additional Comments: When pushing, the force comes from the pressure put into the rear calf. Do not fully straighten the rear knee, but put force into the belly of the calf. This drives the heel into the ground and drives power up through the body to the point of contact. Sometimes this will push the rear heel back, especially when doing a *fajin*. In the final stance, the rear knee is bent, but it is in the process of extending, not of flexing. The power is expanding, not collapsing. Tuck in the coccyx. The tucked position transfers power from the rear heel and calf through the body in a bow stance or counter stance. This differs from the normal bow/horse position, which is more rounded in the hips and natural in the waist.

Early 20th Century Shanghai

It is during the 'between the wars' period that Shanghai started to take on its familiar look, and gain its reputation. The 1920s and 30s were the famous 'best of times, worst of times' in Shanghai. Called the most polyglot city in the world, it took in all comers. In 1916, the population of the Settlement and French Concession was 164,521 Chinese and 5,912 foreigners (Japanese, British, American, German, Portuguese, and more, from thirty nations). A quarter of that Chinese population officially worked in foreign employ. There aren't numbers for the many more in foreign employ who lived outside the Settlement. In 1920, the post-war population was 759,839 Chinese and 23,307 foreigners, a big jump in both. (Statistics from Pott, A Short History of Shanghai, 1928, page 211.)

The foreign population was not made up of empire builders. The city was a treaty port, not a colony, and was run by the middle class – policemen, civil engineers, clerks, teachers. American arrived in force, and changed the character of the foreign lifestyle from cricket and the races to dances and big cars. Shanghai was filled with foreign and Chinese rich and poor – gangsters, warlords, businessmen, revolutionaries, dancehall girls, and refugees.

The Chinese that flocked to the new city lived mostly in the International Settlement, the French Concession, Hongkew, and the area surrounding them, which also grew of its own accord. Writing in 1928 about the origins of Shanghai, Mr. Pott said, "The haphazard way in which the roads were constructed accounts for the utter lack of system with which they were laid out, and makes it difficult for strangers to find their way about." (*A Short History of Shanghai*, page 76). I can second that – years later, it was still confusing.

Around 1918, large, modern department stores and hotels, with electric lighting, started to go up on Nanking Road, nicknamed Da Ma Lu, or 'Main Street.' And in the 1920s, apartment buildings, also characteristic of the downtown, were built to accommodate the growing number of middle class foreigners and Chinese. Shanghai's wonderful collection of Art Deco buildings date from this time.

The Bund has its expanse of space only because any building was originally required to be thirty feet from the tow path along the river. Of the roads running up from it, only Kiukiang Road (Ropewalk Road) was built to a twenty-five feet width. The other major parallel roads – Peking (Consulate Road), Nanking, and Hankow (Customs House Road) – were only twenty feet wide. The Bund was built up after WWI, in the early 1920s, as the row of imposing stone and ferro-concrete buildings that we either hate or love. The creek between the Settlement and the French Concession was culverted and became Edward VII Avenue (Avenue Edouard VII on the French side's signs), a major east-west road. Jessfield park was created on the outskirts, laid out in the English gardening-park manner.

Post WWI, the character of the foreign population started to change drastically. After the Russian revolution, Shanghai experienced its first wave of foreign refugees, as it took in thousands of penniless White Russians. Destitute and homeless foreign refugees without papers crowded in – some women becoming dancehall girls and prostitutes. Later, a flood of Jewish refugees escaped the buildup against them in Nazi Germany, and settled largely in Hongkew, changing the nature of that part of town.

The Chinese population in Shanghai was a skilled workforce in the manufacture of cotton and silk when the rest of China was still making things by hand. There was a growing middle class, many educated in foreign languages, and working in management positions. The Chinese population was increasingly nationalistic and looking for participation in the city. Most of the population of the Settlement and French Concession was Chinese, but they did not have a place on the Council in the Settlement (though they did in the French Concession since 1914). Shanghai continued on as a city governed largely by the foreigners. After the May 30th incident in 1925, the Chinese felt they needed to get control of their city, and strikes and disputes with the police occurred more and more often. In 1928, three Chinese were finally elected to the Council.

The characteristic *shikumen* and *lilong* housing of downtown Shanghai date from this time, as more people, foreign and Chinese, moved in to the city. The *shikumen* were built for the working classes, mostly in the north and north-eastern corner of the city (Chabei and Hongkew). They lacked indoor plumbing and electricity, but were an improvement on the shantytowns. The *lilongs* (terraced townhouses) and villas were for the middle and upper-middle classes, and usually had plumbing and electricity. These were in the central International Settlement and southwestern corner, into the French Concession. Both *shikumen* and *lilong* housing were built for single family occupation but were often sublet to fit in more people. This layout of the city remained for quite some time, and the lifestyle of the alleyways, the lively street life, and Shanghaihua – the distinctive urban language– was part of the definition of being Shanghainese.

Living in Shanghai gave access to foreign ideas, books and foods, which a growing class of Chinese intellectuals, educated in the West, appreciated. European café culture ensured a café seemingly on every street, perfect meeting places for casual interactions. The ability to move between cultures was another aspect of being Shanghainese.

The city was a glorious mix – not just bars, brothels, and dance halls. On Kiukiang Road (now Jinjiang Lu), for just one example, were a number of small printing presses and bookshops – including Evans & Sons, which published books, magazines, sheet music, scrolls, and the 'Shanghai Girl' advertising calendars that I've always loved. Cheek by jowl were the *Association Amicale Sino-Belge* and the headquarters of the pro-Mussolini Anti-Communist Entente. Holy Trinity Cathedral and School, number 219, were the prestige buildings of the neighbourhood. Now dwarfed by surrounding buildings, its bell tower having been used for years as offices, and its spire dismantled by the Red Guards during the Cultural Revolution, Holy Trinity Cathedral has been refurbished and re-opened as a cathedral in 2017. But I am most fascinated by the British Women's Association, in amongst all that, at No. 9. Though not an enthusiastic cook or seamstress, I would have enjoyed taking part in the cake bakes and jam-making and knitting sessions, and especially the annual badminton tournament, which was apparently fierce. For more fun facts, see Paul French, *The Old Shanghai A-Z* (2010).

At first the Japanese residents lived mostly in Hongkew, peaceful citizens like the others, their restaurants offering an evening out for a Japanese meal. Unfortunately, the government of Japan had other ideas, and would eventually take over Shanghai as part of their bid to take the entire country. Even though the war with Japan was already affecting Shanghai by 1932, many foreigners stayed because they had nowhere else to go. They put up a good fight, but in 1943 it was no longer a treaty port, but was controlled by the Japanese.

Not until the end of the war with the Japanese, in 1946, was Shanghai given back to the Chinese. It became a Chinese city governed by the KMT, the Guomindang, which made it a launching site to escape to Taiwan, rather than taking a final stand. Many Shanghailanders had left before and during the war, but some stayed, and some came back. It was their home, even without extrality, and with the threat of the Communists winning the civil war. As Jean Bowie Shor described 1946 Shanghai in *After You, Marco Polo*, "Postwar Shanghai …. was jammed with Jewish refugees, and American troops, and rich Chinese fugitives from the areas already overrun by the Communists, and people without 'visible means of support' who might rightfully be called international adventurers." "Everyone assured everyone else that Shanghai's future was bright, that things were going to be all right, but nobody believed it. The shadow of doom lay over the city. Yet I loved my years in Shanghai. …Shanghai was wicked and riddled with graft, but it was alive and vibrant, and there was no boredom there." (McGraw-Hill Book Company, New York, 1956, p.7.)

Many Chinese businessmen and Shanghailanders stayed on in 1949 with this optimistic attitude, that they had lived through a lot, and were not convinced that things would change all that much. They were willing to give the Communists the benefit of the doubt. Changes at first were gradual, and couldn't be argued against – stabilizing the currency, clearing out prostitution and rickshaws, closing up nightclubs and ballrooms, and dividing up houses to take care of more families. As businesses started being taken over, and private property taken away, more and more realized that it was time to leave their homes if they had some place else to go. For some, who had been born in Shanghai, 'going home' to England was unsettling, to say the least.

Yilu: The First Form

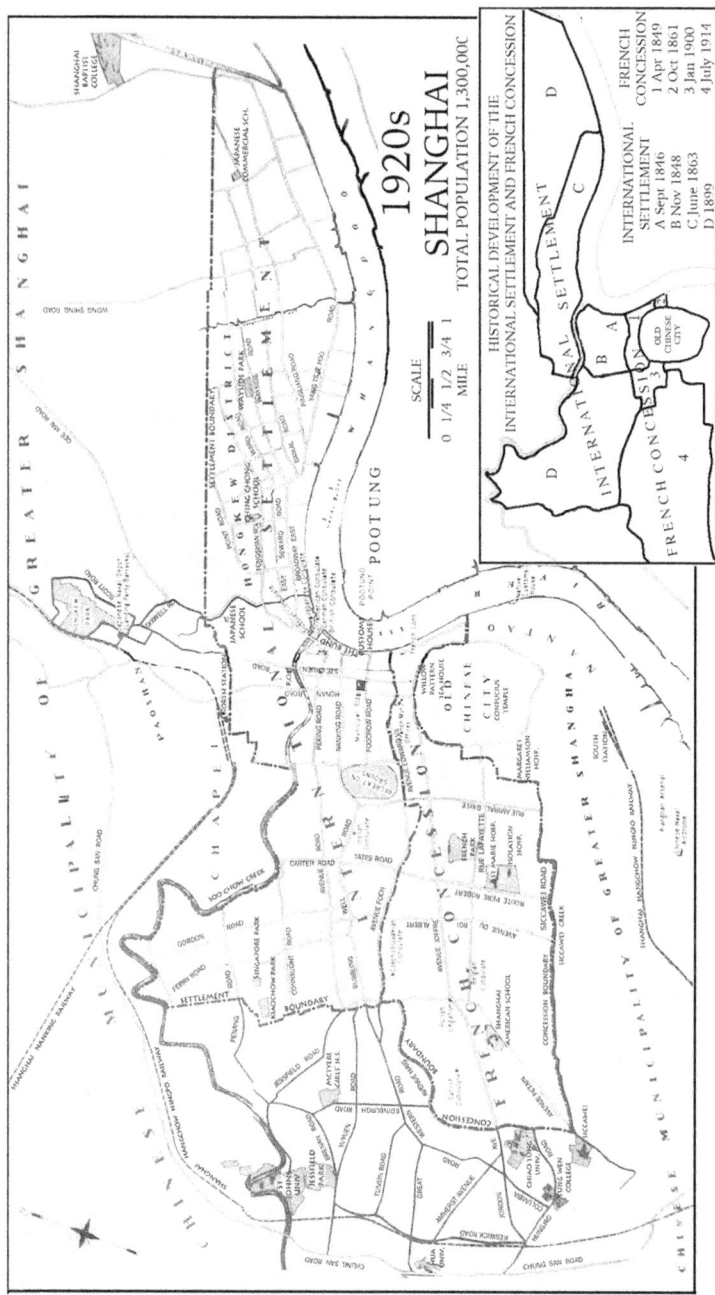

Greater Shanghai, 1920s. You can see by 1920 that, although the boundary of the International Settlement has been finalised, Jessfield Park and St. John's University are well on the outside of it, as were many houses and places of entertainment between them and the boundary.

34. **Needle At Sea Bottom**   hǎi dǐ zhēn   海底针

Overall Movement: Roll then step forward to an empty stance, reaching down to the ground.

Footwork: Coil back and forth in the horse stance, step the left foot across to a high empty stance, then step the right foot forward to a low empty stance, sitting with the left thigh parallel to the ground. Both feet point straight forward in the final empty stance.

Breakdown of Movements:

Part One: Turn the body slightly left, coil the right hand palm up and bring the left hand in past the waist. Turn right and reach both hands to the right. Turn left and *cai* to the left, palms facing out and down. Photos 34a and 34b.

Part Two: Turn left, open, then draw down. Lower into horse stance, bring the hands down to *cai* low to the right, coming well down onto the left knee. Pull (*cai*) across to the middle then up to a high empty stance, bringing the left foot across in front of the right (east). The palms are up, the left in front of the head, the right turned over in front and above the head. Photos 34c, 34d, and 34e.

Part Three: Step the right foot through to a low empty stance, touching the ball of the foot on the ground. Without moving the arms in space, circle the palms around still facing up, coiling the right hand until it faces forward at the waist. Lower and *shunchan* the right hand to the right foot with the palm facing forward (this is in my notes, though since I always extended the hand forward rather than down, I must have learned it that way). Extend the left hand out to the rear, *nichan* so it faces back. Photo 34f.

You may also roll the left hand back and up with a framing block, see photo on the following page.

Yilu: The First Form

In the shift from right leg onto left leg, the hands go directly into position. Twist both hands, the right going directly down, the left going down then back behind the body or bracing up.

In the final empty stance, do not bend the left leg so far that the knee passes the toes. Use the back to put power into the strike like a bobbing toy. The left thigh should be parallel to the ground. The back is flat but not upright, it tilts forward so that the top of the head is tilted.

Direction of Movements: Step and strike east.

Possible Applications: Release a grip, the right hand extends directly down after it coils. Then control with the left hand and stab with the right. Or step in between the opponent's legs, reaching in between them in preparation for a throw.

Internal Connections: The left and right *cai* in parts one and two demand a firm rooting in the lower body, otherwise there is no power in the movement. Maintain this rooting for the low strike of part three.

About the Name: This is the traditional name for an empty stance with the front hand diving low. It has to do with the Monkey King roiling the sea with his staff (it is not searching for a needle at the bottom of the sea). In some styles it is done as a high stance, leaning over. I have seen it done this way in this form as well, standing quite high and leaning forward to touch the right hand to the right foot.

Additional Comments: If you cannot yet or can no longer sit on one leg until the left thigh is parallel to the ground, then I think it is better to not reach the hand to the right foot. Push forward at knee or even waist height, to keep your eyes on the opponent and your connections feeling strong. I think it is more important to keep the head up than to really go to the sea bottom. You should never take the names too seriously. In fact, it really is better to learn the moves without the names so that you are not influenced by them. Later, once you are comfortable with the movements, it may help you to ponder on the names.

As you can see from this photo from Victoria in the 1990s, even when I sat easily on the left leg, so could easily touch the foot, I still preferred to keep the back upright, the hand high, and the eyes up.

35. **Three Through The Back** sān tōng bèi 三通背

<u>Overall Movement</u>: Grab, pivot and do a vertical throw.

<u>Footwork</u>: Coil into a high sitting stance, pivot and land in a 60/40 stance.

<u>Breakdown of Movement</u>:

Part One: Coil into a high sitting stance (*zuopan*), but don't sit into it. Turn the body to face south. Coil the right palm, keeping it facing up until it gets under the jaw. *Shunchan* the left arm so that the palm sweeps around with the arm fairly straight. Do not stop here, as you will lose all momentum. Photo 35a.

Part Two: Step the right foot around to the back and bring the left hand in towards the face (the movement can also be done with the left arm straight throughout). Pivot on the left foot and sweep the right foot, stamping the right foot when it lands behind and hit out with the left hand with a chop. Pull back with the right hand. Photos 35b and 35c.

<u>Direction of Movements</u>: Turn from facing east to facing west.

<u>Possible Applications</u>: Grab the opponent's wrist with the right hand. Support his arm with the left hand. Turn, trapping the opponent's arm over your left shoulder, for an elbow break or throw.

<u>Internal Connections</u>: The body pivots around the *dantian*, with the upright alignment of the body allowing for power to be transmitted either through the arms or into the back shoulder. So you must first find the vertical axis of the body before turning in order to keep the *dantian* stable during the spin.

<u>About the Name</u>: In Chen style this movement is usually called *shan tong bei* rather than *san tong bei*. This is perhaps because of oral transmission. In this case, it might be because of the 'sh' sound. Most Chinese outside of Beijing do not make the proper 'sh', 'ch', and 'zh', sounds, so '*shan*' (闪 dodge) and '*san*' (三 three) sound almost the same. In Shanghai, if I called sifu '*shirfu*' they thought I was showing off, I had to call him sifu like everyone else.

The primary feeling is to use the back, to keep the arms connected through the upper back. Because our Yilu has both *san tong bei*, and *shan tong bei* (move 87) perhaps the name this time is intended to say the that the power of the technique goes three times through the back – that there is first a strike, then a turn, and finally a completion of the throw – each technique fully utilizing the back.

When using the 'three' character, it implies that the movement goes through the back three times with the setup and turning.

Additional Comments: Just before pivoting, first put power into the shoulder as if someone grabbed your hand. Then roll around as if someone pushed down on your back from behind, to roll off his strength. Put power into the right shoulder.

Cai Yuhua stays down into this move, with a sneaky trapping action into the throw. Although I said in part one to not sit further into the sitting stance, you can definitely go right down. I think I may have forgotten that the move was done this way, as this is more like my original notes. Cai Yuhua does a much tighter coil into the jaw than the way I usually do it, which is very cool.

Once I almost hit someone when I turned around quickly with *Santongbei* – he was standing that close. Although no native of Shanghai was uncouth enough to stare at a foreigner normally, a foreigner practising in a park was, and still is, good entertainment value. I was easily distracted when training, as people commented about me, strolled up to get a closer look, or asked me (in the middle of practice!) if I could help them learn English.

Sifu said to ignore them, that it was pride rather than politeness that made me feel the need to respond. He said he always acted dimwitted if people bothered him while training, and eventually they would go away. Another case of taking training into life – to let pride go – sifu said it was pride that made me want to show that I spoke Chinese, even if it was to tell people I didn't want to talk to them.

Having people watching and commenting was hard for me, and I still don't like practising in public places with people around. While constant commentary from passersby about your skills during training was annoying, I have to admit enjoy hearing a surprised voice say, 'hmm, she's got some real skill.' My favourite thing that I've heard while practicing, though, was in Victoria's Playfair park, "Shh, don't bother them, they are doing quiet karate."

36. **Hide The Hand And Punch** (for the second time, alternate version)
    yǎn shǒu hóng chuí   掩手肱捶

Overall Movement: Advance slightly, coil to prepare, and punch.

Footwork: Bring the right foot in by the left and stamp, lifting the left foot by the right ankle. Land the left foot forward to a horse stance. Roll in the legs then push into the right leg to punch. When stepping directly into horse stance instead of circling the feet, use a shovel step. Land the foot while already slightly shifting the centre of gravity forward, so that the foot slides slightly.

Breakdown of Movement:

Part One: Stamp the right foot, lifting the left foot at the right ankle. Close the arms, settling the right fist into the left palm in front of the body. Photos 36a and 36b.

Part Two: Step the left foot directly into a horse stance. Circle the hands, keeping them together, gradually turning to hide the right fist behind the left palm. Do the circle with the *dantian* and legs, not the hands. If the body circles properly, the hands will follow along. They do not move much spatially, and the right fist surface points in the direction to which it will punch throughout the circling. Photos 36c and 36d.

Part Three: Punch with the right fist, dropping the left hand back to the belly. Drive the punch from the body and right leg. Photo 36e.

Direction of Movements: Step west and punch to the north or northwest.

Possible Applications: If the opponent comes at you from the right, cover his attack with your left hand. The further up his arm you cover, the more control you have over him. Bring your right foot in quickly to advance the left foot very quickly towards him and punch. The shuffle step is more hidden than a normal step and also serves to compress energy into the rear leg if you keep down as you bring the foot in. This gives more power and acceleration to the punch.

Yilu: The First Form

<u>About the Name</u>: Chen Xin differentiates the name of this move from the first punch (move 18), calling it Play With The Hand And Punch 演手捶 *yan shou chui*. This name suits this alternate performance, because the fist is not hidden, and you play with it before punching. The pronunciation is the same. This punch and the third repetition (move 88) go more directly into the punch, and into the fist surface than the first Hide The Hand.

<u>Additional Comments</u>: The first punch (move 18), in the first section of the form, winds around before the punch, as the first section focuses on the power flow. Now you are almost to the first Travelling Hands, when the focus is on being more practical. Present the fist directly in the direction in which it will punch. Keep the fist surface pointing in that direction as the hands circle together. Draw a small circle with the hands, keeping the knuckles forward, just following the coiling in the legs. The fist is presented in the palm, so the *fajin* is short. The punch travels directly in a corkscrew, it is not a rolled punch.

Here is the punch from the front.

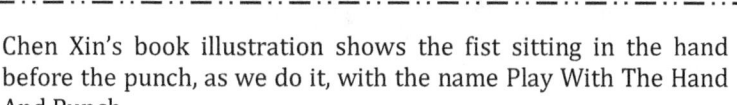

Chen Xin's book illustration shows the fist sitting in the hand before the punch, as we do it, with the name Play With The Hand And Punch.

Chen Xin, Yanshou chui, page 244.

37. Tuck In The Robe Casually (second time, alternate entry)
lǎn zhā yī   懒扎衣

<u>Overall Movement</u>: Start out with a drop back and jump forward, then settle into Tuck In The Robe posture (move 5) as before.

<u>Breakdown of Movement</u>:

Part One: Drop back onto the right leg, bringing the right arm back and up to hang the fist slightly above shoulder height, thumb side down. Place the left hand on the right forearm. Photo 37a.

Part Two: Continue to *nichan* the right arm, curl it down to the rear, keeping it fairly straight, then bring it forward past the body to drill forward. Keep the left hand on the right forearm. Leap forward to the west, by stepping the left foot forward then pushing off to land on the right foot. The hands drill forward while you are in the air. Clench the left hand lightly so that it also drills forward, sitting at the right elbow. Photos 37b, 37c, and 37d.

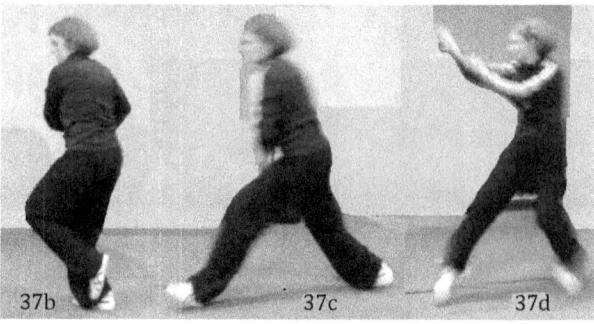

Part Three: Land softly on the right foot and land the left foot behind it, touching the toes down lightly. Unclench the hands immediately but softly upon landing, and sink them down to pull lightly. Photos 37e and 37f.

Part Four: Step the left leg back then step the right foot forward, and bring

Yilu: The First Form

the hands through and across – in other words, continue on as you have done before to Tuck In The Robe, in move 5. Photos 37g, 37h, 37i, 37j, 37k, and 37l.

Direction of Movements: Jump to the west, turn, and finish facing south with the right hand to the west.

Possible Applications: Part one, the jump: Keeping the left hand on the right forearm, you do a small grappling move. You have to twist the right forearm around a bit to come through without releasing your left hand, which results in releasing any opponent's grip. Drive forward to knock the opponent off balance, grab and throw.

Tuck In The Robe works well as a throwing stance particularly after the jump in, stepping in to control and throw. The contact point is the whole body, using the right leg to off-balance the opponent, the left hand to control, and the body and right upper arm to complete the throw. The stance must be firm to do this, as the opponent would roll over your right thigh.

Another possibility – the left hand grabs and the right hand strikes to the neck. Use the elbows to control and twist, then snap the palm to the neck.

Tuck In The Robe may tuck the right arm in under the opponent's armpit, across the chest in direct contact. Your left hand starts out above, so it grabs his arm and pulls it down. You need to get your right shoulder in tight to his armpit and get your right leg tight to his leg. The contact point is your body and upper arm, not your hand. Twist his arm with your left hand to get him a bit up onto his toes, to make it easier to throw him.

Internal Connections: The left side of the body needs to support the right side, as the right arm is extended. It needs to remain relaxed, but be firm, directing power in a balanced way.

Additional Comments: You may drop back quickly to the right leg, using the spring back from the punch. You may do a light *fajin* backfist with the right fist in the air.

Some people leave the left arm slack, letting the elbow open out. Chen Xin described the placement of the left arm as we do it, "Settle the shoulder, close the elbow forward, place the fingers in front of the ribs with the back of the hand up, and the thumb behind."

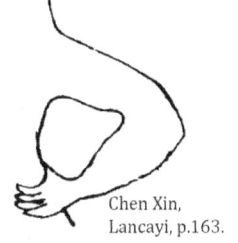

Chen Xin, Lancayi, p.163.

Yilu may be practised at different speeds, each speed developing different qualities and understanding. A comfortable speed is about thirty minutes. Slow can be an hour or more. Fast can be three minutes. (I have never seen or tried it in that time, that is what sifu said. I don't actually believe him on that.)

To do Yilu slowly, feel every space in every cell of your body and seek out all the connections. It feels like you are going fast, as every single minuscule adjustment is felt. You may momentarily stop in the final posture of each movement, and if you do, you must start moving without any break in feeling, connection, power, or energy flow. This is practising 'stillness within movement, movement within stillness.' When doing this you may space out at some point during the form and forget where you are. Don't worry about it, you do not have to do the entire form for the training to be effective. The whole form can take over an hour, but you usually naturally stop at some point before then.

To do Yilu at normal speed, relax and enjoy the movement, paying attention to the energy and power flow, but not stopping. Do the form carefully, carry on mindfully but freely, and *fajin* in the normal places during the form. The actual time you take doesn't matter that much. If you find you are taking only ten or fifteen minutes, though, you are rushing and not being mindful. I find thirty to forty minutes is comfortable. That is the speed that my natural oscillations give the smooth connections to the moves. Different people have different a tendon-ligament setup in their bodies, so times will vary.

This is why I have difficulty with people who say you should do Yilu ten times a day. James and I tried it once. After eight hours we had managed seven times. We took an hour off for lunch, and about ten minutes in between forms. There is no way we could have done ten in one day, much less ten every day. The main thing is not how many you do, but steady, mindful practice over the years.

To do Yilu at fast speed, *fajin* on every movement. If your coiling energy is perfect, then you can *fajin* any time without any feeling of distress. The places where you normally *fajin* are really just convention, and to ensure that most of the time you have a proper balance of softness to hardness. Fast speed practice is <u>not</u> just doing the form normally, but fast. The method is to do extra *fajin*, and all remaining non *fajin* movement is slow and comfortable. So there is no way it could be done in three minutes

To do Yilu at a speed somewhere in between normal and fast, do extra *fajin* where you normally don't, but otherwise perform as usual. Do not ever just 'go through' the movements quickly.

Yilu: The First Form

38. **Seal Off, Shut Down** (for the second time)   rú fēng sì bì   如封似闭

<u>Overall Movement</u>: This time you may go more directly into the press than you did in move 6.

<u>Breakdown of Movement</u>

Part One: Coil in the legs and coil the right hand back, coiling in both arms. Press forward with the forearms, right palm facing out on the outside, left palm facing up, still close to the body. Photos of James, 38a and 38b.

Part Two: Bring the left hand closer to the right forearm, pull then press with both forearms. Photos of James, 38c and 38d.

Part Three: Coil and pull again, bringing the hands closer to tuck the back of the left hand inside the right forearm for the press. Photos of James, 38e and 38f.

Part Four: Fold the left hand over the right forearm, reach the right hand out then roll it in, then press out with the right forearm inside, both palms facing in, wrists joined. Photos of James, 38g, 38h, and 38i.

Part Five: Continue on as in move 6 or go directly into the big pull. Photos of James, 38j, 38k, 38l, 38m, 38n.

Direction of Movements: Step and push to the southwest.

Practical Applications: Control the opponent's arm and press out with both forearms. If he should grab the arms, grab his hand with your left hand to press it onto the right forearm, then do a joint lock. by placing the right hand on his wrist and rolling both to fold his wrist over, keeping it pressed to your right forearm with your left hand.

   Be sure throughout the form that any draw-across action with the hands is done hand-to-elbow distance apart, to build the habit of controlling the wrist and elbow of an assailant (James is fighting a pretty big guy in photo 38k).

Internal Connections: Both arms are extended, so the body needs to settle and support them from the rear, to balance power through the body.

Additional Comments: Follow the line of the middle finger to see the line that the hand is taking. It should always be a circle. Always make sure the hands are describing circles, then move the circles further into the body.

> Don't worry if you are doing the form with a training partner and are not in synch. Do your moves in your own time, especially the *fajin* moves, and you can get back in relative synch on the following slow moves, as the speedier person slows (not stops) to wait for the other. It is more important to listen to your body than to stay together with training partners. If they are your friends they will wait, as you would wait for them. In addition to changes in pace, longer or shorter versions of moves are handy for catching up or waiting without breaking rhythm. Training together is not to march in unison, but to have company.

39. **Dantian Transforms** (for the second time) dān biàn 丹变

Overall Movement: This is the same as move 7. Photos of James, 39a, 39b, 39c, 39d, 39e, 39f, 39g, 39h, and 39i.

Direction of Movements: The torso is facing south; the left hand is to the east.

Possible Applications: Concentrate on the shifting power lines going from bow stance to bow/horse stance. Finding the difference between them is of vital importance in being able to apply all techniques in bow stance and bow/horse stance.

Additional Comments: This repetition is an excellent time to focus on the difference between a horse stance, a bow stance, and a bow/horse stance. The confusion comes because in Chen style this final stance is sometimes called a bow stance and sometimes a horse stance. A Chen style bow/horse stance has weight is slightly shifted to the front leg instead of being fifty-fifty as in a horse stance, and the feet are turned towards the weighting. It is technically a horse stance because the hips are parallel to the line of the stance, not turned. A Chen bow/horse stance facing south with the left hand being the primary attack will have the hips and shoulders facing south, the weight towards the left leg, and the feet pointing southeast. The right foot may point south, but not open more than that.

A horse stance applies power directly to either side. A Chen bow/horse stance applies power more towards one side. A smooth bow stance applies power to the front on the same side. A counter bow stance applies power to the front on the opposite side. There is always a balance of power into the rear arm, along the power line of the stance.

As Cai Yuhua started going regularly to Switzerland to teach and sell his art, he gradually transformed his house. First a fridge went in. Then he built a toilet and shower room in the shed. Later, he built a second storey. This made two large bedrooms upstairs, one for Xiaolan and him, one for their daughter. The big downstairs room became the all purpose work room, taken over by art. The upstairs rooms had much more natural light and air movement than the original rooms, so the changes were qualitative, not just quantitative. He made racks on the balcony for airing everything in the sun, as well.

He also built a second kitchen with gas powered hotplate instead of the coal fired cone. His parents used the first kitchen, so they became essentially two households. Breakfast at home was leftovers from the night before. When the fridge arrived, although that improved the health risks, it didn't really improve breakfast as such, since the food wasn't covered in the fridge and then wasn't warmed up.

In the 1980s I wasn't a coffee drinker, but in the 90s, after I had been to Europe and introduced to espresso, Cai Yuhua had also been to Switzerland and had an Italian style stovetop espresso pot. By then, coffee beans were also available in the fancier shops. Heaven was sitting on my stool in the courtyard with steamed buns and an espresso after a good morning's training. Life's simple pleasures are always the best, and just that little notch above rudimentary makes so much difference, especially when you have been happy with rudimentary. In fact, I seldom take a shower without giving a thought to enamel basins, dribbling hoses, and cold water. Not that long after the final renovations (all done by Cai Yuhua by hand), the neighbourhood was torn down and everyone relocated.

Yilu: The First Form

40. Middle Travelling Hands   zhōng yùn shǒu   中运手

<u>Overall Movement</u>: Circle the hands together as you move directly to the left, right, and left again.

<u>Footwork</u>: Step three steps with the left and right feet to the east, west, then east again, stomping on each incoming step. Pick up the feet from the upper legs, keeping the lower legs relaxed. This keeps the stepping more under control. Circle your weight around the edges of the feet.

<u>Breakdown of Movement</u>:

Part One: Release from the preceding Dantian Transforms, coiling the right hook slightly to face right as you settle left, then open the hands and bring them across to the right. Bring the left foot in. Photo 40a.

Part Two: Step the left foot to the east in a circular motion, bringing the foot forward then back to inline. Draw the left hand across at nose height, palm facing out. Draw the right hand across at belly height, palm facing out, thumb up. As the lower hand (in this case, the right hand) gets to the opposite side (in this case, the left side) externally rotate so the palm comes up, finishing the line to the little finger, then medially rotate and circle the wrist, taking the power to the index finger side. The hand describes a circle around the index finger. Make sure not to bend at the proximal finger joint. Photos 40b and 40c.

Part Three: Step the right foot in to a close parallel step, taking a circular line back then forward, stamping on landing. Circle the hands in the same way, towards the right, snapping them across quickly with the stamp. The stamping is optional, but preferable. The speed change goes with the stamp, so if there is no stamp, the rhythm stays even. Photos 40d and 40e.

Part Four: Continue on, to do three steps, left foot taking a large step and right foot a small step to travel across to the east. On each step the right foot will stamp. The hands circle slowly to the left with the step then quickly to the right with the stamp. Photos 40f, 40g, 40h, and 40i.

129

Part Five: On the final step to the east, circle the incoming foot (the right) a bit further away and do an extra full circle with the hands. Do not stamp on this step. Photos 40j, 40k.

Part Six: Do the same actions for three steps back to the west. This time the right foot is drawing the larger step and the left foot is coming closer and stamping. The hands continue to circle exactly the same, except they move slowly across to the right with the step, then quickly to the left when the left foot stamps. Photos 40l, 40m, 40n, 40o, and 40p.

Part Seven: Do the same actions for three steps back to the east. This time the left foot is drawing the larger step and the right foot is coming closer and stamping. The hands continue to circle exactly the same, except they move slowly across to the left then quickly to the right when the right foot stamps. Photos 40q, 40r, 40s, 40t, 40u, 40v, 40w, 40x, 40y, 40z, 40za, 40zb, and 40zc.

Yilu: The First Form

The connecting action can be considered as the end of this move or the beginning of the following move. Photos 40zd and 40ze.

Direction of Movements: The torso is facing south throughout. The stepping goes to the east, then west, then east again.

Possible Applications: The circular stepping is meant to trap the opponent with the feet. The hands control and throw. Use the power of the body, not the arms. Use the momentum of the opponent to draw him in the direction that he is already going. This technique is practised pulling in both directions, with the feet going out and coming in, so that you are able to apply it in any situation.

Circle the hands in round, vertical circles, do not pull straight across. The hands draw individual circles that interlock. Keep the hand circles within the line of the stance at all times. Do not go out to a straight line with the line of action. If you draw circles, you set up the line that you can lead an opponent along. You do not need to change to a straight line to *fajin* at any point in the technique. Throughout the body, there is no place that is not round or making circles, so "there is no place that is not a fist." Any application can be done anywhere along the line of the circle. A small *fajin* will be enough to send the opponent off. If you keep in the circles and *fajin*, the force is naturally directed straight, like throwing a cricket ball.

Internal Connections: This action calls for and develops a high degree of diagonal connection from the feet through the body to the hands. All movement comes from the body, passing diagonally through from one leg across to the opposite arm, but also to the same side arm, as both are travelling in the same direction.

The first section of the form, up to this first Travelling Hands, concentrates on establishing a strong structure and setting the rules of movement in Taijiquan, developing the *chansi* power throughout the body. The entire first section is soft, with only a few *fajin* actions. The stamping during this first Travelling Hands serves to wake you up, should you have become a little too much one with the universe, and prepare you for the following more applicatory parts of the form. Do not stamp hard, and be sure to keep the foot flat.

About the Name: This first time is called the Middle Travelling Hands because the upper limit of the hands is at the mid-range, at nose height.

The second Travelling Hands is the upper, at eyebrow height. So the Travelling Hands that are in the middle of the form are called upper (which in Chinese also means the first) because the hands are at the highest height of the three repetitions. The third Travelling Hands is called the lower, and is done at belly height. A bit confusing at first. In Chen Xin's book the names *shang, zhong,* and *xia* are with the usual meanings, first, middle, and last.

The use of 'travelling' 运 *yun* instead of 'cloud' 云 *yun* may again be due to oral transmission – both are pronounced *yun,* though with different tones. In my mind, 'travelling' makes more sense. 'Cloud' is also commonly used, though, for this type of circular brandishing motion in martial arts, with the feeling of clouds passing in the sky. It is important that the movement of all limbs continues without any break at all, so that the power can be unbroken within the body.

Also interesting to note, is that there is a similar sounding technique in Chinese wrestling, called weeding, which is written 耘 yún. This weeding power is a rounded crossing power used to pull the opponent over. Combined with a snap, it is a strong crossing power for a throw or take down. I wonder if this were not the original term, later changed to more common words.

Additional Comments: Keep the power in the palms, like circling around the inside of a washing basin, keeping the palm in contact at all times. You can practice with a plastic washing basin nailed to a tree. In China in the 1980s everyone had a washing basin, so this was a good idea, but I didn't want to put a hole in mine, so never did this.

Watch the top hand's middle finger throughout. This focus on the middle finger is not just for this move. Sifu said, "Watch the middle finger like you're watching a mosquito." What he meant was that you should look lively and interested, never just stare at the hands. He had never had to train with blackflies, which is pretty dire, no matter how 'zen' you try to be. I have yet to complete a slow and relaxed form while being tormented by blackflies, even wearing full netting. Once I thought I had, but I had actually left out an entire section.

This photo is me doing Taiji Changquan in 'Laurentian spring' garb.

41. **(Retreating) High Pat On Horse** gāo tàn mǎ 高探马

<u>Overall Movement</u>: Catch, drop back, then bring the arms through forward to control.

<u>Footwork</u>: Step out on completion of the last stamp of the previous move. Bring the right foot around to the front (east) then step it back (west). Then settle to the right leg and bring the left foot to behind, weight on the front leg.

<u>Breakdown of Movement</u>:

Part One: Starting from the last stamp of the right foot and the hands at the right, step the left foot to the east with the foot turned slightly open. Pull (*cai*) with both hands, coming around to the left. Keep the arms rounded so that the pull comes from the waist. Bring the right foot around to the front (east) as you turn, touching it down quite close to the left foot. The hands finish with the right palm up at nose height, the left palm down under the right forearm. Photo 41a.

Part Two: Step the right foot back (west), push the left hand out to the front (east). Drop the right hand slightly behind the body, palm down, with a small *fajin* into the elbow. Photo 41b.

Part Three: Settle onto the right leg and bring the left foot back, touching down near the right heel. Circle the arms around, the right coming through from behind and reaches out over the left. The final posture has the right and left hands about wrist to elbow distance apart. The right palm is down, heel forward, about shoulder height. The left palm is up. Keep the left armpit open, three fingers slightly curled. Look past the middle finger of the right hand. Photos 41c, 41d, and 41e.

<u>Direction of Movements</u>: You are facing east.

<u>Possible Applications</u>: The left hand grabs the opponent's elbow, the right hand comes through to take the wrist and bend his forearm over for a joint lock. This is a strong controlling action done while seeming to retreat.

An initial backup into an elbow strike is included.

Yilu: The First Form

Internal Connections: The movement is completed with a closing action as the body pivots around the *dantian*. Direct power throughout the body from the left foot into the right hand. This differentiation of weighted-leg and power-leg is quite common during the form – a strike is not achieved from a weight shift, but usually is pushed through from the less weighted foot. (The exception is when using the push into the foot that lifts the heel, this foot is usually weighted.)

The complexity of the meridian connections continues through the form, as the moves repeat and the actions continue to stimulate the entire body. It is best to just let this happen, and not think too much on it.

About the Name: The final position is like you are holding a horse's head to control it, one hand on the chin (or the reins) and the other on the forelock (or the bridle). The word *tan* is the common wushu terminology for the palm technique of reaching forward to strike fairly flat. It is like reaching into a cookie jar, tilting the jar with the other hand.

This first time through High Pat on Horse, the technique is retreating. The left leg comes back and the push is done as it completes a retreating action, putting the power into the right shoulder and giving more body turn.

Additional Comments: If you *fajin* into the right elbow and let it continue, the right hand will snap quickly in, ready to reach forward.

If there is a way to make something more expensive, I will find it. I was supposed to go to China on June 4th, 1989, but the tanks in Tiananmen Square and protests all over the country made this untenable. The clever plan of scratching out the date on the plane ticket in June 1989 (in those days tickets were paper, in triplicate), substituting 1990, was discovered by the travel agent in Shanghai in 1990. I made it there on the old ticket, but in those days, you had to confirm tickets ahead of time, and the agent in Shanghai noticed the change. I had to buy, at the full price of $800, a new ticket home. I had to go to the Bank of China on the Bund to get cash on my credit card, which took just about all day. What a beautiful building! I had never been inside. It was almost worth the price of the ticket to see it. I had never been so happy that they gave away credit cards like candy in the 1970s. The next time the card saved me was when I paid the massive fine for the visa violation in 1996.

I was a teaching assistant in the Asian Studies department at the University of Victoria in the 1990s, so managed to get a foot in the door for university funding. By handing over (probably breaking some law) some translations I'd done for an engineering company on the Three Gorges Feasibility Study in the mid-1980s, I won favour with someone with enough power to land me a cushy job at Huadong Normal University in Shanghai, lecturing on Quebecois French a few times a week, with a few lectures in the Physical Education department.

I got room and board, so wasn't a drain on Cai Yuhua's family for the autumn months of the 1996 trip. I would drop by after training to chat, and often stay over on weekends. The bike ride to training took forty-five minutes, and was pleasant in the early morning, though not so nice going back after. I hated getting up at 4:30 for training, but I needed to eat something beforehand if I were to survive until second breakfast. I tried sleeping in and not eating, but would almost pass out during training. It was fun riding the bike through quiet streets, though, and the ride to training is always a part of training that I enjoy.

Teaching at the university was an enjoyable job. I had a great time with the French classes, teaching incomprehensible Quebecois to the students. I had prepared with quite a bit of research about the development of the language and the history, and had brought along some traditional music, so my classes were fun for the students, too, not the usual boring rote memorization. Also, the material would not be on the exam.

My talks (in Chinese) at the Physical Education department went well, too. I will never forget the looks on their faces when I described the government support of our Olympic athletes, and why they had to work nights to continue their training. The conversation went something like this. I wrote down the monthly support stipend. "Do you mean daily or weekly?", 'No, monthly." "Oh, so you have left it in US dollars, so it is six times that amount?", "No, that is in Chinese yuan." They didn't know whether to laugh or cry. Laugh, because they were Chinese and their athletes were properly supported and were going to beat the Canadians hands down. Cry because they were sports people and after all and did have feelings for fellow athletes.

Yilu: The First Form

42. **Right Stab The Foot**   yòu chā jiǎo   右插脚

Overall Movement: A right slap kick, moving to the east.

Footwork: Step the left foot forward (east) with the foot turned out slightly. Lift the right leg fairly straight into a slap kick.

Breakdown of Movement:

Part One: Step the left foot forward with the foot turned slightly out. Bring the left palm over with a slapping action (*pazhang*) and coil the right hand back. Photo 42a.

Part Two: Bring the right elbow across to the left hand, and prepare the right leg to kick. Photo 42b.

Part Three: Right slap kick to at least shoulder height. The slapping hand has impetus forward, not just down onto the foot. Keep the left hand at the right elbow. Kick more from the hip than the knee – this is a snap kick, but it rises and drops fairly straight. Photo 42c.

Direction of Movements: Kick to the east.

Possible Applications: Grab your assailant with the left hand, then strike and kick. The left hand folds over to gain control if possible. Then you can grab his wrist or elbow with your left arm and keep him under control as you kick and strike with the right foot and hand. Crossing the arms prior to a kick indicates that you can trap his arms in both arms, you do not need to grab during the defense, just cover up. You may kick to the groin and strike to the face. Keep the left hand at the right elbow during the kick to control the opponent or protect your body.

Internal Connections: Lift inside the hip joint to keep the leg close to the body when you kick. This aligns the psoas muscle vertically to make the kick easier.

About the Name: The use of the word *cha* can refer either the foot action or the hand slapping the foot. It means to stab in, so you want to have a bit of forward power, not just up and down, both in the hand and the foot.

In some Chen branches the kick is called 擦脚 *ca jiao* meaning to rub the foot, which emphasizes the hand action and the friction created by the forward movement. Either name is common to describe a front instep slap kick with the hand driving more forward than down.

Additional Comments: You may place the left hand nearer the body under the right arm to protect the ribs during the kick.

> I probably still have the record for having paid the largest visa violation fine in the history of Chinese visa violations. The new rules and new visa stamping system had just come in in 1996. I was teaching at the Huadong Normal University, so thought I had a work visa that was good for three months, as visas had always been for three months before. When I went in to renew it I found out that, a) the stamp 'L' meant that it was a tourist visa, for *luyou*, of course, all foreigners should know that. And, b) it was so far past its due date that the visa officer turned white and ran to get a senior officer. The visible date was the latest date for 'entry after receiving the visa' (the new stamping system), not the date of latest exit (which they used to be). My visa was actually for one month, so I had been in China for two months without a visa. I was offered the choice of, a) being deported, b) going to jail, or c) paying a fine. The third choice was not given until after a few visits, getting more and more worried each time, especially as they kept my passport.
>
> The university wanted nothing to do with it. I found out that they often hired teachers in a grey area this way, but were not about to step up and admit it. Technically, I was not being paid for work, I was given room and board for giving a few lectures. The visa officers wanted to know how I could be so far out of date, and what I had been doing. I was not going to give up Cai Yuhua for anything, even if it meant prison or deportation. I had stayed with his family as usual before I had moved to work at the university for the fall session. I think I was saved by the fact that the visa officers knew that the university did this but did not want to spoil their gig, so finally gave me an extension of a tourist visa with a massive fine, as long as I stopped saying I was working at the university. My credit card again saved the day, as I was able to get the cash from the Bank of China.
>
> I don't remember ever being so scared, or so cognisant of how I could disappear with no one knowing where I was or what had happened to me. I was completely dependent on officers in the visa department.

43. Left Coil And Stab The Foot   zuǒ pán chā jiǎo   左盘插脚

Overall Movement: Sit in a crossed stance then come up into a left slap kick.

Footwork: Land the right foot and sit down into a cross stance with the left knee tucked behind the right knee. Then come up, settle into a high cross stance, and kick the left leg.

Breakdown of Movement:

Part One: Land the right foot turned out and sit down into a cross stance. The body faces south, the attention is still to the east. Separate the hands, then bring them down and up to cross in front of the chest, palms facing in. The right hand is on the outside. Photo 43a.

Part Two: Stand up and unroll the arms, extending them out to each side at shoulder height, settling the shoulders. Kick the left leg to slap without moving the hands. Again, the leg rises fairly straight, with a final snap into the hand. The knee doesn't bend too much, nor does it snap back after the kick. Photos 43b and 43c.

Direction of Movements: Kick to the east.

Possible Applications: Control the opponent after the first kick, then kick again. If the opponent grabs onto you when you do the right kick, trying to take you down, move into him, grab, and turn to tangle his arms up. Drop if you need to. Then control him with your right hand and kick and strike with the left foot (instep, or knee) and hand. You don't have to strike with the left hand, you can use that to control at his elbow to gain space for the kick.

Internal Connections: On coming up from the sit, settle the leg into the hip joint first, so that the leg is light for the kick.

About the Name: The *zuo*, 'left' in the name refers to the kick, not the stance. Usually the *zuopan* (sitting basin) stance is fully named. In this case, because of the left (*zuo*) kick, perhaps fully naming it would sound redundant '*zuopan zuo chajiao*.' Also, names are quick references to remind you of the moves, and as such are two, three, or four characters, not more.

Additional Comments: You may sit down completely to a *zuopan* stance on the ground. You need to put a little energy into the left hand. Although it does not move spatially, it still needs to slap the foot with energy.

> If you cannot yet, or can no longer, kick your hand easily, just slap the shin. Keeping upright is more important than slapping the foot if that would mean leaning. Because of the angles of the legs and arms, if the foot is at shoulder height then the hand should easily reach out to touch it.
>
> To improve flexibility, stretch out the back and legs after practice – when you are warm. Place the foot on a support about waist or shoulder height, hold the foot, and reach the torso towards the foot. Always keep the back flat when stretching for kicks, as if trying to touch the lower ribs to the toes. Do not hump the back to put the torso on the leg. Do this with the leg straight ahead and turned to the side, and it will help with the kicks of Taijiquan, which are a bit angled.

In Chen Xin's book, he often relates the moves to hexagrams. Here is a bit for the kicks (page 261):

"This posture (Right Stab Foot), is with the right hand slapping the right foot. Kicking the opponent with the right foot is the trigram *zhen* (thunder, two *yin* over a bottom *yang* line). Hitting the opponent with the right hand is the *gen* trigram (mountain, one *yang* over two *yin* lines). The opponent isn't there, so you hit your foot with your hand. The foot kicks up and the hand strikes down.

(When kicking with the left leg) the supporting leg is the right one, which is *yin* and the trigram *xun* (wind, two *yang* lines over a bottom *yin* line). When *xun* (two *yang* lines over a bottom *yin* line) is below and *gen* (one *yang* over two *yin* lines) is above, this is the *gu* hexagram. Supporting yourself on the right leg is less stable than on the left, so you need to set yourself as a tree sets itself to withstand the onslaught of infestation."

The advice is good, but why the trigrams and hexagrams have to come in all the time, I don't know. They often make much less sense, and are usually carried even farther than this example. This is actually an example that kind of makes sense. But why is the right foot *yang* when kicking, but *yin* when supporting? We are naturally right handed, and tend to come through to kick with the right foot easier than the left. You can feel that. But equally, I can stand quite well on my right leg.

Yilu: The First Form

44. **Left Thrust A Heel**   zuǒ dēng yī gēn   左蹬一跟

<u>Overall Movement</u>: Turn around and heel kick the left foot to the west.

<u>Footwork</u>: Pivot on the right foot and turn around to the left, then kick into the heel of the left foot.

<u>Breakdown of Movement</u>:

Part One: Turn around to the left, pivoting on the right foot. You may touch down the left foot if you need to, but it is better to turn with the knee still up, as a trapping action. The body now faces worth but you are preparing for a kick to the west. Coil the hands and bring them down in front of the stomach, fingers pointing to each other, palms up. Photo 44a.

Part Two: Form fists and continue to coil them to punch out to either side with the thumb sides down (you may also swing the fists up to the sides with the backfist facing up). Finish with the fists at shoulder height. Lift the left knee then complete a left heel thrust kick to the west with the toes turned up to waist height. Photo 44b.

44a   44b

Part Three (optional): Leave the left foot up, turn right and place the hands on the ground (to the east). Kick the right foot up to meet the left foot at shoulder height. This is a handstand done at an angle so the legs are about shoulder height.

<u>Direction of Movements</u>: Kick to the west.

<u>Possible Applications</u>: Grab the opponent to control before kicking. If someone grabs you from behind, turn and get your knee up to push him away. Push with the heel if you can.

If he grabs your left foot to try to twist your leg or throw you, drop your hands to the ground and kick firmly with the right foot, either to his grabbing hand or to anywhere on his body that hurts enough to make him release his grip. Kick to shoulder height at the highest, as this is the highest anyone would lift your leg, which is why the body is slanted – it is not a full handstand.

<u>Internal Connections</u>: Tuck in the hip to enable the kick to be light and clean. If doing the second kick, keep the back firm. If it collapses the legs will not be able to extend.

<u>About the Name</u>: *Deng* is the common term for a heel kick, and *gen* (heel) emphasizes this. Sometimes *gen* is written 根, the 'root' of your body, with the same meaning. This is the reference to the entire body as a unit, when the feet are the root, the torso the trunk, and the hands the branch tips. This is different from when 'root' is used to refer to the parts of the body and their

Shadowboxing in Shanghai

relationship to each other. In that case, the hip socket is the root of the leg, the shoulder girdle is the root of the arm, and the *dantian* is the root of the torso.

<u>Additional Comments</u>: In part two, you may do a sidekick instead. You may also start the punch with the little finger sides twisted up, then unroll them at the end of the kick so the fist centres are down.

Part three, the angled handstand right kick, is difficult to do on your own, but quite easy and natural if an opponent grabs your ankle. It is more practical than it might appear within the form.

Chen Xin suggests that you can keep one foot on the ground when doing the form, rather than doing the full handstand, as long as you know how to use the move. This makes sense, and is actually do-able.

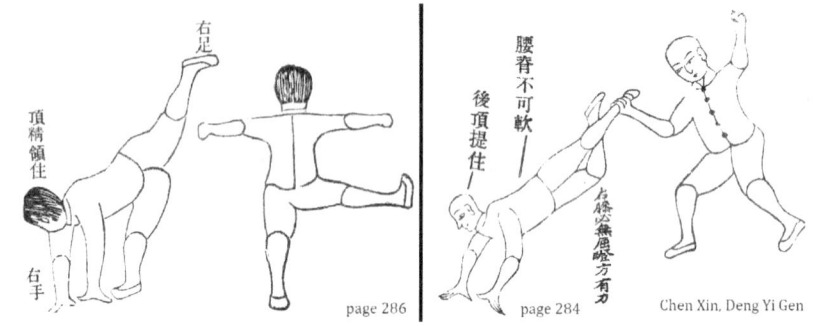

page 286 | page 284 | Chen Xin, Deng Yi Gen

This is when sifu took me aside and explained the handstand to me, especially that it was at an angle, not straight up. He said that it had always been done that way, but he hadn't taught it to the others because 'they couldn't do it, but you can.'

When I told Cai Yuhua, he was pretty skeptical, since they had been with sifu for years. And obviously, if anyone could do a difficult move, it was Yuhua, not me. Yuhua figured sifu had been looking at Chen Xin's book and seen the handstand and found a way to work it in. I don't do it, because, contrary to what sifu said, I couldn't do it either.

Cai Yuhua had warned me when he introduced me to sifu, "don't believe everything he says," which I thought was an odd way to introduce your sifu, but he meant in the 'telling stories' way. This may be one of those instances where sifu's imagination got the better of him. It is, however, a good technique, not as an angled handstand on its own, but when someone grabs your foot you can definitely use it.

Later, Cai Yuhua also recommended to me that I train more on my own, as did Cheng and him. Otherwise, sifu tended to keep changing things, just to keep it interesting for him.

My visa fiasco was resolved by a martial brother. Li, a lawyer, came along with me for my final visit with the visa officers. He was remarkably skilled, and without his help I'm not sure how it would have turned out. He came along with cigarettes on offer and a casual, 'this isn't such a big deal' approach. I took on the 'I don't speak Chinese so well' act (considering my state of mind, it wasn't a stretch of my acting skills), and he sorted it all out. He told me that the officer has such awful writing that he had no worries – once he saw it, he knew he could talk circles around him. They gave me a letter to sign (my first self-criticism letter after sixteen years in China, strangely exhilarating) that stated that I had <u>inadvertently</u> stayed beyond my visa period. This meant that I would not be denied entry in the future. I was so, so relieved when they gave me my passport back, like coming back to life.

Years later this episode came back to haunt me, as the question 'have you ever had a visa violation?' was added to visa applications, and now I have to send a copy of the letter and write an explanation every single time I apply.

With some of my martial brothers, Li in the middle.

45. **Inside Hits**　　　　lǐ biān pào　　　　　　　里边炮

<u>Overall Movement</u>: Horse stance double strike to the NW and SE.

<u>Footwork</u>: Land the right foot and set to a horse stance.

<u>Breakdown of Movement</u>:

Part One: If you did part three of move 44, continue to turn to the right, rotating the right leg at the hip, and land into a bow stance. Hit the right fist down in the same direction as the kick, hitting with the backfist.

If you stopped at part two (which is normal), turn the left foot out, bring it in, and land it with a stamp. Turn the body left and swing the right fist down to hit with across with the heel of the fist. Cross the arms in front of the belly, the right on the outside. Make sure power has been directed down. Photo 45a.

Part Two: Drop the right foot to the northwest into a slightly turned horse stance. The body is now facing southwest, in a stance that is angled. Swing the fists up and over to backfist with the fist hearts up, at shoulder height. The right fist is above the right thigh and the left fist is above the left thigh. Photo 45b.

45a 45b

<u>Direction of Movements</u>: The stance is on the southeast – northwest line, the focus towards the northwest.

<u>Possible Applications</u>: The action in part one breaks the grip of the opponent, then you can move in and hit. The primary attack is the right forearm and fist. If you remain in contact with him after your heel kick, twist and grab him with your left arm. Lower your left leg to move in on him and get your right arm on his torso to take him to your left.

The actual hit, part two, not considering coming from the previous movement, is a strong release from being hugged from behind.

<u>Internal Connections</u>: Gather into the body when closing the arms, to explode out from the core. If the coiling is done properly, the arms will be sent out along the correct lines.

<u>About the Name</u>: 'Inside' means that the power, direction, and placement in relation to the technique of the opponent is from and on the inside. *Pao* usually refers to a double hit, and in this case, it means to either side.

<u>Additional Comments</u>: You may also hit with the front backfist at waist height and the rear backfist at shoulder height. Watch that you do not lean forward if you do this.

Although I would not trade my years of hard training for anything, in my middle years I have come to appreciate the idea of not training too hard. If Taijiquan (or whatever you do) is supposed to enhance your life, it should be one of the high points of your day. If you train just enough that you wish you had a bit more time to continue, then you will look forward to training the next day. This is the way to ensure daily, continual, and lighthearted training.

The problem with this is that while light training makes sense for ordinary people, if you want to be really good, you have to have put in a lot of hard hours. I am firmly in the camp that believes that if something is worth doing, it is worth doing well. Something balanced, smooth, unimpeded, and powerful is just more satisfying than something awkward. You need to be someone who enjoys hard work and doesn't mind a bit of pain and 'eating bitter' if you want to do something well.

But you need to relish the hard work. If you train to the point of exhaustion day in and day out, you get to the point of not caring, and you will no longer improve. There is a difference. In Shanghai, I hated getting up before five, but once I had gotten up and was on the bike and the sun started to rise, I always enjoyed the ride and looked forward to getting to the park to train. In Beijing, at the Physical Culture Institute, I remember months of exhaustion where I only really wanted to sleep. I would drag myself into training in hopes of lengthening the warmup as long as possible. At times I did not even like wushu, it was just my job. Fortunately, I survived those times, and the intense training of the Institute is one of the reasons I was better able to learn in the parks later.

Shadowboxing in Shanghai

46. **Hit the Drum**   jī gǔ pào   击鼓炮

<u>Overall Movement</u>: Repeated coiling, hooking punches remaining in place, angled to the NW.

<u>Footwork</u>: Stay in stance, but turn a bit towards the strikes, and allow the legs to spring naturally.

<u>Breakdown of Movement</u>:

Part One: Coil the hands in to turn over and punch with an inward double hit, left fist heart up, right down. This is a double hit, but is slightly one then the other. First hit with the left fist, then the right. Photos 46a and 46b.

Part Two: Punch left, then right slowly, to the same place, both fist hearts down, and the knuckles slightly hooked in. Photos 46c and 46d.

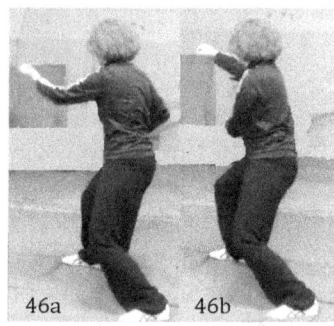

46a   46b

Part Three: Punch left, right, with a quick and small *fajin*. Stay in stance but keep loose and use the natural spring of the legs. Photos 46e and 47f.

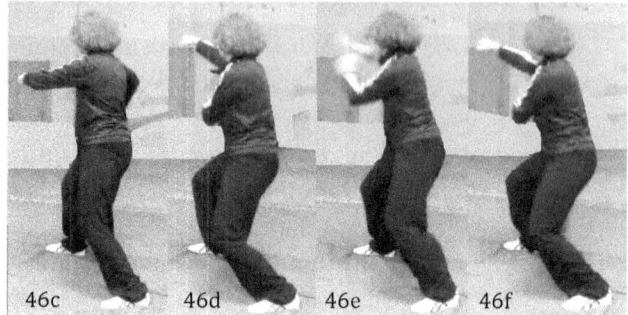

46c   46d   46e   46f

<u>Direction of Movements</u>: The stance stays on the southeast – northwest line, the focus towards the northwest.

<u>Possible Applications</u>: Multiple releases and strikes to the same place, to both sides of the head or ears.

<u>Internal Connections</u>: The punches spring out from the rear leg. The power needs to travel lightly up through the body.

<u>About the Name</u>: This looks like hitting a narrow, vertical drum. You are hitting both sides of the drum alternately. This movement should have a smooth, natural rhythm. The 'drum' stands for the temples or ears, on both sides of the head of the opponent.

<u>Additional Comments</u>: You can do one double strike or three. Make sure you coil the arms well to develop a natural springy power.

There is another way to do this move: The same power and action, but punch right, left, right, left, right, left.

Yilu: The First Form

The first time the left fist comes in, the fist heart is up. For the rest of the punches, the fist eye is down. From the front, note the placement of the left fist in part one and part two.

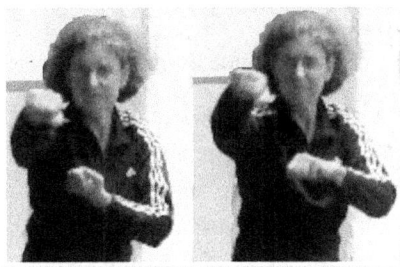

Sifu was also in Jiang Rongqiao's lineage, which included Baguazhang, Xingyiquan, Yang style taijiquan, and Taiji Changquan, among other things. In 2015 I was lucky to meet Jiang's adopted daughter, Zou Shuxian. I arrived in the autumn, by chance two weeks after sifu's funeral service, and there were people in her park that had gone to it. They were happy to talk about Huan Dahai once they knew I was his apprentice, and not just some random foreigner. Zou laoshi said that although his Bagua was good, he was very highly skilled in the Chen Taijiquan that he had learned in a different lineage. She also said that the reason he died so young was his love of drink and cigarettes. He was ninety. At ninety-three, she was still out in the park doing Yang Taijiquan every morning.

I met Madame Zou through another one of those strange meetings. A complete stranger, Hans, had emailed me with some question about bagua translation. Since he was Swedish, and my paternal grandfather came from Sweden, I was super friendly and helpful. It turned out that Hans was married to Jiang Rongqiao's great-grand daughter. We met up in 2015, in Shanghai, and they took me to meet 'gunainai' in the park. On that first trip, we went to a fancy restaurant near the park. On another trip, we visited her house, and went out for noodles. I tried to get a copy of an unpublished book Jiang Rongqiao had hand written, that I copied from sifu, but with mistakes. Unfortunately, she had lost it by lending it to someone.

I went to train with Madame Zou that year, and in later years, but it wasn't as great as it could have been. She would be surrounded by people who didn't want to learn, but loved to chat with a famous master. The chatters would hit on me if I stopped training for a second, so I couldn't really get corrections. In the end, I didn't go to that park much. I felt badly about it, especially with the family introduction, but such is life.

The Longhua Corner of Shanghai

Longhua Park was one of the largest parks in a city of few and small parks. I've seen its name translated as 'Dragon Beauty' and 'Luster of the Dragon.' In 1989, there were from .47 to 1.2 square metres of public greenspace per resident. That meant that if everyone in the city decided to go to the parks in the morning, they would have to be doing standing *qigong*. Fortunately for us, that didn't happen, and we had quite a bit of space for training.

The Longhua pagoda and temple have been there since the year 200, destroyed and rebuilt a few times, the final time in 977. In 1891, Longhua Road was built, oddly, to pass right between the temple and pagoda. The temple and its garden were on the north side, and the pagoda sat on its own on the south side, as now. Both have undergone renovations over the years. The pagoda, particularly, is a major historical site, and protected by law. It is quite special, being seven storeys and octagonal. It was the tallest building in the area for hundreds of years, only supplanted by Holy Trinity Cathedral in 1869.

Longhua pagoda. The slight tilt is not an accident of photography, but part of its charm.

Postcard: Old Shanghai, Shanghai People's Fine Arts Publishing House.

Yilu: The First Form

We weren't the only group training at Longhua Park. Each group had its space – all the regulars knew and no one encroached. Wrestlers trained next to us in the big grassy area and it was fun to watch them falling in the dirt. We were pretty friendly with them, and there was no hint of Taijiquan vs 'real' martial arts. The distinction was between martial artists and the 'music groups' which gradually became more popular. These were bigger groups that did the fan dancing type stuff or whatever. They were mostly in the paved area near the entrance. The martial artists were mostly in the grassy places, came as soon the park opened, and left earlier.

In the mid 1990s, Longhua Park was renovated. A huge Martyrs Cemetery and museum was built in memory of the 1927 Shanghai Massacre – the KMT purge of communists. Tens of thousands of workers, students, and protesters were shot down in the street, and thousands of communists were executed in the temple grounds.

Most of our grassy areas were paved over, and a lot of features were added – a fountain, covered walkways, and more washrooms. Losing our big grassy area, we ended up on paving stones by a covered walkway by a fountain. Instead of remembering moves by where the treeline was, now I remembered by where the fountain was. We didn't really like the changes, training on pavement is harder on the body than training in grass or dirt, and there were more passersby. But at least we had a covered seating area, with just enough space to train straight line moves when it rained. Another good thing about the move was that we were nearer the temple, so could hear the monks chanting. I liked their accompaniment to my "Lustrous Dragon' Taiji.

Longhua Park's history resonates for foreigners, too. Lunghwa was one of the Civilian Assembly Centres set up by the Japanese for the Shanghailanders. From 1943 on, when the Japanese Army took over the city, most foreign non-combatant men, women, and children were interned. Many camps were for single men. Lunghwa camp, in the grounds of Kiangsu Middle School, close to the Lunghwa Aerodrome, was where most families were sent, with 127 'rooms' for families. The internment camps had no facilities – the internees had to build what they needed, and survive as best they could.

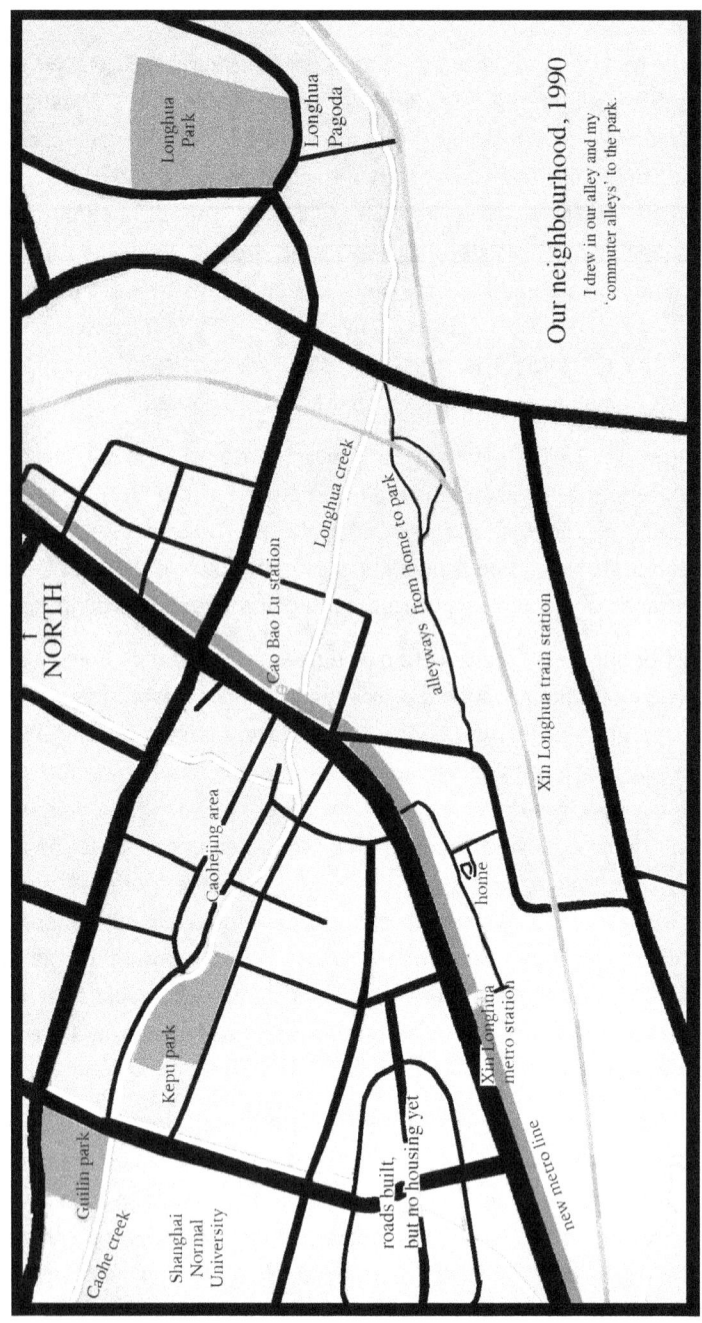

The exciting part of the commute was clambering across the uncontrolled railway crossing, then shooting out across a busy street between intersections. The housing out here was mixed, with villages, small private 'farm houses' like ours, and small apartment blocks.

47. Stab Backwards   dào chā shì   倒插式

Overall Movement: Step into an empty stance, then stand up, twisting away from a drive into the forward heel.

Footwork: Step the left foot forward, then step the right foot forward to an empty stance. Keep the left foot aligned straight to the stance, so both feet point in the same direction. The left thigh should be parallel to the ground.

Breakdown of Movement:

Part One: Step the left foot forward (northwest), and bring the left fist through to punch, fist eye down. Photo 47a.

Part Two: Step the right foot forward to a low empty stance and punch the right fist down, fist eye down. The empty stance is done with both feet aligned, do not turn out the rear foot. The right fist comes through then down inside the right shin. The left fist surface faces the right forearm, tucked slightly inside. Photo 47b.

Part Three: Rise and turn the hips to extend the right heel forward, straightening the right leg. Turn the upper body left. Further extend the right fist to the lower right, drawing the left fist to the chest. The right fist thumb is down and the left fist heart faces in. Photo 47c.

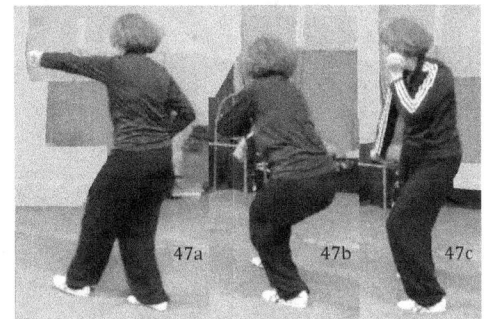

Direction of Movements: The stances stay on the southeast – northwest line, the focus still towards the northwest.

Possible Applications: In parts one and two, go down as if your left hand was grabbed, go along with the action to control and counterattack. Part three is a wrestling move, getting in tight to the opponent and using the body to roll him over the right leg and hip. It can also be a right fist strike to the groin when the body is in contact with the opponent.

About the Name: The backwards hit is action three, driving into the heel, getting power by turning the hip and body away.

Additional Comments: Here is the move from the front.

48. Overturn Rivers And Reverse The Seas   fān jiāng dǎo hǎi
翻江倒海

<u>Overall Movement</u>: Shift back and double strike high and low.

<u>Footwork</u>: Stand up on the left leg and lift the right knee, pivoting slightly so now face directly west.

<u>Breakdown of Movement</u>:

Part One: Stand up on the left leg. Coil the forearms and bring the fists up in tight to the body. The right is on the inside. Photo 48a.

Part Two: Snap the body and lift the right knee. Snap the fists out, right down and left up, arms coiled *shunchan* to their furthest extent. The right fist is over the right knee, the left fist is at the left temple, about a foot away. Both fists snap towards the outside with some downward power. Photo 48b.

48a   48b

<u>Direction of Movements</u>: The stance and focus turn to the west.

<u>Possible Applications</u>: Most effective as an escape from a hug. Since a hug would come from the back, the upper fist may strike the opponent in the head as the release is achieved. The lower fist may be used to strike an oncoming kick, but you need to time this exactly right and hit directly into the soft tissue of the ankle for it to be effective.

It is also useful as a throw of someone trying to grab you from the front. Your right knee can hit his groin while the right forearm takes his left arm down and your left forearm opens his right arm out or goes to control his right shoulder.

<u>Internal Connections</u>: Explode outwards from the centre of the body, so that the power goes both upwards and downwards into the strikes. If the power is gathered properly, the lines that the arms take will come naturally.

<u>About the Name</u>: The movement is small but the power generated is large, like rolling waves. Or, you are powerful enough to make a river run in reverse or turn back the tides of the sea, like a dragon.

<u>Additional Comments</u>: Coil the arms close to the body, do not simply snap out. The arms start out crossed at the belly, bring them up the body then snap out and down from at least chest height.

Here is the move from the front.

Yilu: The First Form

I learned the Taiji Changquan form from my senior martial brother Cheng Jiefeng, who had learned it directly from Jiang Rongqiao. Sifu and Cheng had their own versions of the form, since both had learned it from Jiang Rongqiao, but with different understandings. Eventually they decided Cheng would teach me, because at first Cheng would teach me on Sunday, sifu would spend the week changing it, then Cheng would change it back the next Sunday. Changes are fine when you're working on something, but a little trying when you're just learning it. As it turned out, sifu was happy with Cheng's version, and mostly left it alone. I took three rolls of photos in 1996. I was allowed one roll per weekend as he did the form without pauses.

Cheng, sifu's elder apprentice, was already a master in his own right. He taught at the Traditional Chinese College, and kept theory and practice together. On retirement, he teaches free in a park, there for his own training every day except when it rains. He is an encyclopedia of martial arts, especially *qigong* and Taijiquan styles.

I practised the form for twenty years alone before finding Cheng again in 2015. He was amazed and happy that I still remembered it, though he laughed at what he calls my 'Longfist' way of doing it. He turned it back into what it is supposed to be – Jiang Rongqiao's mix of the power flow and structure of Baguazhang, Xingyiquan, and Taijiquan (though I am convinced of the validity of my Chaquan flavour, considering all the horse stance punches and very Tantui-esque Single Whips). Now. Now when I go, he also has time to show me the applications. I hope one day to get his permission to publish the old photos of him, to go along with my writeup of the form. I have yet to see anyone else who does this form.

49. **Brush The Knee And Plant A Punch** lōu xī zāi chuí 搂膝栽捶
   or **Punch The Ground** jī dì chuí 击地捶

Overall Movement: Land forward and punch straight down.

Footwork: Stamp the right foot then land the left foot to the front (northwest) to a low bow stance.

Breakdown of Movement:

Part One: Bring the right hand around to brush the right knee with the palm down, then lower the right foot to stamp. Photo 49a.

Part Two: Step the left foot forward and shift to a bow stance. Brush the left knee with the left hand, hooking the hand as it passes by (start to form the hook at the little finger). Bring the right fist up and over, then punch down by the left foot. Turn the body left so the left hand is hooked behind the body, facing up about waist height. Photos 49b and 49c.

Part Three: Lower the right fist almost to the ground, then open the hand and circle the palm as if scooping up sand or grabbing something on the ground. Do a full clockwise circle. Complete the circle then hit down with the back of the hand. With this action, the body sinks slightly to take the hand down, rises slightly, then sinks again. Clench the left hand and tuck the fist in to the waist, then twists out so it finishes at the left side of the temple, blocking the head, fist heart facing out as much as possible (little finger side facing the body). Both hands *fajin* at the same time. Look upwards. Photos 49d and 49e.

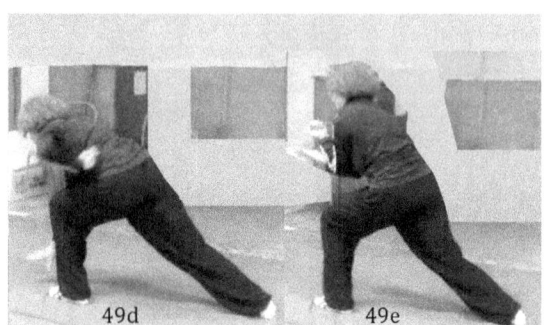

Direction of Movements: Punch to the west.

Possible Applications: Use the right arm to take down the opponent, getting your whole body behind it. You have to watch out for names that make you think you should be doing something that you aren't necessarily doing. It is unlikely that you would want to punch someone already lying on the ground. This action grabs with the left arm, steps in the left leg to control and get as tight as possible to the opponent, connecting with your whole body. Then throw him with the body, assisted by the right arm across his neck.

In action three you could be throwing sand in the opponent's eyes. Both hands *fajin*, but the left is more assisting in getting the power. Although it appears like you are striking down with the back of the right hand, you put power upward into the palm.

Internal Connections: The power need to connect directly through from the rear foot to the head, pressing upwards. In this way the power can transfer down into the fist.

About the Name: Plant A Punch is a name often used traditionally for a punch that drives straight down, especially when the body leans. The technique looks like planting a rice seedling into the ground, and the power should continue through as if 'planting.' Do not think of stopping at contact with the opponent lying on the ground, but of driving right through into the ground. Punch The Ground is a more prosaic name, but describes the same kind of power.

Additional Comments: The stamp can be a quick-step to move forward into the opponent. When stamping and moving a step forward, move everything at once. The stamp helps to propel the body forward. Don't stamp when you are reaching the foot forward, as the angle on the leg is wrong.

The low punch is about four inches off the ground. The fist is turned so the thumb faces in and the fist approaches the left foot. Keep the upper body aligned straight with the back leg, but roll the right shoulder down. Press the meridian point on the top of the head to the front.

You can see Cai Yuhua's alignment during the 'throw sand in the face' snap, keeping the hip set down, and keeping the hand down while the power is sent up, from this angle.

Chen Xin's book includes an excellent discussion on how to press the power into the head to maintain balance and power in this movement. "When I was young my martial elder brothers showed me how to press this move down, pressing down the spine and using it as a firm bridge connecting the upper and lower body, so I could get the feeling of the *qi* connection. But when they twisted in the posture, they both fell over. I realised that to do this posture with the twist, you needed to press up into the head. When the *jing* presses up into the top of the head, the *jing* is directed into the groin area, which becomes opened and rounded and presses both feet firmly into the ground. Then when the torso twists, even a number of men can't hold you down or push you over. My elder brothers thus showed me that when the *qi* makes the feet solid, nothing can interfere with my movement."

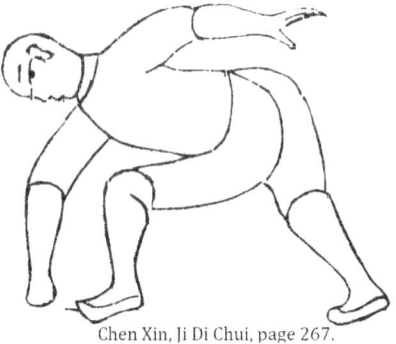

Chen Xin, Ji Di Chui, page 267.

Qi could be called energy, activation, or power, depending on the context. Traditional Chinese explanations of the body do not worry about nuances between energy and matter – there is no clear-cut distinction. *Qi* is energy, the ability to energize, matter on the verge of turning into energy, and energy on the verge of becoming matter, among other possibilities. Similarly, *jing* and *shen* are both physically and non-physically present in the body and mind. It is possible for *jing* to be the source of life, the essence of life, and a fluid which circulates in the body, and for *shen* to be the vitality of the body and mind, the awareness of life, and the human 'soul.' In the Chinese worldview, the *qi* can be stored in the *dantian*, the *jing* in the kidneys, and the *shen* in the heart with no expectation of finding them there with a microscope. What causes movement is not necessarily separate from the movement itself or from what moves. This is one reason why descriptive passages in martial arts books sometimes seem circular to Western logic. The Chinese language does not need to make distinctions that are necessary in English. At the surface level of expression, the Chinese language can use the same word as a verb, noun, or adjective, so the 'topic' being described could be active, matter, or a property.

Yilu: The First Form

50. **Roll Over And Two Rises**   fān shēn èr qǐ   翻身二起
    or **Two Rising Kicks**   èr qǐ jiǎo   二起脚

<u>Overall Movement</u>: Turn around and jump kick.

<u>Footwork</u>: Set first to a horse stance, then an empty stance, then step forward, push off with the right and swing the left leg up to assist the right kick. Land on the left leg.

<u>Breakdown of Movement</u>:

Part One: Do another small circle with the right hand as if grabbing. Sit back on the right leg and turn right. Block up with the right arm. Brace out low with the left arm, extending it well out over the left leg, slightly in front of it, putting power into the heel of the fist. Roll back, turning the left foot in so that the feet are parallel in a horse stance. Photo 50a.

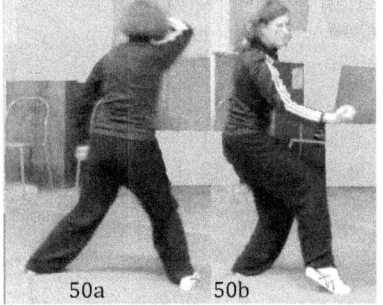

Part Two: Sit back to the left leg and continue to turn to the right (now facing east), bring the right hand down in a backfist. Bring the left fist over to up by the head, rolling the shoulder through from the previous position. Photo 50b.

Part Three: Move forward into the right foot, then drive into it to gain power for the jump. Hook the left hand around the left knee before you take off. Push off strongly up with the right leg. Swing the left knee up then kick the right foot. The arms swing naturally to assist the jump. The right arm swings down strongly then circles up to slap the right foot. The left arm comes forward and down, then swings back and up. Photos of Cai Yuhua, 50c, 50d, 50e, and 50f.

Part Four: Land on the left foot with the right knee still up, ready to go to the following move, don't just drop the foot down. Keep control, keeping the right knee up, so that you can chose whether to do the jump back or a step back into the following move. Photo of Cai Yuhua 50g.

Shadowboxing in Shanghai

Direction of Movements: Jump towards the east.

Possible Applications: The turn deals with an opponent grabbing you from behind. Turning while raising and twisting the right arm releases his grip. Then you may backfist down with the right fist, or press him down with the right arm to aid in the left fist or elbow coming through to strike down.

Jump up and forward to kick with the right foot to the opponent's jaw. The left foot or knee could also be used to strike. You could also step or jump the left foot into the opponent's hip crease to help drive the right foot into a high kick. You don't have to jump up for a high kick, you may jump forward to drive into the opponent with the right knee. Jumping in the form develops the ability to drive into a kick, whether up or forward.

Internal Connections: Lift the *qi* in the body with a rising breath to assist with the jump.

About the Name: Some branches simply call this move Two Rises, *Er Qi*, and that is the important part of the name. Two Rises is traditionally used to refer to a jump single slap kick because both legs leave the ground in sequence, one, two. The left knee first comes up to drive the right kick up. It is thought also that there can be a left kick as well as the right kick.

Additional Comments: If you are jumping, really go for it, taking a large step forward and swinging the arms to push off well into the jump, transferring the horizontal power to vertical takeoff.

Bring the left leg up well, as it can be a first kick, then slap kick the right leg in the air, and land on the left leg after kicking.

If you cannot yet, or can no longer, do a jump kick, take a step forward with the left foot and do a normal slap kick with the right foot, but adding the swing of the arms as you would do for the jump, and holding the left arm out with a hook-hand.

There is no point in trying to jump if you are no longer or have never been a jumper, but never do a movement sloppily because you can't do it. Do an approximation of the movement to the best of your physical and mental ability. Keep the feeling and the power flowing through the movement. If you stop the flow because you can't do an action quite right, then you have to start to store power all over again. There is no point in doing the kick sloppily because it is supposed to be a jump but you are not jumping. If you are not jumping, then do a proper step forward with the same arm movements, and a good, solid, slap kick.

Sifu said that his house didn't have stairs to the second floor. He jumped. He said he liked having a place that his family couldn't get to. Yeah, right. But actually, I didn't see any stairs to the second floor in his house.

Since I was complaining about Chen Xin's use of trigrams and hexagrams in the slap kick moves, I would like to point out that he does lovely little verses about the moves as well. For this move, he wrote (page 277):

Five character verse: "Both feet rise, one after the other. The whole body leaps into midair. If not for the kick to the mouth, how else would you see the red blood flowing?"

Seven character verse: "Vital energy (*zhongqi*) rises to give power up the backbone. Continuous double kicks fly up. Were it not for the ambush to the blood vessels in the east, how could you manage to attack the nose in the west?"

Chen Xin, Er Qi, page 273.

Aside from verses being fun, they suggest that the left foot should be more than just an assist to the right jump kick, but should do a faking or real kick, making this truly 'two rises.'

51. **Beast's Head** (left)　　　zuǒ shòu tóu shì　　　左首头式

Overall Movement: Drop back and settle into a strong stance bracing out with both forearms.

Footwork: Land the left foot, step back the right foot to a cross step. Do not jump back in a hurry, keep the stepping clean. Then step the left foot back and settle into a horse stance.

Breakdown of Movement:

Part One: Land the left foot and step the right back. You should complete the right kick in the air before the left foot lands. Land under control with the right foot tucked in, then push off to do a small hop with the left foot to step the right foot back. Bring the hands up, turning the right hand so the palm faces forward and up, fingers pointing left. Turn the left palm up, fingers pointing left. Photo 51a.

Part Two: Step the left foot back and pull (*cai*) down across to the left, shifting weight to the left leg. Photo 51b.

Part Three: Shift right, pull (*cai*) across to the right, turning a bit to the right. Tuck the right hand in to the body, bring the left palm down along the right arm, and sit back on the left leg. Once the right hand seems trapped under the left, snap it out in a backfist, turning the body into a horse stance. The right fist finishes in front of the nose or lower, the left fist finishes in front of the waist. Both fist hearts face in, though the left may be twisted more to face down and almost out. Brace out with the outside edge of the forearms. Photos 51c, 51d, and 51e.

Direction of Movements: Step back to the west. Face north.

Possible Applications: This is a strong defensive action. If the opponent comes at you for a punch or grab, control his arm and draw it along the line it is already taking. Tuck your other forearm onto his arm above the elbow to

Yilu: The First Form

control his arm and draw it across. You can then draw him back the other way and strike with his face with a backfist. You can also draw him back across and break his arm with a forearm strike.

About the Name: The character for beast (*shou*) sounds the same as that for protect. So it means that it is a protective action – you hold yourself as if facing a beast, protecting yourself from an attack.

This type of double fisted posture is often called something like Protect The Heart, Hit The Tiger, or Beast's Head without much distinction between them. In the 1982 name list this is called Right Side Hit The Tiger. In the 1982 version of the form there is a move called 扑掌 *pu zhang*, Pounce With The Palms, just after the kick, before the Hit Tiger (in the 1982 list, Hit Tiger includes both Beast's Head and Hit Tiger).

Pounce With The Palms probably refers to one version I know that includes a *fajin* double palm strike on landing from the jump. Land the right foot, keep the left foot up, circle the palms down then up and *fajin* into both palms, hopping back naturally on the right foot.

Additional Comments: Action three is a fairly tight posture, the fists are on the midline. You may *fajin* in action three.

> How to cook an eel. First, you've got to kill it by chopping the head off, which is like chopping the head off a hard rubber hose that is jumping around. Then you have to cut it into pieces while the body is still jumping around. I came in on the process at this point. Xiaolan was standing on the neck as Yuhua was trying to get hold of it and chop it up, both laughing so hard it made the task even more difficult. I was horrified that they were chopping up a live animal, but they pointed to the already separated head jumping around on the ground. Cai Yuhua had caught it in the nearby stream.
>
> After that step I have no idea how to cook it, but apparently it is tricky to get just right. Xiaolan cooked it, as she was the eel specialist. Cai Yuhua normally cooked the family meals, so this was a special occasion. She cooked it to perfection, very tasty and tender, but the pieces still jumped when you touched them, which was freaky. I kept dropping them, as they jumped from my chopsticks.

52. **Hit The Tiger** (right)　　　yòu dǎ hǔ　　　右打虎

Overall Movement: Open out, shifting but not stepping.

Footwork: Shift to the left leg.

Breakdown of Movement:

Draw the left fist across under the right elbow, then up along the right forearm. Bring the right fist in, then coil it to hit further out at abdomen height with the heel of the fist. The left fist finishes at temple height, fist eye facing the temple. Shift to the left leg and turn the upper body a bit to the left to roll power into the forearms. Photos 52a and 52b.

Direction of Movements: The stance remains facing north, attention moves to the northeast.

Possible Applications: From the previous defensive position, deflect with the left arm and strike strongly out with the right fist. This action can also be used to break a hug from behind. or from the front.

Internal Connections: The power comes from the body core, to brace both arms outwards, hitting with a well balanced power through to both arms.

About the Name: This position is often traditionally called Ambush The Tiger, or Hit The Tiger. It brings to mind the posture of holding the tiger while pounding on its head.

Additional Comments: Here is the final posture more from the side, to show the alignment of the right arm and thigh.

53. **Beast's Head** (second time, right side) shòu tóu shì 首头式

Overall Movement: Turn around and repeat move 51 on the other side.

Footwork: Lift the right foot then land it where the left foot was, lifting the left foot just before the right arrives. Land the left foot in front (east). Then shift in the stance as in the preceding two movements.

Breakdown of Movement:

Part One: Lift the right foot and turn the body to right, turning to switch in place one-eighty degrees. Lift the left foot and place the right foot where it was, with no hesitation. Land the left foot towards the east. Coil the right palm over to face up and bring the left hand over facing down. Photos of James, 53a and 53b.

Part Two: Pull (*lü*) about halfway to the right, sitting more back onto the right leg. Then tuck the left hand in and bring the right palm over and down the left arm (like swallowing the hand). Left backfist in front of the nose (or lower) and pull down the right hand in front of the abdomen. Sit into a horse stance and keep the move fairly tight. Photos of James, 53c, 53d, 53e, 53f, and 53g.

Direction of Movements: The stance faces south.

Possible Applications: Release a grip on the right arm, using the whole body, then regain control with both arms. The rest is the same as move 51, on the other side.

54. **Left Hit The Tiger** (the second time, the left side)　　　zuǒ dǎ hǔ

左打虎

Overall Movement: Repeat Hit The Tiger on the other side, but not fully.

Footwork: Stay in stance, but roll a bit more in preparation for the following move.

Breakdown of Movement:

Bring the right fist in under the left elbow then draw it across the body as you bring the left fist down. The left fist hits with the heel of the fist at belly height, the right at temple height. This stance is quite open. Do not complete the posture as fully as the first time, but start to settle and coil to move smoothly into the following movement. Photos 54a, 54b (transitional).

Direction of Movements: Facing south, attention to the southeast.

> There is a tendency to over-explain things in Taijiquan, in a misguided attempt to facilitate learning. Books have many lists of errors, and many things <u>not</u> to do. They are all true, but firstly, they need to be learned gradually so that you don't think too much about them while performing. No one can think of that many things at once and not bind up. And secondly, as a maxim in mountain biking says, Never say don't look at that tree. There is no surer way of making your friend hit that tree.
>
> Basic coaching theory tells us is to suggest about three things to try to do, and not to suggest things to 'not do.' People cannot remember more in the heat of practice, and it is much more effective to try to <u>do</u> something than to try to <u>not do</u> something.
>
> Overthinking never helped anyone do anything physical. Playing mind games on opponents is exactly this – trying to get them to over-think and mess up. If we analysed how a bike stays upright as much as people analyse how to do Taijiquan, we would all still be walking.

Yilu: The First Form

55. **Right Stomp With A Palm**   yòu cǎi yī zhǎng   右踩一掌
     or **Right Stomp**   yòu cǎi   右踩

Overall Movement: Move forward with a low kick and strike.

Footwork: Drop down then move forward with a lowed turned out kick.

Breakdown of Movement:

Part One: Coil back, then drop down onto the right leg (but not to full low pouncing stance), continuing the roll of the arms. Coil the left fist in and, still turned over, out along the left leg, unclenching the hand with the thumb on the bottom. Roll the right fist back. Photos of James, 55a, 55b, and 55c.

Part Two: Shift forward and bring the right fist through. Come up on the left leg, but do not straighten it, and kick the right leg low with the foot turned out. Block up with the left arm. Slap the thigh with the right palm, following through to strike to the front (east). Photos 55d, 55e, and 55f.

Direction of Movements: Step to the east.

Possible Applications: Duck and come in with a right kick to the opponent's knee using the left arm to protect yourself and keep the opponent off balance as you move in.

The right hand "throws a dart that is concealed in a pouch on the side." Fighters used to carry these weapons that could be hidden and palmed easily, and the pouch was set up to release them easily. Extend the palm to throw the dart, but don't lift it high. The line of action from the circle of the arm will direct the dart up through momentum. The palm could also be a groin strike if you step in onto the instep instead of kicking. If you kick the knee, you are unlikely to be able to reach the groin with your hand.

<u>Internal Connections</u>: Roll up into the left arm to keep a connection between it and the supporting leg, to give stability and focus in the kick.

<u>About the Name</u>: *Cai* is the common term for a low kick, usually turned out, and usually hitting just below the opponent's knee and sliding down his shin to his foot. The first name gives importance to the hidden palm technique. The second name simply names the prominent technique.

> Taijiquan is an outdoor activity – when it is cold you concentrate on building *qi* and blood circulation, and when it is hot you concentrate on the suppleness of the tendons and ligaments. If you follow the natural fluctuations in weather, your body will develop over time without injury. Also, instead of working always on the same thing, which may lead to staleness, your training changes with the seasons. Performing the same form day in and day out is a lifetime of fascination. You can help the form change your body by allowing the weather conditions to change your focus.
>
> When you train in cold weather, as a rule of thumb, wear just one layer less on the legs than on the upper body. That is, if you wear three layers on top, have two on your legs. One layer on the legs is not enough for much of the year in northern countries. This is the Chinese method of dress, and it keeps the blood circulation warm throughout the whole body. The knees are fragile joints with poor circulation, and need to be kept warm. Westerners tend to bundle up on top and leave the legs with not enough cover. We wear thick socks to keep our feet warm. The Chinese tend to wear thin socks even in the cold, showing perhaps that their logic of warm leg circulation works.
>
> A trick for staying dry when training in the great heat and humidity of Shanghai is to put a small towel down your back inside your shirt. Tuck it into your trousers and loop it out over the neck of the shirt. When you finish training, take out the towel and the back of your shirt and top of your trousers are still dry (in Shanghai the rest is all soaked, but in normal heat keeping the back dry is often enough). This is also excellent for cold weather if you do not have high-tech wicking clothes. It is important to not get wet and stay wet in the cold, as you can easily get a chill when you stop.

56. **Whirlwind Kick** xuàn fēng jiǎo 旋风脚

Overall Movement: Land forward and do an inside turning kick, slapping the foot.

Footwork: Land forward, naturally starting to turn to the right, then do an inside turning kick with the left foot, landing it around to the east.

Breakdown of Movement:

Part One: Land the right foot forward, turned out. Bring the right palm in under the left arm. As you go onto the right leg, the body will naturally turn to the right because of the turn of the foot. Photo 56a.

Part Two: Swing the left leg up in an inside crescent kick, slapping the sole of the foot with the left palm (turn the palm over with the thumb side down and reach out to the foot). Complete the turn while kicking, lifting the heel slightly to pivot on the ball of the right foot. Land the left foot to the east, to complete the body turn to face east. Photos 56b, 56c, and 56d.

Direction of Movements: Land to the east, turning fully around to land again to the west.

Possible Applications: Slide the right foot down the opponent's shin to stomp on his foot or step in to set up your throw. Kick or throw with the left leg, using the left arm to control the opponent crossing his body with the foot behind him, so the left leg moves to the right as the left arm moves to the left in a scissoring action, to throw him down towards his back. You can sweep his ankles or sweep his torso with your leg, keep your arm at his chest height.

Internal Connections: Keep a vertical line through from the head to the supporting foot so that the spin is stable.

About the Name: Whirlwind Kick, also translated as Tornado Kick, is the traditional name for an inside spinning kick. It gives the image of spinning with a force that completely overpowers the opponent.

Additional Comments: Keep the left leg straight during the kick, and swing to its full range. Allow it to swing and drop, do not bend the knee to control the movement after the kick.

Once when I was practising I was a bit confused about a move yet again and asked sifu for help. He said, "Find it yourself, if you find it yourself it is yours. If I tell you, it is still mine."

This lightly made comment stayed with me. Just because he was eating breakfast and couldn't be bothered to get up didn't change the truth of what he said.

I like to teach like that, but these days you have to be 'helpful' all the time, even when you know it isn't ultimately helpful. At some point, if the student really, really can't get it, you should of course step in with a pointer. But if they haven't struggled to find it themselves, you'll just have to make the pointer again at another time.

Anything that I have found on my own, I know, no question. Things that I have made a real mess of, and only then gotten corrected, I remember. Things that I have been told over and over again, well, I wouldn't have to be told over and over if I'd really got it, would I?

This is also one reason why I don't think people should watch videos to learn, or just video themselves to remember. The process is too passive, they have not puzzled over it, thought it through, tried it out, and tried to express it in writing. It is not yet theirs.

57. **Thrust A Heel Behind**   dǎo dēng yī gēn   倒蹬一跟
    or **Right Thrust A Heel**   yòu dēng yī gēn   右蹬一跟

<u>Overall Movement</u>: Heel kick with the right foot with double punches.

<u>Footwork</u>: Bring in the right foot then kick it up to the east.

<u>Breakdown of Movement</u>:

Part One: Once the left foot has landed at the west, bring the right foot in beside it. Open and *shunchan* the hands with palms up to shoulder height. Photo 57a.

Part Two: Lift and hook the right leg in slowly. Bring the hands into the waist, still palms up, fingers gradually turning to point to each other. Clench to fists in front of the waist, and start to coil into the punches. Photo 57b.

Part Three: Heel kick the right leg to the east, putting it out slowly. Punch both fists out to the side at shoulder height, also slowly, fists turned over with the little finger side on top. Photo 57c.

<u>Direction of Movements</u>: Kick to the east.

<u>Possible Applications</u>: Coil the arms to deal with an opponent coming from behind, giving you the opportunity to turn towards him. Catch and push away the opponent with the leg. Hang onto the opponent to push with the foot to strike strongly into him, or push with the hands and foot to push him away. You can hit with your right shoulder, elbow, or fist, depending on how close you are. Similarly, you can kick with your knee, shin, or foot.

<u>Internal Connections</u>: Keep the hip joints tucked in to support the slow kick, tucking up into the *dantian*.

<u>About the Name</u>: *Deng yi gen* is the common traditional name for a heel kick. Because it follows a spinning kick, it is considered to be a kick behind the body, but it isn't really different from the other heel kicks, except that it is dealing with an opponent coming from behind.

Additional Comments: Cai Yuhua does this kick actually a little turned away. As usual, his way is cooler than mine.

Although I was in a poor household in a 'third world' country, the quality of food was actually better in some ways than in Canada, and certainly more natural. One day Cai Yuhua apologized for having made lunch from day-old-noodles. Buying a box of dry noodles as we do would never have occurred to him. Another time he tried out the new style factory raised chicken, which he declared tasted like fish, because they were fed fish scraps. He was used to farm chickens, or chickens and ducks raised at home.

People shopped daily for what they were going to cook that day, so it was always fresh. I've seen people shopping for fish complaining that it looked sluggish in the bucket. Not dead, just sluggish. You bought fish or chicken still alive. The seller would kill it for you if you wished, and clean the chicken.

After I saved a duckling's life by sitting on a stool snuggling it all day after it had gotten soaked in the rain (I know the phrase 'like water off a duck's back,' but you will have to believe me on this – it would have died), I seldom took part in any homegrown feasts. Sometimes I'd come home and a chicken would be gone, and I'd know I'd missed another fabulous meal. After I'd saved the duckling's life, they figured I was so soft hearted that I wouldn't be able to handle eating my friends. That was probably true in the earlier days, and for that particular duck, but I'd been changing with all my visits, had had a few run-ins with their beaks, and was actually looking forward to the chickens as a meal. Black boned chickens are the most nourishing chickens, and I missed out on them.

Yilu: The First Form

58. Capture the Flag And Go Forth With The Drums   qiān qí chū gu
牵旗出鼓

<u>Overall Movement</u>: Do a turned-out kick with hands up in the same direction, then land and double punch.

<u>Footwork</u>: Bring the right leg in, curl it and kick with the foot turned out. Then land and step the left foot forward to bow stance.

<u>Breakdown of Movement</u>:

Part One: Turn to face northeast, bring the right foot in without touching the ground. Bring the fists in to the waist, fist hearts up. Do not release off the twist, but further *nichan* as they come in, so that as you bring the fists through past the waist they change to a *shunchan*. Photo 58a.

Part Two: Kick the right foot to the Northeast, kicking with the heel, with the toes turned out. Double punch in the same direction, the forearms *shunchan* to the full extent. The left fist is in front at jaw height, the right is tucked in at the left elbow. Keep the move slow and controlled. Photo 58b.

Part Three: Land the right foot, then land the left foot forward and move to bow stance. Circle the fists into the waist and turn them over, then extend to double punch to the temples, either slowly or with a *fajin*. The fist hearts are obliquely forward. Photos 58c and 58d.

58a   58b   58c   58d

<u>Direction of Movements</u>: Advance the stance to the northeast. You may also do the kick not turned out, directly to the east.

<u>Possible Applications</u>: Hold the opponent and kick or drive down into his knee while punching. Then land forward and continue with more punches to the temples or ears.

All the moves from here to the Small Grapple are controlling the opponent and moving in on him with one technique after another, combining defense with offense.

<u>Internal Connections</u>: Keep the leg well inside the hip to be able to complete then turn the kick to have power into the step.

About the Name: This is one of the coolest names in martial arts forms. It just fits the action, even without thinking too much about the flags and drums of the battlefield. The image of hitting drums again makes us think of a double hit to the temples.

Additional Comments: You may raise the knee with the foot turned out, and not extend the kick with the two fists. Then when you land, first extend the foot to trample at knee height.

You may also stamp the right foot as it lands. This is best if you have done the straight kick, as the foot is not turned and the knee is in no danger of injury. Use the stamp as a quick-step to move forward.

This photo is of our group (my martial eldest brother, Cheng, in the white shirt) stepping down with the trample.

This is Cai Yuhua doing the parts two to three.

And this is the move from the front.

Yilu: The First Form

59. Brace The Roofbeam To Punch   jià liáng hóng chuí   架梁肱捶

<u>Overall Movement</u>: Shuffle step forward for a high deflection and punch.

<u>Footwork</u>: Follow-in step the right foot to beside the left then step the left to the side into a half-horse stance.

<u>Breakdown of Movement</u>:

Part One: Sink back slightly and circle the fists up, *nichan* slightly, to open, then close. Then *shunchan* and drop the right fist into the left palm at the *dantian*. At the same time, stamp the right foot in just behind the left foot – a quick-step to move forward. Photos 59a, 59b, and 59c.

Part Two: Step the left foot to the left. Bring the hands up to about chest height together, further *shunchan* the left arm and allow the right hand to follow it. The left hand is in a 'character eight,' or V shape. Lower and close the forearms then *fajin*. Punch the right fist out with the fist eye up. Deflect out and up with the left forearm, clenching the fist. Photo 59d.

<u>Direction of Movements</u>: Step to the north, punch to the east.

<u>Possible Applications</u>: You have just hit high, so the opponent will probably come in low. Cover up the attack with your forearms, then you can roll the left deflection up and get the right punch in.

<u>Internal Connections</u>: Drive power from the right heel and calf through the body into the arms, transferring power rather than using a weight shift.

The rolling action prior to the punch practises the absorbing of forces into the body to pop them back out again, along a line established by that taken in the gathering. The sequence from here to the Small Grapple all work on this principle.

<u>About the Name</u>: This refers to when you need to brace up a bridge or a roof beam with a post, without losing support at any time, to be able to work on it. The action of the left arm, controlling the opponent upwards, is what allows the right hand to punch through underneath.

The connection between fighters is often done through the arms, bridging the gap between then. Because the arms are often used in this way, in the martial arts the word bridge '*liang*' has come to mean techniques of the forearm. So the name can also be translated as 'brace up with the forearm and hit with the other fist.'

Additional Comments: Wait until the deflecting block has started to roll out before punching. The left arm deflects to allow the right fist to land the punch.

This is the opening and the final punch, from the front.

> Tourists to China often come back with stories about public toilets, about which I have many, but I don't pass on, as I feel it is a pretty silly way to describe your trip. And, since they never had to deal with a *matong*, they really don't have a clue. A *matong* is a big wooden chamber pot in the corner of the room, emptied and cleaned every morning. This was Cai Yuhua's job, one that he did daily and uncomplainingly. This was quite common in the old downtown area of Shanghai with lack of plumbing in housing, a completely normal part of life.
>
> In our case, it was in the living room, as there really was just the one family room. Later it was moved to the small room between the entrance and the main room, where there was a desk and space to squeeze in a single bed for visitors when the others were full. The family thought I was a bit odd in wanting to be alone when I sat on it, but got used to my foreign quirks. There was a low screen that shielded it, but I just couldn't plunk myself down and carry on a conversation. Now I think it might have been better for my character development for me to have adjusted to their habits.
>
> The best improvement Cai Yuhua ever made to his house was building a toilet/shower room in the garden shed. The shower was cold water that trickled down, but it was lovely having a private room for cleaning up. I didn't mind squatting around the outside drain brushing my teeth, and the nightly basin foot soak in the courtyard was a social event, but full body washing and toilet are kind of nice to do alone. People who complain about going outside to an outhouse do not get any sympathy from me. Running across the courtyard through mosquitos or rain to a private room was a treat.

Yilu: The First Form

60. **Palm Strike Below**   xià jī zhǎng   下击掌

Overall Movement: Move forward again and brace with the right arm as the left arm strikes low.

Footwork: Follow-in step the right foot and step the left foot into a half horse stance.

Breakdown of Movement:

First open and close the forearms as in the preceding moves. Place the right fist in the left palm. Circle in the right foot to beside the left foot and continue to circle forward to the east. Then step the left foot forward into a half horse stance. Open the hands, the right high in front of the head, the left low in line with the left knee. This is a low strike with the forearm and heel of the palm or fist. Photos 60a, 60b, 60c, and 60d.

Direction of Movements: Step and strike to the east.

Possible Applications: Move in tight to the opponent, control with the right arm, and press in with the left leg and arm, striking or throwing.

Internal Connections: Keep a strong bracing line through both arms, expanding through the body.

About the Name: Another straightforward description of the action.

Additional Comments: You may drop almost into a low pouncing stance and thread the left palm along the left leg.

I have the habit of doing this with closed fists, and can't remember if I was taught that way, or if I've just developed the habit because it feels good and makes me thing I'm doing Bajiquan.

This is the alignment, seen from the front.

61. **Greet The Face With A Hand** yíng miàn shǒu 迎面手
    or maybe **Greet The Face With An Elbow** yíng miàn zhǒu
    迎面肘

Overall Movement: Coil again then roll through and advance, putting pressure to the forearm.

Footwork: Quick-step the right foot in, to push the left foot forward, then follow in with the right, with the possibility of another forward step.

Breakdown of Movement:

Bring both hands back, coiling, and roll through, stepping the right foot up, the left foot forward, then doing a follow-step with the right. *Shunchan* the left forearm to its fullest extent to brace forward, placing it vertically. Press the right middle and index fingers close to the left elbow crease. Photos 61a, 61b, and 61c.

Direction of Movements: Advance to the east.

Possible Applications: Press into the opponent's chest, moving forward with constant pressure. Keep the forearm vertical, put power to the front edge of the elbow, and press with the full forearm assisted with your other arm. You can do a further follow-in step with the right leg and drive the opponent further back, just keeping a solid pressure in the arms and not losing contact with his chest. Sifu was often quite casual about corrections, but he was very definite that the forearm must be vertical here, so that the elbow is in contact.

Internal Connections: Roll back into the body but keep a connection through the arms to maintain pressure before the press forward.

About the Name: Some of the names show a sense of humour that I enjoy. The use of the word 'greet' is the same as to greet a guest at the door.

This is also an example of how errors creep in to the name lists. In my copied name list I have written 手 (*shou*) but in my notes on the form I have written 肘 (*zhou*) and I do not remember if this is because sifu ever referred to the move as *yingmen zhou* instead of *shou*. In pronunciation, *shou* and *zhou* are pretty close.

Most copied name lists are just that – copied. The originals are given to the student, hand copied, and returned. So mistakes can occur if the character is not written clearly, if the character is one the student does not recognize, if the student writes down the wrong character for any reason, or if the teacher verbally says something different from what appears on the name list.

I am confident that 手 *shou* was in the name list, as it is almost impossible to mistake that character. I have no idea whether or not 肘 *zhou* is a mistake, but I think it is, as although it is an elbow technique, you do not lift the elbow to face height. You do strike with the elbow, though, laying it into his chest.

<u>Additional Comments</u>: You may take another step forward with the left foot after the main strike, to extend the movement further, keeping the pressure on.

In my notes it says to step the right foot in front of the left before the strike, but I do not remember doing this. I remember always a quick-step up to behind the left foot.

> This form has a number of movements that involve switchover, shuffle, and quick steps, to quickly move in without losing the power of your technique. This is because you usually start out a bit too far away from your opponent to be able to throw or grapple effectively, though you may be able to strike. Also, the opponent is likely to move back when he perceives an attack coming in. So you need to be able to move forward quickly while maintaining contact with and control over your opponent.
>
> Getting in close and keeping close is key to gaining control over an opponent and taking him down or away. When the body is in contact, you have a lot more control, and he has a lot less options, than if you just grab and keep a distance. For example, laying the body against his and using your upper arm to control his head and take him down is a lot more effective than trying to grab his head to pull.

Speaking of greetings, when people ask 'who's there?' the correct response is *shi wo*, 'it's me.' It works even when you've been away for five years. When I turned up completely without warning at the gate after years away (you can't see the person on the other side), Cai Yuhua's mother called out 'who's there,' I said 'it's me,' and she opened the door immediately. If they don't recognize your voice, you're not someone they want to open the door to. If you have to say your name, they would prefer that you say so from the outside so they can decide about you.

62. Little Grapple And Hit   xiǎo qín dǎ   小擒打

Overall Movement: Move forward again, coiling the arms together with an embracing action.

Footwork: Sit back slightly, quick-step forward to a sixty/forty stance, sit back again and turn the left foot in.

Breakdown of Movement:

Part One: *Shunchan* the right hand, keeping the index and middle fingers on the left elbow. This makes the left arm *nichan*, starting a sweeping action. As the left hand sweeps down, coil the right hand back, sitting back slightly. Photo 62a.

Part Two: Quick-step in with the right foot, then move forward to the original stance and bring the right fist around, the backfist facing left, placing the forearm on the left palm. You may *fajin*, but the sequence is smoother if you don't. Photos 62b and 62c.

Part Three: Sit back to the right leg slightly, turning right and turning the left foot in. Start to coil the right fist under the left forearm. Sit back to the left leg, bringing the right fist out from under the left forearm, the fist heart up. The left hand stays on the right forearm the whole time. Photo 62d.

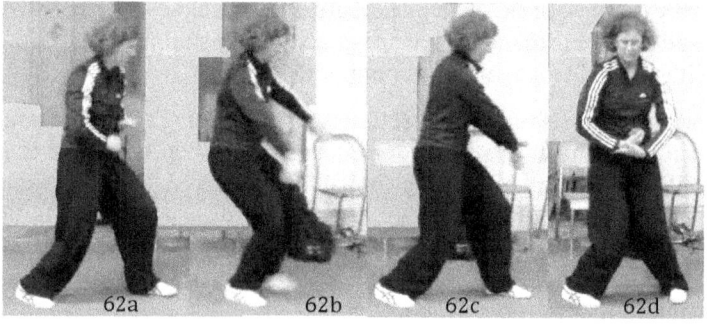

Direction of Movements: Advance to the east, then turn to the west.

Possible Applications: Parts one to two move in on the opponent, grabbing him around the waist to force him off balance and bend him backwards. Grab your right forearm with your left hand to better squeeze him. You must move in to complete contact with the torso, and make sure not to lean forward to possibly fall down with him. Part three serves to practice getting out of grabs to the arm, using weight shift, turning, and coiling.

About the Name: Parts one and two combined is a strong and effective grappling technique, but part three is the 'little grapple.' Some Chen branches call this movement Little Grapple And Control *Xiao Qinna*, without the Hit, which is equally as appropriate.

I am glad that I did so much of my living and training in China in the days before the internet. Although it meant that I lost contact with my sifu and friends in Shanghai afterwards, it also meant that I had the full experience while I was there. No distractions, no contact with the outside world, only letters to friends and family, carefully written on thin blue airmail letter-envelopes.

Cai Yuhua's sister and niece would drop by often. His niece used the home as an after school homework stop, taking care of her grandparents while they took care of her. She was the kind of kid that gives you hope for the future.

The people wandering in and out became my friends and family. On one of my later lengthy visits, one of his apprentices (in the tie on the right) had opened a restaurant, so we had a constant supply of pre-cooked meals. He did a particularly good cucumber salad, which I have never been able to duplicate.

You couldn't ask for a better bunch of guys than Yuhua's apprentices.

63. **Hold The Head And Push A Mountain** bào tóu tuī shān 抱头推山

<u>Overall Movement</u>: Double straight push.

<u>Footwork</u>: Turn and settle into the left leg, then step into a right bow stance.

<u>Breakdown of Movement</u>:

Part One: Turn right, sitting on the left leg. Continue the small circle of the right hand and open both hands over the right knee, palms facing up.

Part Two: Turn right, opening the palms up and around at shoulder height, blocking out with palms up. Settle further into the left leg. Photo 63a.

Part Three: Step into a right bow stance, bring the hands in to the chest, and double push to chest height, balancing power into the upper back. Push into the rear calf, directing power to the centre of the body without shifting the weight too far forward. Photos 63b and 63c.

<u>Direction of Movements</u>: Push to the west.

<u>Possible Applications</u>: Turn around to deal with an attack from the rear. Open up the arms to break the grip of an opponent then move in to push strongly on the chest.

<u>Internal Connections</u>: Expand into the push, getting the power from a transfer from the rear heel rather than a weight shift to the front leg. Feel a direct line from the heel to the hands.

<u>About the Name</u>: The dictionary, non-martial, meanings of *baotou*, hold the head, are; one) to cover the head for protection; two) to interlace the fingers behind the head; and three) to clasp the head in the hands in dismay.

All suggest that the hands are brought well up to the head, if not behind it. This reminds you to always do an entering or controlling action to get the opponent off balance before attempting an attack. It also reminds you to keep your hands up when you bring them in.

Push The Mountain is the common traditional name for a settling double push that intends to uproot the opponent. This is a strong push, uniting the force of the whole body, as if trying to uproot and push a mountain far away. To push a mountain, you must first sink down. You should think of what is the controlling move and what is the finishing move of all the techniques. They may be tightly integrated, but you can't just attack and hope the opponent will go along with you.

> The head is always naturally upright and the torso is vertical in almost all postures. You must sink into the hip joints so that the body remains upright on its own. You cannot let the hips be tight and then tighten up the torso to hold it straight. Applying power within yourself and to an opponent depends on settling and releasing deep within the pelvis and through to the ankles. There is no need to write this for each movement, it should be done without thinking about it, as a natural part of the movements and postures. The ankles play a much larger role than is usually recognized.

The heat of a Shanghai summer has to be experienced to be believed. Training finished at seven am because after that it was too hot to do anything. Our clothes were completely soaked with sweat before the first time through the form. The upside of that is that my body learned to sweat through every single pore.

'Sleeping' meant lying on a plank (too hot for mattresses) sweating and waiting for morning. 'Waking' meant moving and breaking out into even more of a sweat. Weeks of sleep deprivation due to the unrelenting heat of August 1990 made me move out of Cai Yuhua's home and get a room with air conditioning in a relatively nearby residence at Shanghai Teachers University. It was more than I could afford (I think $20 a night), but after going all the way to Shanghai it didn't make sense to be too tired to think straight, much less to listen to sifu and train. I had a Japanese roommate who chanted Buddhist prayers every day, relaxing for naps. I found a great spot for training on the flat roof in the afternoon, shaded and cooled by the lines of drying sheets, seen only by the residence's laundry workers, who soon got used to me. I spent many happy hours on the rooftop doing our *chansijin* exercise.

University residences in China are all locked the same way – a cable bike lock looped around the door handles from the inside. This means you can't get in or out between the hours set by the institute without getting the doorman up. Chinese are pretty early risers, so this wouldn't normally be a problem, but to make training I had to be on my bike by 5:30 am. The doorman hated me and I swear would change his sleeping spots on the sofas scattered around the lounge just so I couldn't find him.

64. Triple Palm Exchange   sān huàn zhǎng   三换掌

<u>Overall Movement</u>: Push right, left, and right palms.

<u>Footwork</u>: Stay in place, but roll and shift to put power in the pushes.

<u>Breakdown of Movement</u>:

Part One: Settle then shift a bit to back into a bow stance. Push the left palm out, fingers pointing up, palm facing right. Turn the right palm up and pull in under the left elbow. Photos 64a and 64b.

Part Two: Shift a bit to a horse stance. Push the right palm out, palm facing down, fingers pointing left. Pull the left palm in under the right elbow, palm up. Photo 64c.

Part Three: Settle then shift a bit to a bow stance. Push the left palm out, fingers pointing up, palm facing right. Pull the right palm in, palm up. Photos 64d and 64e.

Part Four: Shift a bit to a horse stance and start to push the right palm out, starting out the following move.

<u>Direction of Movements</u>: Push to the west.

<u>Possible Applications</u>: Release grabs and come back to push repeatedly. The opponent is trying to get control of your elbows or wrists so you coil with alternate hands to break his grip and get a grip on his main attacking arm. If you get his hand or wrist, push on his elbow to roll it over. If you get his elbow then strike to his body. Don't forget that the movements in a form are usually

done quite large. These multiple pushes to go their full extent so that you can find the power from the legs and body. When using them, the movement is more likely to be very small, just enough to tie up the opponent, and then finish him off with a sharp *fajin*.

Internal Connections: The power into the pushes comes from the rear leg. Shift the stance to direct power more effectively. When pushing to the *shun* hand – the same side – it is best to be in horse stance to drive power to the side. When pushing to the *ao* hand – the opposite side – it is best to be in counter bow stance to drive power diagonally through the body.

A horse stance applies power directly to the side. Up until now, most horse stances in the form have been open horse (front leg turned forward) or bow/horse (weight to the front leg, feet parallel and angled). In those, the power goes to the side, but not directly, so the arm is aligned with the thigh, which agrees with the scapular line. A full horse stance uses parallel feet and a centered body, and the power is applied out to the heel line. Once again, when changing from the bow stance to the horse stance, the entire body readjusts to bring power in the most efficient way from the rear leg. This involves a realignment in the hip socket and a replacement of the pelvis, among other things. The power must balance in the upper back.

About the Name: The pushes roll so that the palms exchange places without losing contact. Mike, one of my students in Victoria (and my Aikido sensei), renamed this move Three Annoying Pushes because he never figured out how to connect them.

Additional Comments: Keep the elbows down. Use the natural spring in the legs, releasing the push and the pressure in the legs without losing connection, in order to push again in a smooth, rhythmic manner.

> Especially in the 1980s, everything in China was hand made and repaired over and over. Cai Yuhua's step-mother was constantly mending something. One day she discovered my torn shirt (true Canadian quilted plaid shirt jacket, lovingly ripped and aged) and painstakingly mended or patched every single tear. Needless to say, I was pretty embarrassed at what she had done for me.
>
> Her fingers were an amazing testimony to hard work, gnarled and twisted by years as a teenager of grabbing silk worms from boiling water in the silk factory. I spent a fair bit of time with her always, chatting with her as we sat around cleaning vegetables, washing clothes, or soaking up the sun on the little stools in the courtyard. She was the second wife of Cai Yuhua's father. She had taken care of his wife in her last days, and he had found her indispensable and kept her on. They got on well together, he quiet, her chatty.

65. **String Of Pearls Strikes**   lián zhū pào   连珠炮

<u>Overall Movement</u>: Press out, drop back, then strike forward with a wedging hit.

<u>Footwork</u>: Shift back, drop down, then advance the right foot and follow up the left foot with a stamp.

<u>Breakdown of Movement</u>:

Part One: After the right palm pushes out, bring it back in to meet the left forearm. Then shift forward and press out with both forearms together (*ji*), palms facing out. Photos 65a, 65b, 65c, and 65d.

Part Two: Drop down, almost into a low pouncing stance (turn the left foot straight), pulling down and across, turning the palms up. Photos 65e and 65f.

Part Three: Open up the hands similar to Seal Off, Shut Down, and come up on the left leg, leaving the right leg open. The stance is an open T stance, leg open. Photo 65g.

Part Four: Step the right foot forward and do a *fajin* double hit or block and hit to chest height. The right palm is facing west, the thumb side down, to hit with the edge of the hand. The left palm faces the same direction as the right hand, fingers pointing up, under the right forearm. Follow in the left foot to stamp with the *fajin*. Photos 65h and 65i.

Yilu: The First Form

Direction of Movements: Strike to the west.

Possible Applications: Catch, control, then move in and strike.

Also, an application is not necessarily a *fajin*. From this it is obvious that thinking about one application while doing a technique would make the form too set in stone and inhibit your finding the power within a move. If you don't have good bodywork, the application wouldn't work. If you do have good bodywork, then there are a multitude of applications that will work.

Internal Connections: Roll inside the body for the back and forth movement, don't just move the arms.

About the Name: Continuous Pearls, Pearl Necklace, or Hanging Pearl Curtain are common traditional names for a move that appears smooth but manages to get in a few techniques. The image is that of a string of pearls, one following the other without pause.

Additional Comments: Do not lift the foot to stamp. Do a sliding friction stamp.

Internal styles demand that you breathe always through your nose.

One reason is that the tortoise breathes slowly and evenly through its nose, and lives a long life. So, what works for it must be good for us.

Another reason is that you should never be panting and over exerting when doing Taijiquan, Baguazhang, or Xingyiquan. You should be able to generate power without huffing and puffing, and making a lot of noise.

Another reason is that the tongue should remain lightly on the palate to keep the channels connected through the body, and if the mouth is open you can't really do that.

Yet another reason it that this keeps the mouth from drying out. In the West, we tend to drink during exercise, but in China they tend to drink before and after. And when a form takes forty minutes to get through, you are certainly not going to stop for a drink.

Within this regular breathing, at times you use the breath to assist the move, such as exhaling strongly to *fajin*, and lifting the breath for raised moves. Never force breathing to fit the moves, let it assist the movement naturally.

66. **Single Whip** (third time, alternate version)   dān biān   单鞭

<u>Overall Movement</u>: Coil and turn back to the east in bow stance single whip posture, rolling the power continuously through the body.

<u>Footwork</u>: Lift the left leg, step back, then roll within the stance until you are in a bow stance facing east.

<u>Breakdown of Movement</u>:

Part One: Push the left hand further along the same line (west) and bring the right hand back to the left forearm, palm facing the forearm. Photo 66a.

Part Two: Hook the right hand and hit with the back of the wrist out on the same line, to head height. Bring the left hand in to the *dantian*, palm facing up. Photo 66b.

Part Three: Lift the left leg and do a digging step to the rear (east). Coil the left hand at

the *dantian*, palm still facing up. Then thread the left hand out under the right forearm, then circle it under the right hooking fingers. Coil in the body and shift in the legs to do this action, first to the left leg, turning in the right foot, then to the right leg. Photos 66c, 66d, 66e, and 66f.

Part Four: Draw the left hand across to the east, shifting to a bow stance. Coil in the body and shift to the left leg. Stay in a bow stance, facing east (do not shift to horse stance). Photos 66g, 66h, and 66i.

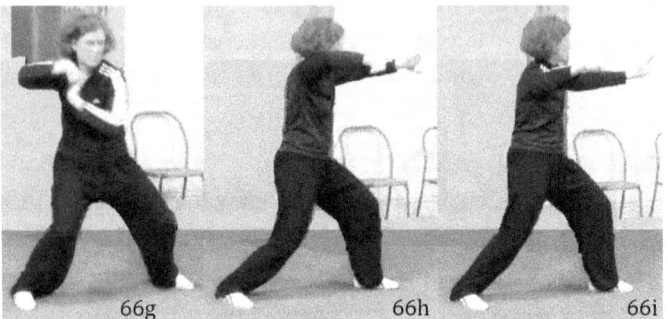

Yilu: The First Form

Direction of Movements: Facing east.

Possible Applications: Strike with the right backhand, then control and grab with the left. Hang on with the right and move in to whip out a strike or throw with the left arm.

Internal Connections: There are three coilings within the body, with small weight shifts, to maintain the connection between the hands.

About the Name: This time the Single Whip stays in a bow stance as a Single Whip and does not turn to Dantian Transforms.

Additional Comments: When you open to the Single Whip posture, push back with the right heel and roll the right hook-hand to vertical, to settle to a bow stance.

The body is beautifully balanced in Single Whip. The five bows of the body are first pulled open and then settled into the *dantian*, maintaining the openness. Single Whip (and Dantian Transforms) is like a crossroads in the form, coming frequently to set and balance the body before heading into the next section. Always take the time to open settle well, with a fully balanced 'big opening and big closing.'

Single Whip has always been a popular move in the Chinese martial arts. It simply looks and feels good, whether in *aobu* or *shunbu*, turned or straight on, open hands, hook, or fists. Here are some variants. From left to right: from Qi Jiguang 1560, from He Rubin 1628, from Tales of Heroes 1862, from Chen Xin 1921, from Zhang Wenguang's Chaquan 1985, and Cheng Jiefeng (Taiji Changquan) 1996.

Late 20th Century Shanghai

The population of Shanghai in 1953 was 6,204,400. Government leaders did not trust the Shanghai intellectuals, businessmen, well-educated students, and people who spoke foreign languages. Shanghainese, as a whole group, were never trusted by the Party even though the communist movement started there (because the communists were able to meet within the protection of the Enclaves). Shanghainese were too skilled, too well educated, and too affected by foreign habits. Many thought coffee was a normal drink. Stores had shop windows with displays of goods. Bakeries sold Russian bread, French croissants, and English sponge cake.

The Party saw Shanghai somehow as both a parasitic city where waste and consumption outweighed production, and as a place full of skills and capital that could be extracted. In the early days of the PRC, factories and expertise were moved from Shanghai to the interior, as part of the strategy to prepare in case of invasion of the coast. Shanghai paid massive taxes, essentially funding industry in the whole of China. By 1956, the leaders realised that it made more sense to have industries on the coast, and Shanghai's well-trained workforce and infrastructure were utilized. This development of heavy industry brought into the city pollution with it.

The Party, continually concerned with controlling the Shanghainese, had special treatment for the high school students of Shanghai during the Cultural Revolution. About a million and a half were sent to the countryside from 1968 to 78, 'to learn from the peasants.' Many were able to return home in 1978, but many spent the rest of their lives trying to get back.

When I started going in the 1980s, the population was about 11,860,000. Shanghai was still expected to support the rest of the country, send people out to teach, and fund the interior, in short, make great contributions to China without expecting anything in return. Although it was one of the cities opened in 1984, it was not allowed to grow, as any 'excess' capital was taken to help the provinces.

The heavy industry made the Shanghai that I lived in foul (and this is not even getting me started on the noise). When I was there in the 1980s and 90s, Shanghai's air pollution did not even meet China's not-very-stringent air quality standards. Chronic nose and ear infections, lung diseases, and cancer rates in Shanghai were the worst among China's cities. And you could see this. The air pollution was not hidden emissions, but airborne particulate – we literally never saw the sun. You could look straight at it with no danger to your eyes. Seventy percent of the smoke in the air was coal dust. Factory chimneystacks were bad enough, but small stoves that burned cheap briquettes, such as we used at home, released fumes at ground level – a miasma that hung undispersed throughout residential neighbourhoods.

As for the water, even in 1985, more than ninety percent of industrial and residential liquid waste went into the drainage systems completely untreated, and from there to the Huangpu River. The Huangpu (the drinking water supply) became an anaerobic black and smelly slough for the summer – four months of the year on average in the 1980s.

The groundwater was equally contaminated. Our little farm, like the others, would use groundwater for watering. From this to contaminated soil, and probably to contaminated vegetables. We had a fresh-water well, but always boiled the water.

The commode that we used was normal for the city. Downtown, many old areas would store the contents of their commodes in leaky containers to be picked up by night soil collectors, either in carts or barges. Unfortunately, the barges that took the night soil out to the farmers were the same that brought food in from the farmers.

The government realised that heavy industry within a city wasn't working, and in the 1970s, started to build satellite towns to move the factories out of the downtown. Although necessary, it was not well done. These first satellite towns were Soviet style apartment blocks with no entertainment and no transport to the city, since the workers were all moved out there as well. It is no surprise that the workers did not want to move there, and lose their Shanghai *hukou* (residency permit) and way of life.

In 1949, downtown housing was 42% *shikumen*, 19.8% 'new-style' *lilong*, 14% shacks, 9.5% villas, and 4.3% apartments (stats from Xu Mingqian, City Context: the development of Shanghai City, 2004). Most of this housing, originally intended for one family, though often sublet, was divided up further. The *shikumen* came to house one family per room ('one family' often including three generations), with many rooms subdivided, stairway platforms becoming a room, and hallways becoming kitchens and storage areas. Rooms with tall ceilings could have a mezzanine type room added.

In 1980, the per capita living space in the city core was 4.4 square metres. During the 1980s, the poorer, more overcrowded, areas were cleared, apartments built, and the residents rehoused in them. The old areas were essentially slums, with no running water. Demolition of their homes put the residents into more modern apartments, usually in the same place. Suburban housing areas were developed to house some of the residents, giving the residents more spacious living quarters that were not too far out of town.

Downtown streets were built for a time when traffic was carts and carriages, and was always bustling. Traffic was already an issue in the 1920s, with "motors, trams, buses, ricshas, hand carts, bicycles, wheelbarrows and pedestrians using the same thoroughfares" (Pott, A Short History of Shanghai, page 278). Traffic signals were introduced and some streets made one-way as early as then.

In the 1980s, this street layout was essentially unchanged. The map was about the same as pre 1949, just with different street names and no foreign enclaves. The tallest buildings were still the old ones. Off the main roads ran lanes, with the original *lilong* and *shikumen* housing. In terms of architecture, not that much had changed. In terms of lifestyle, after years of Party rule, there were no cafés and few bakeries, just in foreign hotels or special areas. The European café culture that came in the 2000s was new in the rest of China, and in fact, in North America, but was a return to normal for Shanghai. In Beijing, cafés still feel artificial, and the people act like they are doing something special when they sit in a café. In Shanghai, there are many local cafés, not just international chains, and they are almost all excellent.

The long bamboo laundry poles sticking out over the street, and the life overflowing from every doorway gives Shanghai's laneways a more vibrant feel than the Beijing closed-off courtyards and walls that I was used to. I visited quite a few families in my trips, and always thought these *shikumen* and *lilong* lanes a cool urban environment. A lot of life spilled out into the lanes, especially in the hot weather, and the sound of the alleys was Shanghaihua. There were fewer cars and more bikes and busses than pre-1949, and of course, no rickshaws, but it still felt pretty crazy. You could pass the time watching cyclists and pedestrians wend their way around and through the snarled up buses. Although there were not that many cars, the noise and fumes from the ill used trucks, cars, and busses were quite enough for me.

The look of downtown Shanghai was shops below, housing above, laundry in the middle, drying in the city's fumes (photo from 1996).

Downtown in the 1980s and 90s, once you got there, was actually quite quiet, not 'pedestrianized streets' but naturally just lacking in vehicular traffic.

In the 1980s, Shanghainese wore the same uniform of green and blue Mao suits as the rest of China, but there was always a subtle way of being more stylish. It was clear, coming down from Beijing, which was the hip city and which was the hick town. By the 1990s, the comparison was even more pronounced.

Downtown Shanghai, 1996. Note the man in suit and tie, arm in arm with a woman, a man purse tucked comfortably under the other arm. Not your average PRC citizen at that time, but normal in Shanghai.

As soon as Shanghai was allowed to do business again, it flourished. Pudong was declared an Economic and Technological Development Zone in 1990, and building started, with huge investment from the central government, working together with the skill set of the Shanghainese. Shanghai was still being used, not being helped. In 1991 it was still giving three quarters of its revenue to the central state.

By 1990, the population was about 13,342,000, giving a population density in of 22,003 people per square kilometre (of the whole administrative area, and probably not including the migrant workers). That was a density ten times that of Beijing, with its wide avenues and large parks. The urban core was more a density of 100,000 people per square kilometre, and higher in the old Chinese city. The per capita living space was 6.6 square metres.

Shanghai had grown from 1843 to 1949 with migrants from the local area, speaking a dialect of the Wu language, and quickly learning Shanghaihua. After 1949, housing restrictions prevented movement within the country. Shanghainese stabilized through the 1980s, over an extended Shanghai metropolis, with relatively few Outlanders.

In Shanghai during the 1990s they used to say, 'don't go away for the weekend, you'll never find your house when you come back.' This wasn't just a joke. The 1990s saw massive downtown projects, such as elevated expressways, metro lines and stations, and shopping malls, which called for the demolition of most of the remaining *lilong* and *shikumen*. The 1990s also saw a new approach to inner city clearance. Rather than slum clearance for urban renewal and the betterment of the residents, it became demolition and relocation. The new high rise buildings that replaced the housing were much more modern and expensive, out of reach of the displaced residents, who were given compensation enough to relocate out to the suburbs, but not enough to buy in to their old area. The 1990s '365 project' eliminated 3,650,000 square metres (365 hectares) of slums and 3 million square metres of *lilong* housing. Pudong was developing as a massive new housing estate, and the super skyscrapers to show off the New Shanghai started to go up.

By the late 1990s, real estate started to privatise, so urban renewal gave way to property development. By 2001, residents could legally be put out by force. By 2004, over 70% of *lilong* and *shikumen* housing had been destroyed. Those who can afford the new high standard apartments – mostly upper-middle-class Putonghua speaking Outlanders, attracted by the job market, and encouraged by the changes in residency rules – have moved in. Even without getting into the corruption and violence sometimes involved, demolition and relocation were hard on the residents who were moved against their will. Relocation has broken up the cohesion of the Shanghainese, who in many cases are no longer surrounded by people speaking Shanghaihua.

During the 1990s, the only other regular woman in our training group lived in a *lilong* house just across from Longhua park. I would go to her place some weekends to help her daughter with English. It was cozy, and only the one family lived in it, so her family was very comfortable. The toilets at the end of the lane were relatively clean. It was certainly not a slum. These lanes are all gone, redeveloped into a faux-Chinois tourist area around the temple and strange, empty-feeling streets lined with high rises.

67. **Forward Beckoning** qián zhāo 前招

Overall Movement: Advance and sweep the hands across and out, up and down.

Footwork: Bring the right foot in, circling by the left and out to a *kaibu*.

Breakdown of Movement:

Bring the right hand around at shoulder height, palm facing the front, fingers pointing out as the hand comes around, then up as the hand comes down. The hand sweeps across then *nichan* and continue down the left side. Bring the right foot in beside the left foot then step out to the right. Drop the left hand then bring it up inside the right, *shunchan* to at least head height on the left side. At the end of the action, release some of the pressure between the two hands to slap with the back of the left hand. Continue to circle the right hand to arrive at the right side. Stand more on the right leg. Photos 67a, 67b, and 67c.

Direction of Movements: Face east.

Possible Applications: Step in, releasing the opponent's grip on your left arm with the right cover. Then drop the opponent over your right leg with your lowering arm. Or keep him under control with the right hand, and roll him back over the left leg with your left arm.

It can also be a backfist with the upper hand, responding to an attack from the rear.

Internal Connections: The power flows to the index finger of the left hand and the little finger side of the right hand. Rise and breathe in to put power up into the hit. Wait to feel the power flow, keep the arms connected to each other and release the hit into the high hand when the time is ripe. Listen and feel the hands.

About the Name: The action of the upper hand is like raising it to beckon to someone. The far regard also gives the idea of beckoning to someone far away. Chen Xin uses the character 昭 *zhao*, meaning to look. This is probably a dialect meaning. Most Chen branches use the character 招 *zhao*, meaning to beckon. Chinese beckoning is slightly different from Western beckoning – the hand is held up at least shoulder height and the palm faces down, then the straight fingers flex towards the ground a few times.

This can also be translated as Forward Trick, or Front Provocation as 招 zhao also means a martial trick or posture. The name implies taking care of something that is in front.

Additional Comments: Do not look at the hands with your eyes, look with your ears, especially to the high hand. When I asked sifu about where to look, he said look (*kan*) with your ears. The eyes stay forward, and the entire body looks and listens to the movement towards the side, making this a very spaced out movement if you're not actually throwing someone.

Here is the move from the front.

I learned the Baguazhang that sifu had learned from Jiang Rongqiao. I learned it from Cai Yuhua in the 1980s, and sifu corrected it in the 90s, and taught a group of us the Bagua sabre. Sifu taught with his cane, we grabbed bamboo sticks from the ground. He didn't need a cane for walking; he just carried it in hopes of being attacked and whacking someone with it. I seemed to be the only one who could tell in which direction the cutting edge was supposed to be, so I was the one everyone looked to. He couldn't remember the moves until he had been fed second breakfast with some drinking involved. We managed to recover the entire sabre form week by week by treating him on Sunday mornings after practice.

Shadowboxing in Shanghai

68. **Backward Beckoning** hòu zhāo 后招

<u>Overall Movement</u>: Step around and repeat the movement on the other side.

<u>Footwork</u>: Step the left foot around to face west, and shift more to the left leg.

<u>Breakdown of Movement</u>:

Part One: Step the left foot around the right, hooking in, turning on the spot to face west. Sweep the left hand over and *nichan* and open down by the right hip. Thread the right hand up inside, *shunchan* and put power to the back of the hand. Shift mostly to the left leg. Photos 68a, 68b, and 68c.

Part Two: When you feel extended up to the right, release the power so that the hand further extends. Photo 68d.

<u>Direction of Movements</u>: Face west.

<u>Possible Applications</u>: Dealing with an opponent coming from behind, turn around quickly. A low throw or a high hit.

<u>Internal Connections</u>: The power flows through the body between the index finger of the rising hand and the little finger side of the lowering hand.

<u>About the Name</u>: This is the same technique, but turning around to deal with someone coming from behind. Similarly, it can also be translated as Backward Trick, as 招 zhao also means a martial trick or posture.

<u>Additional Comments</u>: Make sure you are hitting to the same spot as the previous movement, as if it is the same opponent.

Here is the release of power, from the back.

69. Wild Horse Tosses Its Mane   yě mǎ fēn zōng   野马分鬃

<u>Overall Movement</u>: Advance four times from a crouch with a lifting, driving action.

<u>Footwork</u>: Shift to the right leg, lift the left knee then extend the leg to advance into bow stance. Then crouch with the rear knee almost touching the ground, then lift the rear knee, then advance into a rear weighted bow stance. The difference between a rear weighted bow stance and an open horse stance is that a bow stance will always have the pelvis turned to face the line of action, while the horse stance has the pelvis turned to the front. Do this to advance three times. Notice the distinctive use of the crouching stance in the movement. Chen's small frame Taijiquan (*xiaojia*) also uses this stance and footwork, which I find interesting.

The first Toss The Mane posture goes directly into the stance. After that, there are three choices for footwork: 1) stop directly into stance; 2) push forward and bring the rear leg in with a stamp; and 3) push forward, bring the rear leg in then advance the front foot to extend the move further. The third option covers more distance.

<u>Breakdown of Movement</u>:

Part One: Shift to the right leg, bring the right hand down to control and press out, palm facing out at shoulder height. Bring the left palm in to the waist, palm up. Raise the left knee, then extend the leg to press into the ground. Extend the left hand at shoulder height, pulling back the right hand at shoulder height. Photos 69a and 69b.

Part Two: Circle and press the left forearm out. Roll back the right hand to lift, then circle down and up. As the hands circle, shift slightly back to the right leg, turn the left foot out, then shift onto the left leg and lift the right knee. Complete the circle of the right arm with the elbow outside the right knee. Step the right foot forward and shift to a rear weighted bow stance. Photos 69c, 69d, and 69e.

Part Three: Shift back to a half squat, back knee almost touching the ground, setting well into the leading hip joint. Circle the rear hand in a vertical circle, almost touching the ground as it comes through. Coil the leading arm to half circle and half press, finishing with the palm turned out by the head. Step the left foot forward and shift or shuffle-step to a rear weighted bow stance. Photos 69f, 69g, 69h, 69i, and 69j.

Part Four: Repeat action three on the right side. Photos 69k, 69l, 69m, and 69n.

Part Five (optional): Repeat action three.

<u>Direction of Movements</u>: Stepping moves to the west, angling slightly on each step.

Possible Applications: The leading forearm deflects and lifts the opponent's arm, keeping it under control. Your other palm and knee can then stab his chest and groin. Then drive forward with a low kick and pressing throw. The first strike is with the upper arm, the follow up is with the whole body.

Or, press with the upper arm, step in and strike or throw with the upper back and shoulder.

Keep the leading arm up as it coils, so that you press the opponent and duck under with the low stance, sneaking the rear arm in to make contact. The ducking action sucks the opponent in, he thinks you are weak and dropping down. This sets up for your counter attack.

Internal Connections: Drive the rear heel back to send power to the arms, shoulders, and upper back. Settle well into the hip joint in the crouching stance.

About the Name: This is an excellent image of a horse running and tossing its head, quite heedless of any hinderances. It is repeated to both sides, up to four times, freely moving amongst opponents like a wild horse.

The neck of a horse is extremely muscular. If you wrap your arms around its neck, one toss of its head can lift you right off the ground and toss you strongly away. I have had to hold horses this way to assist veterinarians and it is impossible if the horse doesn't want to cooperate. At the very least you get dragged around, in fear of getting tangled up in its equally strong legs and hooves. If you lift your feet off the ground in hopes of saving yourself from the hooves, the horse simply picks you up and walks away with you.

Additional Comments: I have in my notes three stances to right, left, right stances; and also four stances to right, left, right, left stances. As long as the movement is done correctly with proper power application, exact choreography doesn't matter. Going on to the following move is different depending on which side you are on, but both ways can be done smoothly.

I do these moves to slight angles, alternating directions, but I also have in my notes to go in a straight line. To go in a straight line you need to clearly turn the leading foot more, before stepping forward.

Here is the final posture from the front.

70. Six Sealings, Four Closings (for the third time, alternate version)
liù fēng sì bì   六封四闭

<u>Overall Movement</u>: Finishes the same as Seal Off, Shut Down, but with a different action prior to the push, moving forward into it.

<u>Footwork</u>: Sit into a cross stance or full sitting stance, then step the right foot forward and shift forward to a front weighted empty stance.

<u>Breakdown of Movement</u>:

Part One: Pull (*cai*) down to the left then across to the right. Turn the waist fully to the right, turning in the legs to sit into a low resting stance. Keep the back straight. Pull (*lü*) down on the right side very low, the right palm facing up, the left palm facing down, almost on the ground. Photos 70a, 70b, and 70c. (keeping fairly high, which is an option).

Part Two: Step the left foot forward and sit fully into a cross sit stance, either on the ground or slightly up. Turn the hands over and pull (*lü*) down, very low, in front, turning the body left. The right palm faces down and the left palm faces up. Photo 70d.

Part Three: Continue to pull (*lü*), coiling the left hand to the left, keeping the palm facing down. Stay low as long as possible. Then open both hands to an outward reverse deflection, palms facing up at the neck. Come up on the left leg, bring the right foot in to meet it, then step the right foot into the double low push of the Shut Down. Bring the left foot in behind the right to complete the push. You may push off the left leg for a jumping step to the side. Photos 70e, 70f, 70g, and 70h.

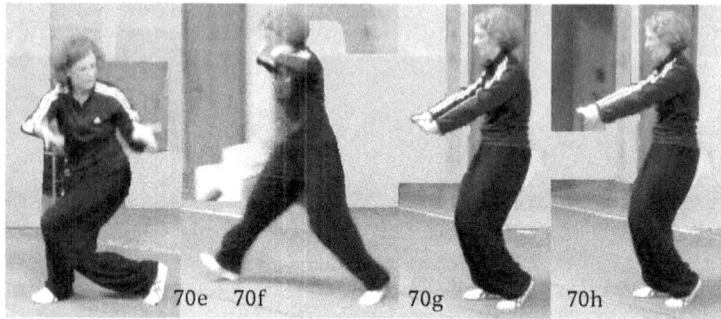

Yilu: The First Form

Possible Applications: Control the opponent and take him down completely to the ground, going down with him to maintain control and press his arm onto the ground. The push is the same as Seal Off, but there are extra controlling actions and a jump, which makes it more aggressive, charging to the attack.

About the Name: This repetition of Seal Off, Shut Down is done starting out from a low stance, and coils to the back before standing up into the rest of the actions. The actions thus go in all directions – six relating to your body: up, down, front, back, left, right; and the four cardinal directions: north, south, east and west. This give a complete shutting down and off of all egress.

Some interpret the name to mean six on one side and four on the other, not completely shutting off. When it is thought of this way the arms do not push evenly, but push with a sixty/forty balance. This would give an apparent opening for the opponent to come into, which would set you up for using Single Whip.

Additional Comments: You may *fajin* with the push, doing a low stamp with the left foot. In this case, it will be flat.

If your last Toss The Mane is on the left side, turn right and pull (*lü*) back. Then go directly into the press down. As the left hand comes level with the left foot, bring the right hand over to control the opponent's shoulder. Tuck the left hand in towards the face, bring the right hand around, then step the right foot forward to push.

Sometimes your teacher's pointers make a huge difference to the entire power flow of the form. Sometimes they don't. You seldom know which pointer will be important when it is given. This is one of the reasons why you should not pick and choose the things that 'work for you,' especially when just learning. Each system has its own way of doing things that fits in with its overall power flow. There isn't a right way and a wrong way. Well, of course there is a wrong way, but there are a number of right ways that work according to the overall concept of each style. The point is, that you can't know which is which for a while.

71. **Dantian Transforms** (for the fourth time)   dān biàn   丹变

Overall Movement: Start the same as move 7, finish the same as move 66. Photos 71a, 71b, 71c, 71d, 71e, 71f, 71g, and 71h.

Direction of Movements: Torso angled south, left hand and foot to the east.

Possible Applications: Catch and control the opponent, then step in and throw down, continuing to control. If the first throw doesn't work, readjust to drive the left elbow more into the centre of the opponent, keeping the thigh in contact.

About the Name: The name is Dantian Transforms, but this time it is done as a Single Whip , for a smoother transition to the following move.

> A rounded crotch is achieved by pulling in the knees slightly (*kou*) and opening the hip joints from the back. These actions, done together, flatten the back to the appropriate position. Doing a wide stance does not open the crotch – that is, just having the loin area seem really open is not a rounded crotch. The usual understanding in Xingyiquan and Baguazhang, and our Taijiquan, of 'rounded crotch' means that the back of the hip joint is open, which is done by closing in the knees. If the knees are open, the front of the hip joint is open, but the back of the hip joint is shut.

Yilu: The First Form

72. **Double Chop** shuāng pī zhǎng 双劈掌

<u>Overall Movement</u>: Turn to the west, release a grip, and jump to land with both hands chopping.

<u>Footwork</u>: Shift left, right, then, sit back to the left leg, them jump straight up. Push off with the left leg, raising the right knee. Land left, right with a one, two sound.

<u>Breakdown of Movement</u>:

Part One: Shift forward to the left leg and roll the right arm under. Roll the right arm *nichan* so the hook faces up or right. Shift a bit to the left leg and slide the left hand along the right arm to the right wrist. Slide with the fingers on top and the thumb underneath the arm. Photos 72a and 72b.

Part Two: Sit back to the left leg and coil the right hand inside, pressing with the left hand on the wrist, so they end up with the right on top and the left underneath. Photos 72c and 72d.

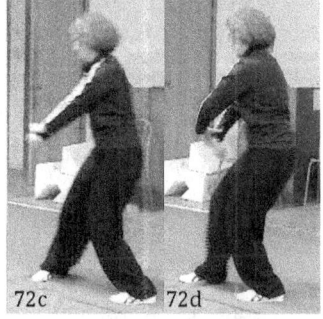

Part Three: Jump up, pushing off the left leg and lifting the right knee. Lift the hands with the jump, palms facing up. The right hand comes up the inside and extends out in front of the left. Land on the left foot first, quickly followed by the right foot. Chop with both palms down at the same time as the feet land, right hand still in front. Photos 772e, 72f, and 72g.

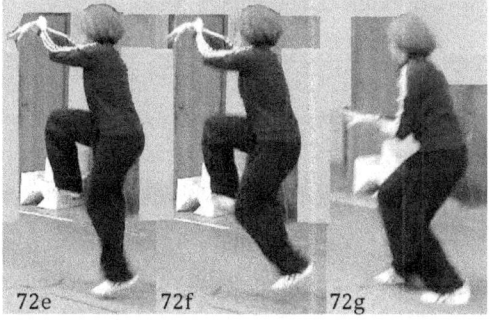

<u>Direction of Movements</u>: Facing west.

<u>Possible Applications</u>: First break a grip on the right wrist, then control the opponent's hands, twist them over and chop to break while stamping on him. You are turned, the opponent grabs your right arm, so you twist it under to make him think he has control over you. Readjust your body around your

203

fixed arm, bringing your left hand in to assist in breaking the grip of the opponent. Then use both arms to grab his arm or arms, turning his elbows to lift then striking down strongly.

Internal Connections: Lift the *qi* a bit to lighten the jump, breathing up.

About the Name: Another clear naming by the action, a double chop with the palms.

Additional Comments: The stance doesn't change structure with the jump and landing, keep the weight back to the left leg.

Here is the move from the front.

Most people who know me think that the most disgusting thing I've ever done is to step into a rotting pig up to my knee. I have, however, jumped from a height with a bicycle into a field freshly spread with night soil (it was dark both times).

This was when I was staying at Shanghai Normal University, near Guilin park, heading back each evening after supper at Cai Yuhua's. Shanghai is far enough south that the days are fairly even length, something I never got used to, so it is darkish by 8 pm, even in the summer. Normally I scooted across the big road, wended my way through Caohe village, then along the canal-like Caohe creek. When there was a lot of traffic, I went down the big road on the wrong side (wide bike lanes, no problem) to the stop lights to get across, then along some boring empty roads, built with development in mind. On that route, in the darkness, I thought I might try a short cut across a field and leapt down into it from the road with my bike.

Being in it up to my thighs was not enough. I had to slide my arm up to the shoulder down my legs to reach my feet to get my plastic sandals back after they were sucked off by the muck. I destroyed the plumbing of my room washing off the mud, and the plumber told me that that kind of mud is night soil, not just mud. The stain never came off my favourite striped shirt, and the bicycle was thickly coated in sticky goop. That is probably the worst thing I've ever done to a bike.

Yilu: The First Form

73. Jade Maiden Throws The Shuttle   yù nǚ chuān suō   玉女穿梭

<u>Overall Movement</u>: Leap forward with multiple strikes, then turn to prepare for the following movement.

<u>Footwork</u>: Step the right foot forward then push off to leap forward (west). Land on the left foot, then land the right foot behind in a back-cross stance. Pivot around to the right and prepare the right foot to step.

<u>Breakdown of Movement</u>:

Part One: Step the right foot a big step forward (west), turned out. Extend the right hand forward (west), stabbing with the fingers. *Nichan* slightly so the thumb side is down.

Part Two: Push off the right foot to leap forward (west), going for height more than length. Extend the left palm forward with the fingers up and the edge of the palm forward. Bring the right hand up and back to block up, palm facing up. This is the in-air position. Keep both arms within the Taijiquan posture rules – do not overextend the left arm or lift the right elbow in a long fist type 'block and push.' Photo 73a.

Part Three: Land the left foot, then land the right forward (west) behind the left foot in a back-cross step. Maintain the hands in position on landing. Then turn around to the right, bringing the hands around, bracing around and arriving in the initial action of the Tuck In The Robe Casually – the right hand down at the right leg and the left hand up at the left side. Photos 73b, 73c, and 73d.

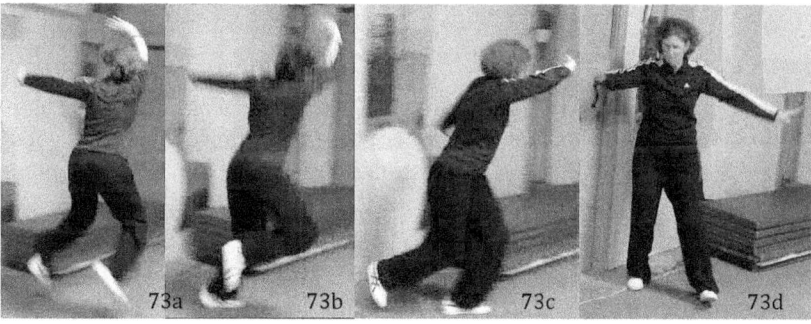

<u>Direction of Movements</u>: Moving to the west. On turning after the landing, face south.

<u>Possible Applications</u>: Attack directly forward, using the legs to put power into the hands. Drive forward with multiple direct threading strikes. Move quickly. On landing, turn to throw the opponent to the ground. You can get better control over him by threading your hands along his arms. Get in as close as possible for the throw, spinning him around your body.

<u>Internal Connections</u>: Lift the *qi* to lighten the jump.

About the Name: This name is traditionally used for this type of hand action, one reaching forward under the other, usually with open palms. This action resembles the action of a shuttle being thrown through the threads on a loom. One hand needs to create a space for the other to thread in, like the threads are spread on a loom before shooting the shuttle through. The name would have come into being when most homes had small weaving looms, so the image was a clear one.

'Jade Maiden' is the traditional reference to a beautiful young woman, due to the lightness of the colour and the smoothness of the surface of fine jade. Pale faces are valued in China for both men and women. Ruddy faces mean the person is out working the fields or otherwise working outside, while pale faces indicate a more cultured lifestyle. The name is thus often translated as Fair Lady.

The term has also come to mean a skill done beautifully.

Additional Comments: You may also push the left hand out flat with the edge of the palm forward on the first step instead of on the jump.

You may also jump for a combination of length and height.

Here is another photo, it is hard to catch a jump, even when taking clips from a video.

73

Chen Xin wrote a nice little verse for this move (page 326). "The Jade Maiden in the Heavens works with her golden shuttle. It comes and goes, weaving silk attire. He who understands the central place of Taijiquan, will run as a rabbit and fly as a bird (as fast as the sun and moon travel)."

Once, after we'd gone to the area around the new metro station for a restaurant supper, and were walking back along the dark lane. I was walking alone with sifu, and he started talking about *"zamen liangong de"* (we, who train martial arts), which I thought was a little odd and out of character. Later he told me someone had been following us closely enough to be stalking, and he was giving them warning that they shouldn't mess with us. They slunk off into the dark, so sifu didn't get to play with his cane. He would have been happy to, but awareness and avoidance of danger is a better martial skill than fighting.

74. **Tuck In The Robe Casually** (for the third time) lǎn zhā yī 懒扎衣

<u>Overall Movement</u>: Go directly into stepping the right foot out and draw the right hand across. Continue on as usual. Photos 74a, 74b, 74c, 74d, 74e, and 74f. See also move 5.

<u>Direction of Movements</u>: Facing south, right hand to the southeast

<u>Internal Connections</u>: Do not think of where the *qi* is going. When you do the moves correctly then the *qi* will naturally flow to the right places. The correct movements and positions will unblock your body, and then the *qi* can flow smoothly. Otherwise there is a risk that it is just your imagination that moves the *qi* or even that the *qi* will not be appropriately used.

> You need to search for the point of final extension in each posture. One practice is to stand in the final position and move the arm in and out, trying various ranges and degrees of rotation. The point where the index and middle fingertips tingle is the starting place. Then relax a bit so that you do not maintain this tingling, but keep the same energy. This is a different place for different people, so each person needs to test each position on their own. You must not copy your teacher by rote, but must look for the feeling.
>
> Do not do too much in a stationary posture, it is the movement into and out of the posture that give you the correct feeling. Extend into the posture, expanding rather than collapsing, to maintain a certain degree of flexion. Even during movements where the hand comes in towards the body, flexing the elbow considerably, figure out how to do this with a feeling of extending the arm.

75. **Seal Off, Shut Down** (for the fourth time)　　　rú fēng sì bì
　　　　　　　　　　　　　　　　　　　　　　　　　　　　　　如封似闭

<u>Overall Movement</u>: This can be done the same as usual (see moves 6 and 38), but is usually done with a quicker coiling, leaving out anything not directly moving forward, and done with a *fajin* in the press, and a jump into the push.

<u>Breakdown of Movement</u>:

Part One: This time bring the right hand down and join the left to it right away, to press with the forearms together, right palm out, left palm in, missing out the two single forearm presses. Then coil the left hand to trap on the right forearm, draw back and *fali* with both forearms, both palms facing in, right forearm inside the left. Photos 75a, 75b, 75c, and 75d.

Part Two: Then continue on as usual, drawing back then pressing forward, down, and up. You can choose to go back and forth or go directly to the double *an*. You can also choose to stay in stance or bring the right foot in beside the left and step back out again. Photos 75e, 75f, 75g, and 75h.

<u>Direction of Movements</u>: Push towards the southeast.

<u>Internal Connections</u>: Training any martial art involves training cognitive, motor, emotional and spiritual aspects, and the internal styles emphasize training the deep sources of these. Traditional styles have integrated all the elements needed to fully develop the practitioner, so training the style itself with an awareness of all its aspects will bring this development slowly and

sequentially – each element comes when the time is ripe. By the time the practitioner has progressed to emptiness the form is integrated into the body/mind. The form is not lost, instead, when the practitioner has finally reached the stage of 'having' the form, she is no longer 'there' to have it.

Possible Applications: Coil the right wrist/arm around the arm of an opponent, changing from a weak position to a strong position. Then trap the opponent's hand on your right arm by pressing it down with your left hand, and use the elbows to roll his arm over with a wrist lock and a take down. The final posture is a push down and away. The final rise of the hands pushes into the soft belly to get under the ribs and then dig up into the floating ribs.

All non-stepping moves roll around the edges of the feet. This is what creates the *chansi* power in the legs.

Whenever moving within the same stance, roll around the knees and ankles without shifting the feet. Roll to get feeling from the big toe to the little toe, around the outside of the foot to the heel, then back along the inside of the foot to the big toe. This roll goes from one foot to the other, drawing an infinity symbol (∞) around the edges of the feet. A vortex power is developed that coils up the legs. It is harder to get the *chansi* power in the legs than in the hands, so you have to pay special attention to this.

Practice the form very slowly to search out and get this feeling in the legs. Later, when you do the form faster, you will be able to keep the feeling. If you only ever do the form fast, you cannot find the feeling of the circling around the feet.

Keep your fingers together, the thumb slightly apart but with the root pulled in. Pay attention particularly to the index finger, that it does not separate from the others.

Keep a rounded line through the wrist and fingers, keep the palm stretched, but do not flex at the fingers except for specific hooking or punching techniques. This enables the *qi* and blood to reach the fingertips. If the wrist bends too much in either direction then the circulation of *qi* is blocked.

Keep the arms both extended and rounded. If they are too bent they become square. If they are too straight the power is lost. You must always keep the elbows and shoulders settled down. You need to be completely relaxed in the upper body for the legs to be steady.

Shadowboxing in Shanghai

76. **Dantian Transforms** (for the fifth time)　　dān biàn　　丹变

Overall Movement: The same as usual (see moves 7 and 39), so be sure to keep fully attentive. Photos 76a, 76b, 76c, 76d, 76e, 76f, 76g, and 76h.

Direction of Movements: Facing south, the left hand to the east, the right hand to the west.

Internal Connections: Settle into the stance, taking your time and settling down after the vigorous combination of Wild Horse, Double Chop, Throw The Shuttle, the spin to Tuck The Robe, and the quicker Shut Down. Do not let the high energy of the preceding moves get you excited and carry over into the following moves.

Additional Comments: Here are some photos of detail of the coiling.

Yilu: The First Form

The difference between the *chansi* of Chen style and the *chousi* energy generation of Yang style is this: *chansi* is like the silkworm coiling and twisting to create silken threads, while *chousi* is like someone pulling silk out from a cocoon. *Chousi* is a smooth, uninterrupted power. Smooth circles are *chousi*.

Chansi coiling is within the body, each joint of the body coils. If you don't coil then you can't *fajin* in the manner of Chen style. The spiraling coils create the lines for the *fajin*. The circles drawn by the middle finger in all the actions of the form are not smooth circles, but are the culmination of the *chansi* power through every joint of the body.

I managed to get a photo of sifu coiling in this move. He seldom led a practice, so this meant that I had to decide between following along or stepping out to take photos. I usually opted for following along, little thinking I would want photos for a book thirty years later.

Shadowboxing in Shanghai

77. **Upper Travelling Hands** (for the second time, alternate version)
shàng yùn shǒu 上运手

Overall Movement: Step sideways from west to east, back to the west, then back to the east, circling the hands in front of the body.

Footwork: Step the left foot to the east in a circular motion, forward, then back to the line, lifting the leg from the hip. Place the foot down toe first, feeling the weight shift around the outside of the foot as you shift across to the left. Press up with both feet so that you are essentially doing a horse stance on the balls of your feet, heels raised quite a bit. Settle the left foot and bring the right foot in and place it close to the left foot. Press up again, so you are essentially doing a *kaibu* stance on your toes. Settle onto the foot that stepped only after going through the raised stance, do not shift gradually across. Do three steps to the east, repeat the same stepping on the opposite side for three steps to the west, then repeat again three steps to the east.

Breakdown of Movement:

Part One: Step the left foot sideways to the east, then bring in the right foot parallel nearby. Press up with the feet and draw the hands across and around with the same movement as Middle Travelling Hands (move 40), except at forehead height. Keep the elbows down. Keep the fingers together. Extend the hands well to the front, especially the rising hand. Turn the waist well, keeping the top of the middle finger in front of the forehead, this should keep the armpit open. Almost push out, keep power pushing away from the body by sticking the *qi* to the upper back. Keep the arms rounded, but extending. Settle down one foot then the other as you move across.

Photos 77a, 77b, 77c, 77d, 77e, 77f, 77g, 77h, and 77i.

Yilu: The First Form

Part Two: Step the right foot sideways to the west, then bring in the left foot nearby. Press up with the feet and draw the hands across and around with the same movement as Middle Travelling Hands (move 40), except at forehead height. Settle down one foot then the other as you move across. Photos 77j, 77k, 77l, 77m, and 77n.

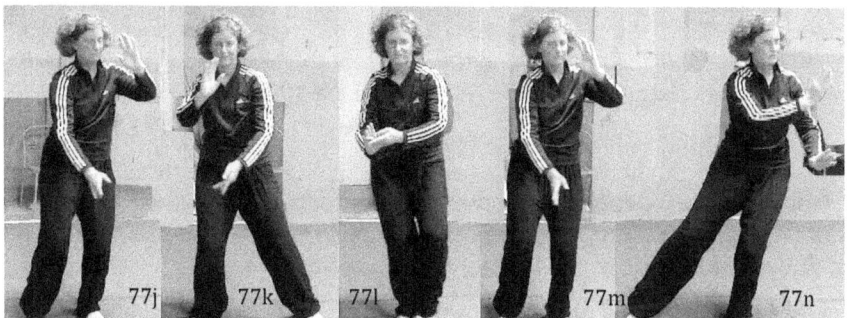

Part Three: Step the left foot sideways to the east, then bring in the right foot nearby. Press up with the feet as you draw the hands across and around with the same movement at forehead height. Settle down one foot then the other as you move across. Prepare for the following move with a slightly more frontward draw on the final step. Photos 77o, 77p, 77q, 77r, 77s, 775, 77u, 77v, 77w, and 77x.

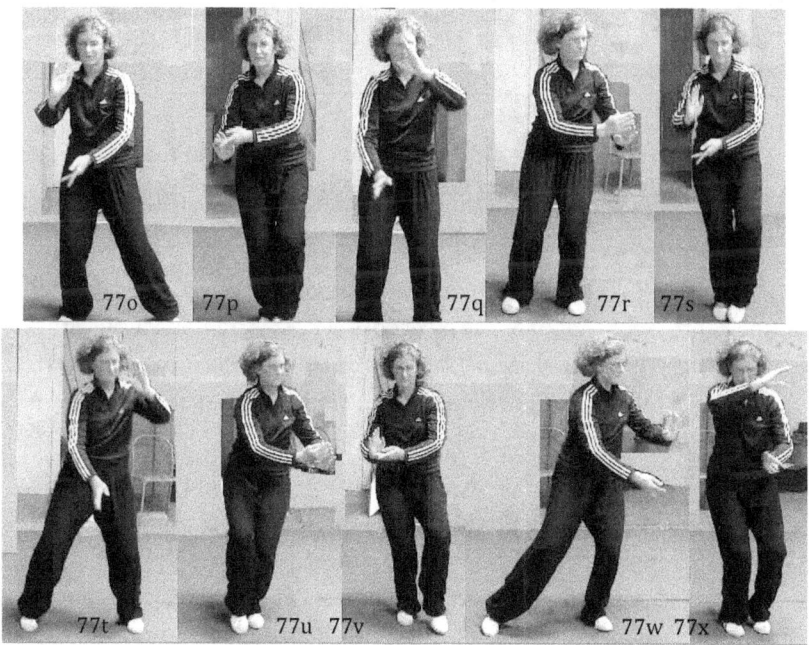

<u>Direction of Movements</u>: Facing south, moving east, west, then east again.

Possible Applications: Controlling by stepping, drag the opponent to either side, depending on his attack. Go along in the same direction as he was going already.

Internal Connections: Lift the palms and stick the *qi* to the upper back. This allows you to roll the hands over without losing power, also to roll the palms over without breaking at the wrist. Sticking *qi* to the upper back puts *peng* power into the front and back, so the line from the back to the arm elongates without them changing position relative to each other.

About the Name: This is the upper of the Travelling Hands, meaning the hands pass by higher than the other Travelling Hands. The three Travelling Hands are middle, upper, and lower, in that order. Usually *shang*, *zhong*, and *xia* mean first, middle, and last, so the name is slightly confusing until you know they refer to the hand height instead of the order.

Additional Comments: It is hard to see what is going on with the legs in the photos. Here is the stepping from the side. At the midpoint, both heels are up.

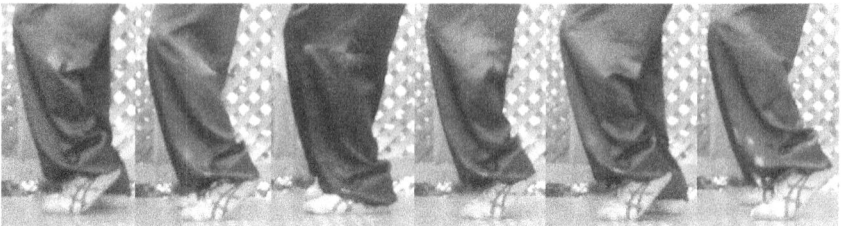

> Watch the hands when they are in front, but listen to the hands as they move out to the sides, do not watch them with the eyes.

To make good Chinese scrambled eggs, beat the eggs well and toss them into a very hot pan. The mix cooks almost instantaneously with a quick stir – don't overcook. For egg and tomato, cook the eggs first. Then take the eggs out, cook the ginger, onion, and tomatoes, and then put the eggs back in just at the end.

When Patrick came back from Shanghai in 1989 and visited me in Vancouver, he was very proud of his egg and tomato cooking talent. He threw everything in all together. When I next saw Cai Yuhua he laughed, saying they had been stuck eating Patrick's mess so as not to hurt his feelings, laughing, "I mean, how hard is it?" I couldn't feel superior to Patrick – the only 'cooking' Yuhua allowed me was cleaning vegetables and picking rocks out of rice. My cooking skills came from watching from the doorway and applying later, on an electric stove.

Yilu: The First Form

78. Double Swaying Lotus   shuāng bǎi lián   双摆莲

Overall Movement: Pull through in horse stance, then do an outside crescent kick with the right leg and drop onto it, pushing the left foot out to a half-split stance.

Footwork: On the last step with the left foot, take a larger step. Shift into horse stance then come up to prepare for the kick, bringing the right foot in loose. Kick the right foot in an outside swinging kick.

Breakdown of Movement: Part One: On the last step left, take a larger step and circle the hands to the right. When the hands get to the right side, pull (*lü*) down to the left side, sitting into horse stance.

Part Two: Stand on the left leg, pull (*lü*) up to the right side, bringing the right foot in. Photos 78a and 78b.

Part Three: Take the hands over to the right, preparing to swing left to slap. Bring the right foot up then swing it out to the right, slapping with both hands, first the left, then the right, with two crisp 'pa pa' sounds. Keep the leg straight, swinging it to full range, so the foot lands to the rear. *Shunchan* the right hand (thumb up) and *nichan* the left hand (thumb down) to slap the outside of the foot with the palms. Angle the ankle so that the slaps are on the foot, not the edge of the shoe. Photos 78c and 78d.

Possible Applications: Get the opponent off balance with the pulling, then throw, trapping him between your arms and right leg. You don't have to lift your leg high, it can be a low sweep as well.

About the Name: *Bai* means 'swing,' 'slash,' or 'wag,' as in slash with the tail (*baiwei*), so *bai jiao* or *bai tui* is a swinging kick.

An outside crescent kick is traditionally called *bai lian* 'swaying lotus' instead of the more prosaic *bai jiao* 'swing the foot.' In some styles the kicking leg comes in to cross before kicking out, so the kick comes from a half lotus squat, which may be why the kick is referred to as a lotus leg.

The 'double' refers to the double slap, not to a double kick.

> Training with Cai Yuhua in the other park that we went to when it was just us training, one day, as he did this move I saw a flash of a jumping outside crescent kick and drop directly into the sitting splits. I asked him about it after he'd finished the form, and he said, "My back hurts today, I didn't want to hold the stance." So that is an option, if you are ridiculously strong, coordinated, and flexible.

When I was there in the 1990s, Cai Yuhua and Cheng Jiefeng both trained on their own at a small park across the way from Guilin park.

This later became the huge Kangjian park, with bamboo groves, waterways, and lots of training spots. I trained there with Cheng from 2015 on. The park lacks covered areas for rainy day training, and one wet autumn I made friends with a lady who did solid Yang style. We shared one of the few covered spots on those rainy days when no one came to class. She was there on her own, enjoying her form, every day. Her daughter lived in England, and I was on my way there, so that was something we held in common. That is the other nice thing about Kangjian park. Half the people in the park are teachers at the university across the road – educated, well travelled, and often with relatives abroad – who see me as a person, not just a foreigner.

Yilu: The First Form

79. **Leap The Mountain Peak**   yuè cén   跃岑
    or **Fall In To The Splits**   diē chá   跌叉

Overall Movement: Drop into a half split, keeping the arms extended.

Footwork: Land the right foot directly after the kick, and tuck the left foot in behind the right knee. Lower yourself on your right leg and extend the left leg along the ground.

Breakdown of Movement:

Part One: Stamp the right foot on landing, bend the knee, and tuck the left foot in behind the right knee. Swing the hands down, up, and over to strike down in back fists, left in front and right in back. Photo 79a, done in the Canadian prairies.

Part Two: Drop on the right leg, reaching out the left leg (east). Drop into a half split, hurdler's position, with the left fist upright over the left foot and the right fist up behind to the right. Photo 79b and photo 79, of Gilbert in Victoria.

Direction of Movements: The stance is on the east-west line, the torso angled southeast.

Possible Applications: If something went wrong with your attacking kick, drop immediately to the ground and drive the left foot into the opponent's leading shin. Only use this technique when you are really in trouble, because it is a risky one. Keep the right arm up to protect you from counter attack, but if you drop completely to the ground he won't be able to reach you at all. You can use the same technique without dropping down, if your first throw (the outside kick) didn't work and you are still attached to him, turn the other way and take him down with your left arm. Drop your body to put your weight into taking him down.

If you cannot get his shin, try to get your left leg in between his legs. It is also a practice in the skill of going down and getting back up again without losing control, if you know you can drop down and still apply power forward and up, you are more comfortable in throwing situations.

About the Name: The posture, although on the ground, looks like you are leaping a great distance. It looks like the posture a hurdler takes in the air. The second word of the name I have in my notes as 夯 over 山. This does not exist in a dictionary, but 岑 cen, 山 over 夯, means a mountain peak. There is a possibility also that this was a miscopying of the character 岔 (chà), which means forked, and is the posture the legs could be said to take.

The name given in the 1982 list is *diecha*. The original meaning of *die* is to stumble or fall, so in this context it means to drop down quickly. The word 叉 *cha* means forked, more as in the prongs of a fork. *Diecha* is a more standard term for a seated split posture. Also of interest, a dialect meaning of *cha* is to block up, or jam.

Additional Comments: Some do the half-split stance with the right knee up, some with the right knee on the ground. Keep the body behind the left leg, don't go forward and stress the right knee.

The extended foot turned up, instead of a normal drop stance, is because of the idea of kicking the opponent's leg. The extending leg needs to stay firm. Following the outside crescent kick as it does, it really is a right-left kick combination, so the drop should immediately follow the first kick.

If you can't drop down, step out with the left heel to step on the opponent's foot.

Be sure to keep the right foot flat when it stamps. The foot is coming down from a height, so wait before putting impetus into the stamp.

Some branches of Chen style like to do a big stamp in the various stamping moves. This stimulates the bottom of the foot, which is the pump from the veins for blood circulation and a gathering place for the end/beginning of meridians for *qi* circulation. We often do a heel-lifting push into the foot (such as in Pound With The Pestle and White Goose Flashes Its Wings), so have less need to do this extra stimulation. We do a lighter stamp, which is easier on the body.

If you cannot yet, or can no longer, do this half-split hurdler stance, sit down as well as you can onto the right leg into a drop stance. Do not slacken your spirit and become discouraged because you can't do the move fully. Do something properly, perhaps even a half horse stance. Don't cheat in any way to force yourself into the stance. Always keep your supporting knee tracking with the foot.

Yilu: The First Form

80. **Sweep The Shin And Double Strike**   sǎo jìng pào   扫胫炮
    or **Sweep The Main Hall With The Leg**   sǎo táng tuǐ   扫堂腿

<u>Overall Movement</u>: Come up on the right leg, step forward and sweep kick, bracing or striking with the arms.

<u>Footwork</u>: From the half split, come up on the right leg. Step the left leg forward, slightly turned out. Sweep a full circle with the right leg, so end up facing north.

<u>Breakdown of Movement</u>:

Part One: Come up on the right leg, turning right and keeping weight on the right leg. Roll (*nichan*) both arms over to turn the fist hearts upwards and twist the left leg inwards to help get the power transfer. Photo 80a.

Part Two: Step the left foot forward, slightly turned out. Continue to roll the left arm until it comes back around (*shunchan*) to drill forward. Photo 80b.

Part Three: Sweep a full circle with the right foot, going around until it lands to the east of the left foot in a *kaibu*, facing North. Sweep the right arm around with the leg, palm facing down. Circle the left palm to face down. Strike the right forearm into the left palm (or do a double brace) as the right foot lands. Photo 80c.

<u>Direction of Movements</u>: Facing north, right foot to the east of the left foot.

<u>Possible Applications</u>: Sweep the opponent, keeping control with the arms. You can either brace with the forearms or control with a grab to help take him down.

<u>About the Name</u>: The first name is one of the practical names, sweep with your shin and double hit his chest. The second name, with the Main Hall, refers to the chest. The acupoint Jade Hall is in the centre of the chest.

<u>Additional Comments</u>: I usually do this with a double bracing of the arms (as shown in the photos) instead of a slap. In this case the left fist is *shunchan* in front of the chest, forearm vertical, and the right fist is *nichan* at the thigh, forearm also close to vertical. Put power to brace out with both forearms.

If you cannot do a full-circle sweep, you may do a half-circle, stopping at the same place.

Here is the move from the front, showing the double brace.

I went back to Shanghai in 2015, the first time since 2001, and fell in love with the city. With the extensive new metro system, you could get around without becoming too frazzled. For the first time, I was out and about in the old Chinese city, the French Quarter, and the old International Settlement, eating in restaurants and visiting famous sites. Thanks to the map app on my phone, I was able to wander around with the ability to sort myself out when I got lost. I stood in shock as people waited for the green lights before crossing the streets. I took in films in the famous Cathy cinema. I checked out local restaurants, cafés and noodle shops without ever finding a bad one. With the new lines of the metro system, my various hotels were never much more than an hour away from Kangjian park, where I trained every morning.

It was great to meet up again with Cai Yuhua and Patrick, after years of being out of contact. Patrick had been a proud Shanghailander for years, now with an almost grown family. I went back in 2016, 2017, and 2019, and the first flush of enthusiasm is not wearing off.

21st Century Shanghai

The population of Shanghai by 2000 was about 16,408,000, by 2010 about 23,019,000, and by 2020 about 27,795,000. The municipality has spread, obviously, to include more outlying areas.

In my Shanghai of 2015-2019, the sun shone, the sky was blue, and the air was soft. My weather app on my phone told me when there was an inversion day, when the smog hangs in the air, but really, it was nothing compared to what we lived through day after day in the 1980s and 1990s.

I like the Chinese-foreign mix of Shanghai. If it hadn't been for the foreign influence, it would not be the great city that it is today. The Chinese built Shanghai to what it is, but it wouldn't be the same without that initial kick – that grain of sand that made the pearl. I admit that I love the not-Socialist-city feel of Shanghai.

The modern world, with its WIFI, smart phones, and tap payments sits more comfortably on Shanghai than it does on Beijing. With the new metro lines, you can get downtown from anywhere to stroll around a shopping, eating, and cultural core that is lively and engaging. I am not much of a shopper, but do like to stroll, to eat, and to relax at a café. I have yet to have a bad meal in any of the randomly chosen noodle shops and restaurants, or even Lawson's fridge.

I love wandering about. Crossing the streets is safe. Firstly, the streets in the older area are not wide at all. You don't have to scuttle across six lanes while cars turn right in one of the lanes at each end, like in Beijing. Secondly, people wait at the traffic lights. I watched at a broken traffic light for quite some time as no one crossed the road and no one honked. I thought I had been transported to Tokyo.

You are lulled into the feeling that you can get across the street without danger, but silent electric scooters that can go any direction at any time are always there if you step out without scanning in all directions. When you do, the guy on the scooter always looks at you like the near crash is your fault. And I guess it is, if you are distracted enough to be gazing off into the distance instead of scanning.

The metro, improved transportation, malls, and high-class buildings have all come at a cost to the Shanghainese. The government found it easier to demolish than to renew. Often a neighbourhood was destroyed for gentrification, as old traditional neighbourhoods were demolished and new 'old' areas built to please tourists and rich people. The line of condos along Suzhou creek is one such. Surely no one could afford to live there, trendy as they look. The Xintiandi complex is another. I ate there once, enjoying the sun and watching other tourists eating there, who were enjoying other tourists taking photos... I certainly couldn't afford to buy anything at any of the shops. Oddly enough, searching for an affordable restaurant in Xintiandi, I ended up at a courtyard table with an excellent hamburger, so had an East-meets-West meal. I guess if you like an 'old enclaves theme park,' it is pretty good. Better than KFC in the old Shanghai Club, anyway.

Over a million residents were relocated out of downtown Shanghai from 1995 to 2007. Compare that to the 1.3 million people relocated for the Three Gorges Project and the 1 million people relocated for the construction of the Beijing Olympic sites. This means that the Shanghainese were relocated from downtown to the outskirts of their city, and mixed in with newcomers who spoke a different language. The ramifications are much more far reaching than simply moving house. Instead of being a cosmopolitan city, with fascinating architecture, special local cuisine, and a vibrant local vibe, it is becoming a global city not that much different from others – its skyscrapers displacing the people and taking away the sense of belonging or of home.

Ironically, the metro, which caused so much dislocation, allows the relocated people to travel easily into the downtown if they wish, just for the day, and even to commute to work downtown quite easily. The high rises and the elevated highways are disorienting for people who know the old downtown well. For me, not so much, as I always got lost anyway. The actual layout of the city has not changed all that much, if you ignore Pudong, which I do.

Yilu: The First Form

The Bund, the mile long stretch of colonial-reminder waterfront, is dwarfed now by Pudong across the river. In the 1980s and 90s its buildings were still among the tallest around, and now has a nostalgic, out-of-time look to it. On most visits to Shanghai I go up to the restaurant in the Peace Hotel (I can't keep up with its name changes) that overlooks the Bund, get a window seat, and splurge on the cheapest thing on the menu. (Egg fried rice is always on the menu of good restaurants, intended to <u>go with</u> a meal, not to <u>be</u> a meal, but there isn't much they can do about you ordering it alone.)

The hotel has been refurbished (top photo), and the view has changed (bottom photo).

81. Golden Rooster Stands On One Leg   jīn jī dú lì   金鸡独立

<u>Overall Movement</u>: Thread the hands up and down as you stand up on the left leg, lifting the right knee.

<u>Footwork</u>: Stand firmly on the left leg and lift the right knee. Push off with the left leg to jump up. Land the left foot, then the right foot. The right foot stamp is relaxed so that it rebounds and is able to step directly into the following move.

<u>Breakdown of Movement</u>:

Part One: Still facing north, if the right forearm is in contact with the left hand, coil the right fist around and inside the left palm in a small grappling move. If not, go directly to thread up. Thread the right palm up above the head, palm facing up, fingers pointing left. Push the left palm down. Raise the right knee. Photo 81a.

Part Two: Jump stamp, pushing off with the left foot and landing on it as well. Reach the right hand up on the jump, turning the palm forward. Allow the left hand to go up with the right arm, tucking in at the elbow. Then bring both hands palm down in front of the body to press down with the stamp. The feet make two separate sounds, the left, then the right. Photos 81b and 81c.

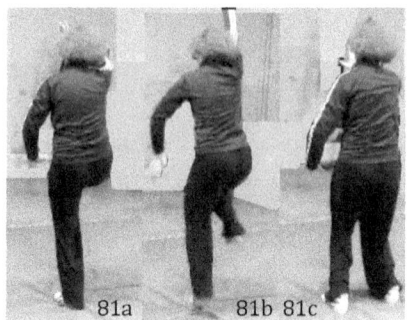

<u>Direction of Movements</u>: Face north.

<u>Possible Applications</u>: Control the opponent then drive up into the jaw and groin. The upper hand can drive strongly into the opponent's jaw. The extra reach and strike down can drive the elbow into his back, as he will be bent forward after the knee to the groin. Come down with the right elbow or pulling down with the right hand, kicking his shin or stamping on his foot. The left hand is available to balance by grabbing the opponent wherever necessary for the variety of techniques. You do not need to strike with the rising hand, you can use it to grab and control to make your knee strike stronger.

<u>Internal Connections</u>: Use a lifting breath to rise, but maintain a steady connection to the ground, sucking into the hip joint to raise the knee without pulling the body off balance. Raise the breath for the jump.

    Settle the body as the hand and knee rise, not just to keep your balance, but to balance the powers and directions through the body.

    The raised arm, elbow over shoulder, gives a strong connection from the hand to the pelvis, through the fascial Deep Front Arm Line. To use the anatomical names, the pectoralis minor and the coracobrachialis muscles

Yilu: The First Form

form this line, which works functionally when the arm is raised above the shoulder. When the arm is at rest, the corner is too sharp to use the connection. Any technique that uses a raised arm to deflect before grabbing and pulling down is allowing this line to connect the grab directly to the pelvis, deep into the body.

About the Name: One-legged stances with an arm raised are traditionally called Golden Rooster Stands On One Leg. Roosters are respected for their fighting ability, and the one-legged stance is an aggressive one showing their readiness to attack. Often a chicken will stop mid-attack on one leg, so this stance in the martial arts is used to show its balance combined with power and intensity.

Additional Comments: The jump has a quick turnover time, it is not a heavy landing. Stand up slowly under control, then jump quickly and reach the arm fully up into the jump. Bring the hands down with a small *fajin*.

Here are photos of the move from the front.

> The chicken that is wandering around in the video made of Cai Yuhua in 1995, from which I extracted the photos shown throughout this book, made me quite nostalgic. Cai Yuhua raised the chickens for food, and there were always some in a large cage. He'd let them out to roam around the yard, with a string attached to a leg. I learned a lot about how chickens fight when I lived there. I would set out a line of snacks for the ants, and then watch the chickens get the ants, in a true example of 'pecking order.' I'd also 'play' with them, with a stick, never my fingers. I never laugh at the use of chickens as a fighting model, their hit is surprisingly strong and masterfully accurate. Quite painful, in fact, when they got you – they figured out that my fingers were attached to the stick.

82. **Heel Faces The Sky** (for the second time, alternate name, other side)
cháo tiān dēng   朝天蹬

Overall Movement: This move is usually done the same as move 81, on the other side.

Footwork: Step the right foot to the east. Bring the left foot across, then stand up on the right foot and raise the left knee. Push off the right foot to jump up, landing on the right foot and slapping the left down on the landing so that it rebounds, prepared for the step into the following move.

Breakdown of Movement:

Part One: Step the right foot to the east and turn the body to face east. Thread the left palm up above the head, palm facing up, fingers pointing right. Push the right palm down. Raise the left knee. Photos 82a, 82b, and 82c.

Part Two: Jump stamp, pushing off with the right foot and landing on it as well. Reach the left hand up on the jump, turning the palm forward. Bring both hands palm down in front of the body to press down with the stamp. Photos 82d and 82e.

Direction of Movements: Face east.

Possible Applications: The same as move 81 unless you lift the foot straight up, in which case you are kicking the opponent in the chin instead of a knee strike. This repetition can be seen as a follow-up of the first knee strike.

About the Name: Although this is usually done the same as Golden Roster Stands On One Leg, with the knee raised, I have been told that it is supposed to be done extending the leg straight up in front of the body – that the sole of the foot is supposed to face the sky.

Some Chen branches use the character for a lamp for *deng*, instead of the character for a heel kick. In this case, the name means that it looks like you are holding a lamp up to the sky. With your hand, not your foot. This is a lot easier.

Here is the action from the front.

In 2015 I met Jarek, of his China From Inside website, and we became immediate best friends. Jarek has lived in Shanghai for many years – he is another foreigner who is a real Shanghailander. He trained karate in Poland in the 1980s, gradually becoming interested in Chinese things. He moved to Beijing to study at the Language Institute for four years, training traditional martial arts while there. He then moved to Shanghai, and has been living, learning, and training there ever since. He travels around China to visit sacred sites, and his writeups of these trips are a perfect combination of thoughtful, funny, and knowledgeable. In person, he is even more so. He is one of the few people who I find interesting talking about martial arts. His Chinese is brilliant, as is his English. Jarek's classical Chinese is better than mine, especially the mid-range not-quite-classical style, so there are quite a few little things in A Shadow on Fallen Blossoms that are there thanks to him.

For someone who would never leave Shanghai, Jarek (on the right) gave Hans (on the left) and I a pretty rough time for our enthusiasm about Shanghai. I met Hans at the same time, and arguing with Jarek bonded us (Jarek loves Shanghai, he just won't admit it).

83. Backup Twisting The Arms (second time) dǎo niǎn hóng 倒捻肱

Overall Movement: The same as move 31. Photos 83a, 83b, 83c, 83d, 83e, 83f, 83g, and 83h.

Direction of Movements: Facing east, move backwards to the west.

About the Name: On the repetition of this move, Chen Xin suggests another name for it, which is more visual. He calls it 真珠倒捲簾 *Zhenzhu Daojuanlian*, Roll Up The Pearl Hanging Curtain. This term is used in the martial arts to refer to absorbing and shooting back power that is coming at you, so is quite a good name. You can see how *daojuan lian* could become *daojuan hong*.

Possible Applications: As you step back, circle the foot a bit. Use the foot to get into the opponent's leg and kick back, pulling him into the throw.

This can also be done as an advancing move, turning to hook the opponent's leg. The hand that is pulling back is on the opponents back, the pushing hand is on his chest, the foot hooks his leg.

The arm moving back can do an elbow, forearm, or palm strike. This is more likely to be used in reaction to a grab from the rear.

I have seen it done as a relatively vertical throw, first moving in to catch the opponent's arm and under the knee. If the opponent grabs your wrist, twist to turn into a grab, stepping in and turning the hip into him. Lift his arm and tuck your other hand down to his knee, then you can tip him over your hip.

Yilu: The First Form

It can also be used as a simple step back and pull the opponent into your hit. Use a stamp on the rear leg to drive power directly from the rear foot to the striking hand.

Here is the move from the front.

We hand-washed our clothes in cold water. Two enamel or plastic basins were essential (wash and rinse or holding basin), as was a low stool. Xiaolan and I spent a lot of time in the courtyard washing clothes, as hand washing piece by piece takes a while. In the winter, this was rough on the hands, but fortunately you didn't sweat so much, or could pretend that it didn't matter so much, so you didn't need to wash your clothes so often. Hanging something up to air worked just fine. In the summer, the cool water was refreshing, and the clothes would dry quickly, so you could wash daily. If you wanted hot water you heated up the kettle, but normally you didn't. Because of the lack of fuel and the effort involved in getting a fire going, Yuhua would normally heat the kettle for drinking water, and for the nightly foot wash, not for washing clothes.

Cai Yuhua always insisted that we all wash our feet every night. This involved boiling the kettle for the hot water, as there was only cold running water, but it was never seen as too much trouble. We filled up our own plastic or enamel basins with cold water and he would come by with the kettle to warm it up, and we would all have a little soak and a scrub. There was no way that anyone would go to bed with dirty feet. When you are in a situation where you can't do a full wash, it is surprising how good it feels to wash the feet.

Shadowboxing in Shanghai

84. **White Goose Flashes Its Wings** (for the third time)

bái é liàng chì   白鹅亮翅

Overall Movement: This is the same as moves 9 and 32, starting out the same as move 32. Photos of James, 84a, 84b, 84c, 84d, 84e, 84f, 84g, 84h, 84i, 84j, 84k, 84l, 84m, 84n, 84o, 84p, 84q, 84r, 84s, 84t, and 84u.

Yilu: The First Form

Direction of Movements: Facing east, then south.

Internal Connections: When stepping, always lift from the hip joint. Don't tilt the pelvis – suck into the hip joint so that the hip flexors (the Psoas muscles particularly) lift the leg easily.

The circles of the feet are a continuation of the coiling around the feet that continues up through the thighs. The arc taken in the step follows the circle that the foot would be doing if it were on the ground.

Additional Comments: Here are parts of the move from the front (showing photos 84k and 84l, and 84q and 84r).

> Stepping within the form is almost always following a circular path, whether drawing the rear foot in, stepping to the side, or stepping back. The infinity sign drawn within the body is seen in the footwork.

85. **Brush Knee And Counter Stance** (for the seventh time, the third non-alternate style) lōu xī ào bù 搂膝拗步

Overall Movement: The same as moves 10 and 33. Photos 85a, 85b, 85c, 85d, 85e, and 85f.

Direction of Movements: Facing east.

Possible Applications: There is a phrase used in Chen Taijiquan: 'If the body is working well, through the whole body there is no place that is not a circle and making circles,' which means that there is no place that does not have the potential to be a 'fist.' A circle is a full three sixty degrees, so this means that a *fajin* can be applied anywhere along the circle – like slamming on the brakes of a bicycle going around a corner means heading off the circle at that point – but a *fajin* slams on the accelerator, like throwing a cricket ball.

Additional Comments: The right hand passes close by the jaw, and the left hand tucks in close to the waist. Keep the power connected between the hands. Keep a coiling power in the arms so that there is an expanding feeling even as the hands move towards the body.

Here are photos of the move from the front.

The various Brush Knee and Counter Stances are a good example of how our branch uses the *shun chan* and *ni chan* a bit differently. The arms are extended by coiling around, both in *ni chan*. Then the left arm switches to *shun chan* and the power rushes in from the hand, through the back, and out the right arm, which also switches to *shun chan*.

Chansijin goes through the whole body. It is often described as the action of the arms, but this is just the outward, visible, appearance of what is going on inside. There is nowhere in the body that is not doing *chansijin*. The main thing is to coil, not just rotate, like a vine coiling around a tree trunk to travel up it – you need to be aware of going away, coming towards, and going around.

In general, *shun chan*, smooth coiling, includes a rotation of the arm such that the little finger turns towards the palm (in English this is external rotation). There is also often a movement of the hand away from the body. The power flows out from the shoulder, around the arm, and to the back of the hand and ends in the fingernails. It also flows outwards from bone to muscle and skin. External rotation of the leg turns the knees outwards, and *shun chan* considers the action coming from the waist, through the hip joints, around the thighs, around the shank, to the heel, and then to the toes.

Ni chan, or *dao chan*, reverse coiling, includes a rotation of the arm such that the thumb turns towards the palm (in English this is internal rotation). There is also often a movement of the hand towards the body. The power flows in from the finger pads, around the arm, to the armpits and shoulders. It brings energy in, gathers, or accumulates power, and can be used to draw in an opponent. Internal rotation of the leg turns the knees inwards and *ni chan* considers the action using the waist, hip joints, thighs, shanks, and feet.

In our branch, we often do a full *shun chan*, going out and around until it turns into a *ni chan* coming back in, and then going out again, still in *ni chan*. We also often do a *ni chan* outwards behind the body. We take the *ni chan* as far as it can go, then unroll it so that the power flows back into the body with a *shun chan* that flows into the other arm. So it gathers energy and sends it back in, which is a bit different from the usual understanding.

Instead of puzzling over if your coiling is *shun* or *ni*, inwards or outwards, double or single, opposite or the same, ask yourself are you going around and around, or just back and forth? Are you feeling power transfer or are you just plunked down? If you are going back and forth, or are stuck, try again, finding the movement and power lines.

86. **White Snake Spits Its Tongue** bái shé tù xìn   白蛇吐信

Overall Movement: Coiling the arms, lift the left knee, then step forward and thread the arm forward.

Footwork: First shift back and forth, then come back to a high empty stance on the right leg. Then lift the left knee, step forward, and follow-in step the right foot with a stamp.

Breakdown of Movement:

Part One: Shake Wings as in move 34, part one and the start of part two. Photos 86a, 86b, 86c, 86d, and 86e.

Part Two: Come across to the right leg and reposition the left leg to a high empty stance. Pull down and across to the middle then *shunchan* until both palms face up, the left hand in front at shoulder height, the right hand at the left elbow.

Part Three: Stay sitting on the right leg. Push the right palm forward, thumb side facing in, palm down. Bring the left hand in, palm still facing up. Photo 86f.

Part Four: Lift the left knee, bring the left palm up to the jaw, then stab it out, palm still facing up. Bring the right hand in to the left elbow, palm still facing down. Photo 86g.

Part Five: Step the left foot forward and stab the right hand forward (east) with a *fajin*. *Shunchan* to stab with a twist, the little finger side on top (or palm up, depending on your flexibility). *Nichan* the left hand to pull back in, palm facing down at the waist, as the right hand stabs. Photos 86h and 86i.

Direction of Movements: Moving east.

Possible Applications: Cover an attack, sit back to draw the opponent in, then drive forward along the midline.

About the Name: The character for a snake's tongue is not 信 but this character is used almost universally in the martial arts to name movements with darting palms. A snake's forked tongue is actually written 芯. The 信 character is common, while the proper character for a snake's tongue is uncommon, and in this case what was probably a mistake because of oral transmission has become the norm.

Additional Comments: Make sure the body stays upright. Extend the right shoulder into the strike but not so much that it drops. Do a sliding stamp with the right foot for the *fajin*.

Here are photos of the move from the front.

87. **Dodge Through The Back** (second time, alternate version)　　shǎn tōng bèi　　闪通背

Overall Movement: Spin around with a flat throw.

Footwork: Step the right foot forward to the east, then spin to set into a sixty/forty stance facing west.

Breakdown of Movement:

Part One: Step the right foot through to the east. Coil the right hand in by the jaw, palm facing up, elbow out to the side. Relax the arms. Photo 87a.

Part Two: Sweep the right leg around and sweep the arms flat around at shoulder height until the body faces west. Stop the right foot with a flat stamp, without lifting the foot. Strike with the left palm down in front (west). Pull the right hand in to the *dantian*. Photos 87b and 87c.

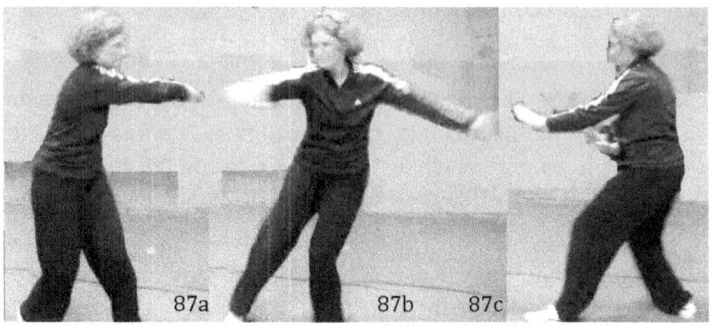

Direction of Movements: Face west at the completion of the movement.

Possible Applications: Stepping in to catch and throw the opponent with a spinning throw. The White Snake move has reached in to strike and grab the opponent already. Get the left hand in, grabbing whatever you can. Step in so that you are not trying to hard to spin him. You can also hit with your right elbow as you turn.

Or, deal with an opponent grabbing from behind, getting your shoulders out of the way and striking with your left hand. If he already has a good grip on you, settle down and spin, driving to his face with your right elbow to release his grip. Then you can strike with your left hand or elbow as you take him down with your right hand.

Internal Connections: The arms must stay connected through the back for either the back or the arms to be effective. The body must be upright to maintain balance and control during the spin, so push up (*ding*) into the top of the head. Keep the hip joints relaxed to swing the leg around easily.

About the Name: This is the usual name in Chen style for this move. It is an effective dodging technique, and uses the back effectively, plus uses the arms as a unit connected through the back.

Yilu: The First Form

The character 閃 *shan* means to get out of the way, to dodge, to evade.

Some traditions use the character 扇 *shan*, which means 'fan,' describing the action as like snapping open a fan. That word is not used here, but it is an excellent image for the action of the whole body.

<u>Additional Comments</u>: Relax the left arm, put power to the right shoulder to hit.

This is considered the second performance of a similar move, move 35, Three Through The Back, although the names and techniques differ. This time, the power is more a flat spin than move 35, which goes overhead.

Here are photos of the move from the front.

In throwing techniques, the farther the better, "like seeing off a guest." In China, when seeing off an important guest, you go along with them as far as possible – right out to the car or bus stop. A lesser or closer guest is seen to the door. I remember gradually changing from a 'see to outside' guest to a 'see to elevator door' guest, to 'see to the door' guest with Di Guoyong in Beijing. The first time I was no longer 'seen to elevator door' was a bit disconcerting, though it is actually a good thing, as it implies a closer friendship.

Let go with the controlling hand for two reasons: Firstly, to avoid badly hurting your opponent. Allow their body to follow a natural trajectory. If you hang on you can do a joint break within the throw, but this is not necessary in most cases. Secondly, that they do not hurt you. A skilled opponent can hurt you with a small *fajin* if they keep in contact with you, even at the moment of falling. If you let go and try to send them a long distance, you can then keep the distance.

88. **Hide The Hand And Punch** (for the third time, alternate version)
yǎn shǒu hóng chuí   掩手肱捶

Overall Movement: The same as move 36. Photos 88a, 88b, 88c, and 88d.

Direction of Movements: Stance is east-west, punching to the northwest.

Internal Connections: Use the power of the landing from the preceding movement to rebound the right foot forwards and connect the right fist into the left palm. Press the right heel back and snap the hips into the punch.

> You must stay relaxed for *fajin* movements. If you constantly practise with hard energy you can injure yourself. If you hit people with hard energy you will hurt them, but the injury you do yourself may be greater in the end.
>
> One way to practise punches is to repeat to four directions. After each punch, coil back, bring the right foot back in to stamp, then set up for the next punch. Practise the low punch, driving the right forearm into the left palm, then practise to medium height, and then practise to shoulder height. For the high punch, turn the shoulders completely, almost ninety degrees to the direction of the punch. The shoulder must extend into the punch, if it pulls back in after the punch then you have lost the power and distance. Snap the hips (*kou kua*) to put power to the punch.

The parks appreciated the regulars. Popular tourist parks, that charged an entrance fee, sold a cheap monthly pass for regulars, to get in when the park opened early in the morning. We had to pay the regular entrance fee if we were late. Our passes had our photos on them so you couldn't cheat. All this organization was for a fee of about one yuan, but it would really add up training every day.

Everyone showed up when they showed up, started practising, called out 'good morning' when sifu arrived, and stopped to ask questions or just to chat when the mood struck. So the hard workers worked hard and the others enjoyed themselves, and we all got along.

Yilu: The First Form

89. **Tuck In The Robe Casually** (fourth time, alternate entry)
    lǎn zhā yī   懒扎衣

<u>Overall Movement</u>: The same as move 37. Photos 89a, 89b, 89c 89d, 89e, 89f, 89g, 89h, 89i, 89j, 89k, 89l, 89m, and 89n.

Direction of Movements: Facing south.

Settle into the stance and think of how cool it looks. Confidence and ease come with being comfortable in the movements. Enjoying the moves helps you to improve on them.

My martial elder brothers told me two important concepts.

My martial eldest brother, Cheng Jiefeng, said that Taijiquan should be stable, comfortable, and aesthetically pleasing. It is important that people watching should feel comfortable and put at ease. This seems simple, but makes a lot of sense. If onlookers are ill at ease watching you, then you do not have smooth power.

My martial second eldest brother, Cai Yuhua, said that your whole body should feel like it is chuckling. Not a big, 'ha, ha' laugh, but a little chuckle. He said there can be no anger in Taijiquan. This is another simple idea. When you get to the fourth repetition of a move, perhaps thinking of these simple things will help keep you focused on the present.

What my martial brothers said about your body applies to your mind/heart as well. Your mind/heart should be comfortable and happy while doing the form. Of course you want to improve, and that is hard work, but you won't improve by being stressed about it. Don't take it too seriously, and don't involve your ego – you won't find the right power that way.

Looking through photos to illustrate the book brought back many memories. You can see the casual nature of our class in the park. The woman behind is doing Tuck in the Robe, discussing it with her friend, while sifu teaches the bagua sabre, done with a cane and a sword, standing in for sabres.

It wasn't just the photos learning in Shanghai that brought back good memories as I wrote this book, but ones from later as well. I found this great photo with Tam, at Playfair Park in Victoria (a time and place remembered fondly by those who were there) which illustrates the light-hearted nature I am talking about. We were imitating the old style 'coach with athlete' photos that were so often in magazines in China, but couldn't help laughing. You can also see in Tuck In The Robe Casually, how the rear elbow tucks in.

Continuing on with the same thought, Chen Xin wrote (page 162). "Every move comes from the mind/heart in your chest. If you are too much in your mind, too fussed, you will lose your rootedness. If you do not use your mind/heart, everything will be slack. You need to find the place in between using your mind and having an empty mind.

90. **Close Off And Shut Down** (for the fifth time)   rú fēng sì bì
如封似闭

Overall Movement: The same general actions as moves 6, 38, and 75.

Breakdown of Movement:

Part One: Keeping the left hand on the waist (pressing the back of the hand into the ribs), twist the waist to the right and bring the left elbow over to the right and draw the right hand in. Photos 90a and 90b.

Part Two: Pull in and press out to the right with both forearms, palms angled up. Photos 90c and 90d.

Part Three: Draw the right forearm in, tucking the back of the left hand inside it, then press forward as they meet. Photos 90e and 90f.

Part Four: Cover the right forearm with the left hand, the right hand hooks, loops in, then continues on to press out (*ji*). The right forearm is now on the inside. Emphasize the right elbow strike first. Photos 90g and 90h.

Part Five: Open the right hand forward to hit with the back of the hand to the side, then pull across with both hands. The right hand comes directly across, palm facing left. Photo 90i.

Yilu: The First Form

Part Six: Hook the right foot in as the hands pass it. Pull across to the left, press, then pull to the centre, in front of the body. Photos 90j, 90k, and 90l.

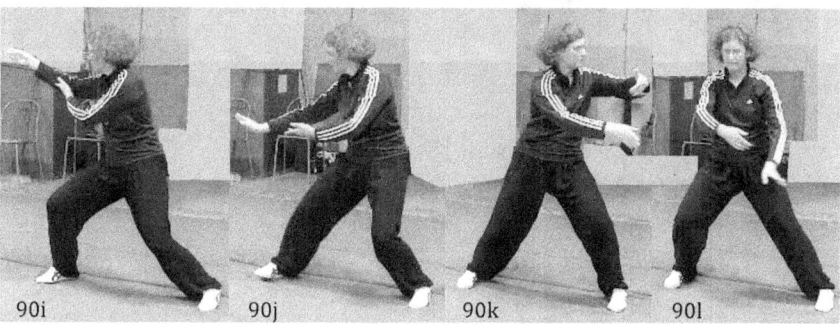

Part Seven: Draw the hands in close to the head, then down the jaw line to the chest, then push out. Continue to *nichan* the palms to press up at the end of the push, power going to the outer edges of the palms. Photos 90m, 90n, 90o, 90p, 90q, and 90r.

Direction of Movements: Facing southwest.

Possible Applications: Sifu described the characteristic action at the end as, "An old man picks up his beard and flicks it into an opponent's face." Not as seriously suggesting that was the application, but to give an idea of the line of power.

The rolling moves train a soft control, coiling around the limbs of an adversary, gradually getting him more twisted into your grip. I was lucky to have my camera with me when sifu spent some time explaining the soft control.

All my activity in Shanghai in 2015 was because we didn't have emails in the 1980s and 90s, and the neighbourhood was torn down, so I lost touch with Cai Yuhua after 2001. The Swiss, years later, got us back together. One day I had a phone call out of the blue. I knew his voice right away, calling on a friend's phone in Switzerland. They had seen my comments on my website about being sad about losing contact. I finally went back to Shanghai in 2015, and I started going back on every trip to China since.

When Yuhua's neighbourhood was taken over by modern housing, all the families had been moved out. I visited them way out, still technically in greater Shanghai, and still in the same corner of the map (a larger map now), at the final stop of line one of the metro, and then a bus ride. They were in a very nice group of bungalows with enclosed yards, bamboo in the back, a garden, large rooms and an upstairs. Very nice indeed for a farmer's son. We both have mobile phones now, and can contact each other to get together when I am there.

Yilu: The First Form

91. **Dantian Transforms** (for the sixth time)   dān biàn   丹变

Overall Movement: This is the same as move 7. Photos 91a, 91b, 91c, 91d, 91e, and 91f.

Internal Connections: The Single Whip (and including Dantian Transforms) is a beautiful example of a move that shows the *yin-yang* structure and feeling of the body. The *yang* side of the body is where the sun hits, and the *yin* side of the body is 'where the sun don't shine.' If you were an animal sitting on your haunches it would be more obvious, as your chest, belly, inner thighs, shins, and inner arms would be under or inside. You can see on yourself that the *yin* side has smoother skin and is the side you prefer to protect from attack, or to attack on others, while the *yang* side has rougher skin and is the side you usually prefer to block with. In Single Whip, while the whole body opens up, the *yang* side rounds and protects the *yin* side. The feeling is of expanding into the *yang* side, then sinking with both open but with a feeling of being protected by the outside. This is called balancing being open and closed.

Possible Applications: There are many. I prefer the full armed, stuck-to-the-body throw, but grappling is an option. The beginning is an obvious grapple, as sifu showed in the photo on the next page.

Pay attention in the later stages of the form that you are still doing the *chansi* power throughout, that the feet are stepping properly, and that the shoulders and arms are staying relaxed, so that everything works together smoothly and the circulation of *qi* and blood is unimpeded.

Push into the rear calf to put power into the bow stance. This drives the heel into the ground and closes the hip, tucking the tailbone in. Do not let the front knee go past the ankle. This ensures that the power goes to the arms and is not wasted into the front leg as too much of a weight shift.

Then push into the left foot and turn the body to the bow/horse stance. Pay attention that the knee does not get pushed forward when you push into the foot. Push directly up and back into the body. Round the loins, closing the knees and opening the rear of the hip sockets, letting the pelvis tilt to a natural position. The power should rise from the legs to the arms, then settle back to the legs.

Relax the upper body and arms so that the power can settle into the legs. Keep the fingers of the left hand together. Leave the right hooked hand relaxed, do not pull it tightly down. Keep the lines smooth through the shoulders, elbows, wrists and fingers.

Here is Cheng placing me in the Single Whip of the Taiji Changquan form. Note my *Huili* Warriors, the best training shoes, made in Shanghai.

Nostalgia and Preservation

Downtown Shanghai, even with the demolition of a great deal of the downtown core, is still a fascinating city of distinctive neighbourhoods. The French Quarter, with its tree covered roads and old houses. The old Chinese City, with its narrow lanes overflowing with life. Huaihai Road, with the classic cinema, brand name stores (which unfortunately took out many classic buildings), local shops, cafés and restaurants. Fuzhou Road with its art supply and book shops. Nanjing East Road is really just lots of tourists, and people trying to make money off them, but the big old department stores gives it an historic feel. Nanjing West Road is a bit of a high rise hell, but with interesting side roads, and leads out to Jing'An temple and park, the boundary of the old International Settlement. The elevated Yan'an road and the cultural desert underneath it takes some getting used to, but at least it takes the traffic up above and provides a bus lane below.

I love to wander the smaller lanes, poke into corners, and look behind walls. I am an enthusiast for architecture, and especially love the treats and surprises that Art Deco apartments have in store for us. I am not alone in this, nor is it an entirely 'foreigner' thing. The draw of the 1930s Shanghai has led to urban planning meant to protect and preserve the remaining old neighbourhoods.

The Urban Planning Exhibition Centre celebrates the old neighbourhoods and explains the preservation plans. Four hundred of the foreign-built houses and apartment buildings, and some neighbourhoods and even trees, especially in the French Quarter, are now protected. There is understanding of the human scale that makes us love the city. Not the bright lights and skyscrapers, but the narrow tree-covered streets, dark in the evening, lit by few and far between street lights, with a feeling of safety and calm.

Displaced Shanghainese are nostalgic for the urban lifestyle and sense of entitlement that being a real Shanghainese gave them. This melancholic nostalgia is for what is no longer there – not the crazy 1930s and the foreign part of its history, but the *lilong* and *shikumen* neighbourhoods, and the culture that went with them.

For quite a while, the history of Shanghai for the Chinese was one of imperialism and oppression. From the 2000s, there started to be a slightly different viewpoint, seeing the Old Shanghai as good as well as bad. Shanghai is losing its character, its special architecture, and its neighbourhood layout and vibe, which were a large part of its lifestyle and language. It needs to remain special in some way, so its history has become more a celebration of the old cosmopolitan city that it is becoming once again. A lot of the foreign tourist draw is the 1930s nostalgia, especially older people who lived there before and want to stroll the streets again. A lot of 'faux' displays play up the 1930s nostalgia. Now it is becoming a global city with nostalgic enclaves for tourists. Although I don't have much patience for faux displays, I do admit to a fascination with the old foreign street names of the enclaves, and present two maps on the following pages, just for fun.

Shanghai was never an 'East meets West' city, but a mix of all sorts. Looking back at the treaty port 'glory days,' is a way of looking forward – expressing that its natural destiny is to be a global city. Preservation, which is certainly good for tourism, may bring investment from those very tourists.

A bit more than the usual performance artists, more like installation art, with the car set up. Tourists really go for the 1930s nostalgia, strolling along the Bund and up pedestrianised Nanjing East Road. There is even a tram that runs up and down the pedestrianised road, which is fun to watch, as the tram sneaks up on strolling people absorbed in their phones.

Yilu: The First Form

Preservation only applies to areas not already gone. The Bund (top photo) will probably always be there.

Most of Huaihai East has already turned into huge chain stores, but I hope that the Cathay Cinema (left) will continue to survive.

Whether called Foochow Road or Fuzhou Lu (below), its shops have always been, and are still are, the place to go for books and art supplies.

Shadowboxing in Shanghai

Old street names of downtown Shanghai, culled from quite a few sources, especially The Old Shanghai A-Z, Paul French, HKU Press, 2010.

Yilu: The First Form

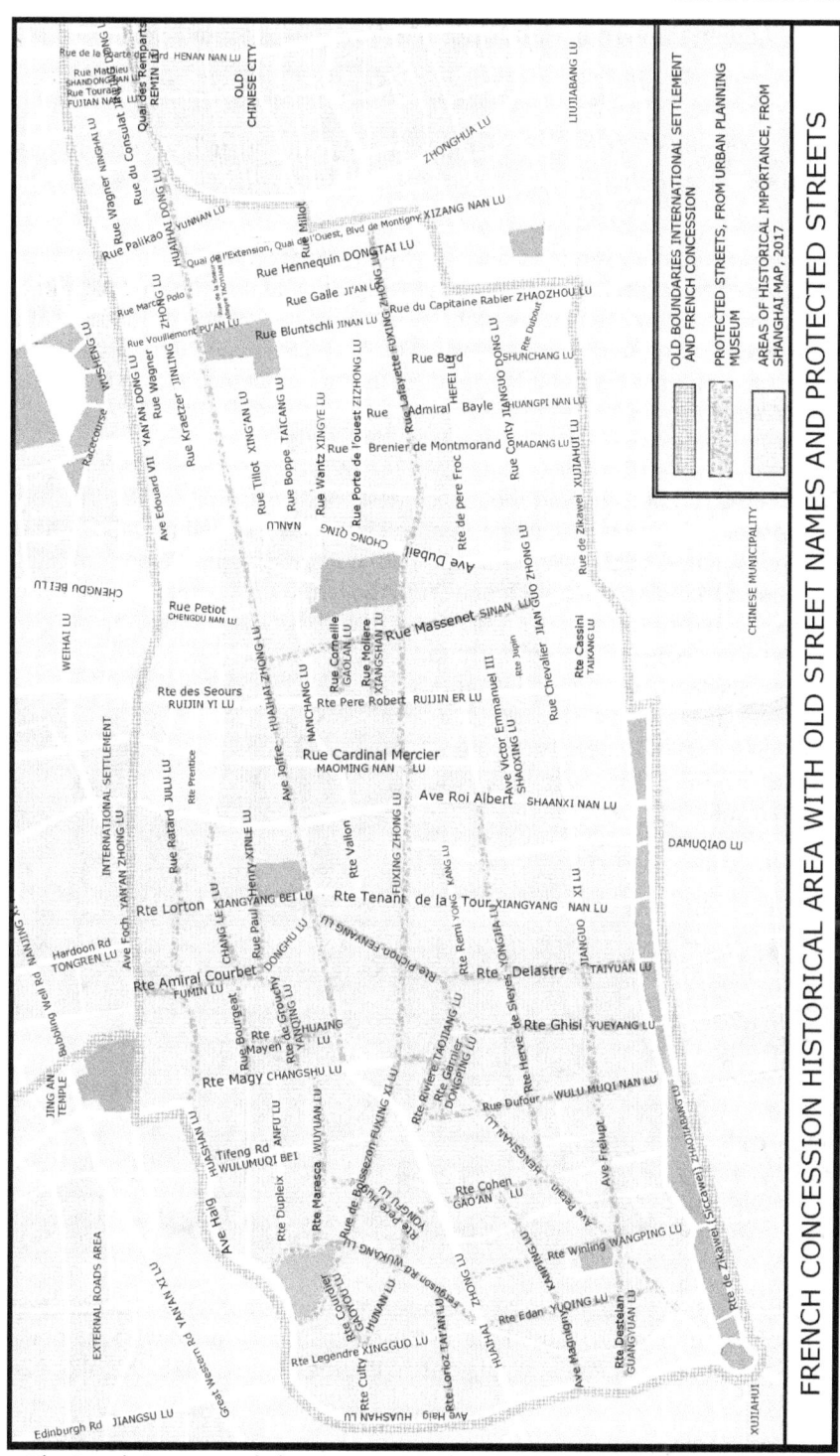

The French Quarter, with the most protected streets, enlarged for a bit more detail.
251

Shadowboxing in Shanghai

92. **Lower Travelling Hands** (for the third time, alternate version)

xià yùn shǒu   下运手

Overall Movement: Circling the hands similar to the other Travelling Hands, but lower, step to the east, west, and east, this time with a crossing step, and keeping the hands low.

Footwork: Step the left foot to the east, circling forward and in, in a sweeping action. Step the right foot to the east, circling back behind the left foot and in to the line of action (to the east of the left foot). Step back to the west the same way, and then again to the east. On the turnaround, jump up directly and turn a half circle in the air, landing in a horse stance facing the other direction.

Breakdown of Movement:

Part One: Circle step the left foot to the east (body is facing south). The foot draws more of a sweeping circle than the previous Travelling Hands. Draw the hands across to the east, the top hand at chest height, the bottom hand scooping. Circle step the right foot behind the left, travelling to the east. Draw the hands across to the west, the top hand at chest height, the bottom hand scooping. The hands push a bit more to the side than in the previous Travelling Hands. Repeat twice more. Photos of James 92a, 92b, 92c, 92d, 92e 92f, and 92g.

Part Two: When the hands arrive at the east, jump straight up with both legs and spin around to the right in the air. Bring the arms around with the body. Land on both feet in *kaibu*, facing north. Photos of James 92h, 92i, 92j, 92k and 92l.

Yilu: The First Form

Part Three: Circle step the right foot to the west (body is facing north). Draw the hands across to the west, the top hand at chest height, the bottom hand scooping. Circle step the left foot behind the right, travelling to the west. Draw the hands across to the east, the top hand at chest height, the bottom hand scooping. Repeat twice more. Photos of James 92m, 92n, 92o, 92p, 92q, and 92r.

Part Four: When the hands arrive at the west, jump straight up with both legs and spin around to the right in the air. Bring the arms around with the body. Land on both feet in *kaibu*, facing south. Photos of James 92s, 92t, 92u, 92v, and 92w.

Part Five: Circle step the left foot to the east (body is facing south). Circle step the right foot behind the left, travelling to the east. Draw the hands across to the east, the top hand at chest height, the bottom hand scooping. Circle step the left foot to the east again, and draw the hands across to the east, the top hand at chest height, the bottom hand scooping. Repeat once more. Photos 92x, 92y, 92z, and 92za.

Direction of Movements: Facing south travelling east, facing north travelling west, then facing south travelling east.

Possible Applications: Crossing the foot behind allows you to apply more power to sweeping the opponent aside. The hands draw more directly side to side than previous Travelling Hands, and the feet are placed to obtain maximum power. This crossing footwork is practical, and you can pick where you will step, according to the situation.

Internal Connections: The previous Travelling Hands focused on the internal connections to find the crossing power within the body. This repetition uses more practical connections. Find the link between the rear foot and the forward moving hands. Use the power shift rather than the transfer of weight to get the line through.

About the Name: The upper hand passes by the body at the lowest level of the three Travelling Hands.

Additional Comments: Lift the legs from the hips, with the lower leg relaxed. Pick the feet up, do not sweep them on the ground. Be sure to draw a circle in front with the leading leg and a circle behind with the back-crossing leg. The placement of the knees will be aligned if you circle. If not, the knee joints can be pinched on landing.

One day I was slightly bothered in the knees while practising, and sifu said, "Circle your foot as you cross back, instead of doing a back-cross step." Like magic, the pain was gone. And, as with many things sifu taught, I had the experience of what happens when you do it wrong, so will never forget how to do it right. Instead of being a detail to remember, the circle step (which I should have been doing to maintain the infinity circle in my stepping) immediately became an integral part of the movement.

Yilu: The First Form

You may drop right down into a horse stance on the turn. You may then do an extra circle, faster, so that the turn has a grand spirit.

Sometimes I jump and sometimes I don't. I have more the habit of lifting my knee and turning, because I like the feel of the press down with the knee lift. I didn't jump on the filming day, so James did a video for the photos of the more standard way to do this move.

If you chose not to jump straight around, first lift the knee and catch, then turn and stamp the foot. Photos of me, equivalent to photos 92j and 92k.

And equivalent to 92t and 92u.

> Chen Xin mentions (page 380) that in this iteration of the move, although it is named Cloud Hands, is also called Travelling Hands.

93. **Phoenix Spreads Its Wings** fèng huáng zhǎn chì 凤凰展翅
   or **Central Basin** zhōng pán 中盘

Overall Movement: Step out and open out from the Travelling Hands.

Footwork: Step the left foot to an open stance, then step the right foot through to a horse stance.

Breakdown of Movement:

Part One: Step the left foot leftward (northeast) to an open stance, hands continuing the Travelling Hands action to the right. Shift more to a forward weighted horse stance and bring the left arm up and over, then apply force downward. Keep the right arm where it was, but put more pressure into it, do not leave it slack. Photos 93a.

Part Two: Turn the left foot out and step the right foot through (southeast) to a forward weighted horse stance. Coil the right arm and bring it through to cross above the left forearm in front of the body. Open and *nichan* both arms out in line with the thighs as you shift forward to the slightly turned horse stance, settling into a *shunchan* at the end. Photos 93b and 93c.

Direction of Movements: The stance is angled on the northwest-southeast line, torso facing northeast.

Possible Applications: Control and step in to take down. Bring the controlling arm over the top of the opponent's arms down to his chest. Or if closer, go over his collarbone to disrupt his balance even more.

Internal Connections: Use the power line from the rear leg into the body, and out to the arms.

About the Name: This move should be centered and large, to fit both names.

Additional Comments: Be sure not to bend the elbows too much when turning the hands, keep the pressure on the outer edges of the arms, like a large bird spreading its wings. This keeps the pressure down low in the back.

Yilu: The First Form

94. **High Pat On Horse** (second time, alternate version, advancing) gāo tàn mǎ   高探马

   or **Capture With Both Hands**   shuāng lǚ zhǎng   双捋掌

Overall Movement: An action similar to move 41, but with the body moving forwards.

Footwork: Bring the left foot in behind the right, into a high front-weighted empty stance.

Breakdown of Movement:

Part One: Settle onto the right leg and bring the left foot forward, touching down near the right heel. Coil the arms around, the right comes back to the jaw then through to the front. Bring the left hand across then in. Photo 94a.

Part Two: Settle into the right foot and push the right hand, pulling in the left hand. The final posture has the right and left hands about wrist to elbow distance apart. The right palm faces down, heel forward, about shoulder height. The left palm faces up, three fingers slightly curled. Keep the left armpit open. Photo 94b.

Direction of Movements: Going to the east.

Possible Applications: Similar to move 41, but moving forward instead of drawing the opponent into emptiness. Keep the right foot solid, the body upright, and the back spread to keep balanced.

Internal Connections: The power is turning through your body to place the same side hand over its own foot, so you need to be careful to not let power dissipate. Be careful to keep the front knee aligned with the foot.

About the Name: The arm actions of the two High Pat On Horse moves are the same, but in the first, the body backs up and catches, while this time the left foot and body move forward. This time, advancing, is more of a catching action than the first time (move 41).

Additional Comments: Note that the left hand's technique is lǚ, a strong pull. Not lǚ, the more common stroking pull used in Taijiquan.

95. **Crossed Kick**　　　　　shí zì tuǐ　　　　　十字腿
   or **Single Swaying Lotus**　dān bǎi lián　　　　单摆莲

<u>Overall Movement</u>: A right spinning outside crescent kick, slapping with the left hand, turning to face west.

<u>Footwork</u>: Step the left foot forward, turned in. Swing the right leg up and do an outside crescent kick. Land the right foot with a stamp and lift the left foot by the right ankle.

<u>Breakdown of Movement</u>:

Part One: Open the hands, pressing out and down, then coming in to cross forearms, the left on top. Step the left foot forward (east) with the foot turned in. Photos 95a, 95b and 95c.

Part Two: Swing the right leg up and out in an outside crescent kick right around to the west-northwest. Slap the outside of the right foot with the left hand when it is at the southeast. Slap with the left hand turned over, thumb down. Let the momentum pivot the left foot further around to the right. Keep the right arm tucked near the body. Photo 95d.

Part Three: Lower the right foot, but don't land it. Bring the left arm around, blocking in with the little finger side of the forearm, fist heart facing in, forearm vertical.

　Snap the body and lift the right knee, snapping the fists out, right down and left up, arms coiled *shunchan*. Hit down with the right fist, *shunchan* to hit down with the backfist, very low (arm almost fully extended). Photos 95e and 95f.

<u>Direction of Movements</u>: Finish facing west. Turn with the step, turn more with the kick, and complete the turn with the strike.

Yilu: The First Form

Possible Applications: Press into the right hand. If it gets grabbed, cross the left hand over it to control the opponent's hand. Pull around and sweep the leg into his torso to off-balance him. Keep the right arm crossed with the left to support it, to try to prevent his grabbing either arm, and to help control the opponent's body. Then do a knee strike or hook him with your right foot and drive the right shoulder into him and strike down into his belly with the right fist.

About the Name: The arms cross like the character 十 before the left hand's slap during Crossed Kick. The arm and leg also draw the character 十 at the moment of slapping. This is a single handed slapping outside kick, so either name is a straightforward description of the kick.

In the 1982 name list, part three is separately named Press Down With The Elbow (压肘 *yazhou*). This action is similar to move 48, Overturn Rivers And Reverse The Seas, but is a more open action.

Additional Comments: Keep the leg straight during the kick, swinging to its full range right around to the back. Tuck in, but do not land, the foot, before the knee strike.

Here are photos of the kick and the final move taken from the other side.

Your daily training is the process, and should enhance your life. If it becomes a chore or a struggle then you need to take a break, not necessarily from your training, but in your approach to training. Do not worry about the end of the process, of becoming perfect. That is unlikely to happen. This does not mean that you shouldn't train very hard. Just don't take it too seriously, and don't take it personally, even if you have dedicated your whole life to your training.

Your heart should be light even when you are working hard. If your heart is heavy then you will not achieve the right feeling, and then you cannot do the movements correctly. If you allow yourself to become frustrated, you prevent yourself from getting it even more.

96. **Hit To The Groin**   zhǐ dāng chuí   指裆捶

<u>Overall Movement</u>: Land and do a low strike.

<u>Footwork</u>: Land the right foot, then the left, and shift to an open horse stance. When stepping down from a one-legged stance into a horse stance, use a digging step, sliding the foot slightly along the line of the stance. In this way you do not need to come down so fully on the supporting leg as if you were to step into the full horse stance without a slide. When the feet are on the ground and then stepping, they almost always circle because they are following the existing coiling done in the legs. When stepping down from a one-legged stance the landing foot moves in a straight line to the stance position.

<u>Breakdown of Movement</u>:

Part One: Coil the right foot a bit to turn out before landing. Stamp the right foot and lift the left foot to the ankle, the body is now facing northwest. Then land the left foot forward (west). Keep the right hand down and bring the left to the right elbow, trapping the right hand. Photos 96a and 96b.

Part Two: Drop down, moving in on the opponent. Cover and control with the left hand and snap the right fist out and up to groin height. Hit with the heel of the outside edge of the fist or the forearm. Keep the wrist loose. Snap the left hand back to the *dantian*, catching the belly. Photo 96c.

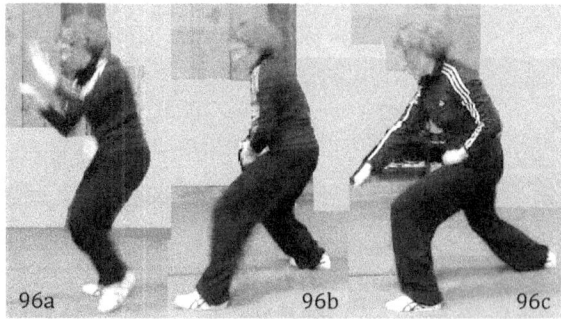

<u>Direction of Movements</u>: To the west.

<u>Possible Applications</u>: Punch up into the opponent's groin. Keep the wrist loose, so if the forearm is blocked the fist might flick up into the groin through momentum.

<u>About the Name</u>: A name that gives the application, pretty explicit. In the Chinese, it is 'finger beating to the groin,' or 'pointing beat to the groin,' which implies that the strike can be done as a fairly light hit, used to set up for the following move.

97. Wild Monkey Presents Fruit — yě hóu xiàn guǒ — 野猴献果
or White Ape Presents Fruit — bái yuán xiàn guǒ — 白猿献果
or Strike The Heart With The Elbow — dǐng xīn zhǒu — 顶心肘

Overall Movement: Roll back, then come forward to the left leg, bringing the fist through and lifting the right knee.

Footwork: Roll back a bit to the right leg, then shift to the left leg and stand up, lifting the right knee.

Breakdown of Movement:

Part One: Turn right, turning well back toward the right, roll the right hand back and up to a high block (*jia*). Roll the left hand over, still at the waist, bringing the elbow to the front. Photo 97a.

Part Two: Turn further to the right. Roll the left fist out to the rear (west), extending it rolled over (*nichan*). Then *shunchan* to press the forearm forward. Turn the body left. Open the right arm to the rear, then roll it through, turning the fist heart up, then extend it out to the front (west). Lift the right knee, extending the fists. The right fist is up in front at nose height, the left is at the right elbow. Photos 97b and 97c.

97a 97b 97c

Direction of Movements: Going west.

Possible Applications: First cover up, deflecting with the right arm and striking with the left elbow. Then catch the opponent with the left hand and step into a right knee strike and right punch to the jaw. The left fist goes out first, so although the final posture looks like a double hit, it can be a grab, control, and hit.

Internal Connections: Coil within the body to roll the left arm into the elbow. This will wrap the arms together, so the right arm rolls back. In this way the grab and punch are smooth, and follow from the preparation within the body.

About the Name: This type of posture with a knee up and both fists presented forward is often called 'white or wild,' 'ape or monkey,' 'presents,' 'a peach or fruit' in many traditional kungfu styles. The posture gives the impression of presenting something, hence the name. Considering the placement of the hand at the beginning of the move, what 'peaches' are being presented is pretty obvious. The use of the ape or monkey in the name reminds people of Sun Wukong, the Monkey King, famous for stealing peaches from the immortals, among other cheeky things.

Shadowboxing in Shanghai

The 1982 list includes a name for part one, using the elbow to strike into the heart of the opponent. This is a close-range technique.

Additional Comments: The right fist passes under the right knee when coming through, so it comes up into the punch.

In 2015, Jarek told me that there is such a thing as a reader's card at the Shanghai library. I just needed to show my passport, I didn't need to be a Shanghai resident, to get the card. With it, you can ask for and read, but not take out, books (many books are not on the open shelves), so I spent hours there. The library is an impressive building in the French Quarter, with its own metro station. The location was great, with cafés, restaurants, tree-lined lanes, fascinating old residential buildings, and walking distance to other metro lines.

Days in Shanghai on that and later visits were basically commute, train in the park, commute, work in the library, commute, collapse, while I worked on A Shadow on Fallen Blossoms and Falk's Dictionary. The library has an enormous reading room that was usually packed, with an assortment of separate desks and shared tables, first come, first taken. I was forced to take weekends off because there was nowhere to sit. You looked up what you wanted in the computer system, then asked for your books, up to four at a time, then waited for about twenty minutes, watching the conveyer belt above the heads of the librarians, hoping for your volumes. In the reading room we all took notes, used the Xerox service, and snuck photos of pages with our phones.

This was so, so much better than the time I spent in the library of Huadong Normal University, when I stayed there in 1996. I was researching Taijiquan history, and had to go through the card index, ask for books and magazines I needed, wait an eternity, then hand copy everything of interest, sitting in a cold and poorly lit reading room.

 The library, an oasis of calm.

Yilu: The First Form

98. **Double Ramming** shuāng zhuàng chuí 双撞捶

<u>Overall Movement</u>: Cover and double hit, advancing.

<u>Footwork</u>: Land the right foot, stepping forward (west), then follow-in the left foot with a stamp.

<u>Breakdown of Movement</u>:

Part One: Still with the right knee up, turn the body slightly left. Circle the fists to the left with the body movement, *shunchan* to swallow them into the chest. Photo 98a.

Part Two: Turn the right foot to kick with the outside of the foot, landing as still turning left. Bring the hands in. Photo 98b.

Part Three: Step the right foot forward (west) then bring the left foot in with a sliding stamp. *Nichan* and strike forward with both fists at about chest height, fist hearts down. Hit slightly inward as well as forward, drawing a flat circle. Extend the fists well forward. The right fist is forward but the left fist is not far behind. Photos 98c and 98d.

<u>Direction of Movements</u>: Going west.

<u>Possible Applications</u>: Cover up an attack then drive straight in to the opponent's chest. Be sure to step in so that you do not have to reach far for the strike.

<u>About the Name</u>: The use of the word *zhuang*, which means ramming or smashing, states that this is a particularly strong strike. The use of the word *chui* indicates that it is a punch not with the knuckles. In general, *chui* is used when punching with the outer edge, the backfist, or just about any part of the fist other than a straight punch into the knuckle punching surface. Often the forearm will be part of the punch as well. When *quan* is used, that usually indicates punching with the knuckle punching surface, with either an upright fist or a horizontal fist, with a clean surface and a clean fist strike.

<u>Additional Comments</u>: Do not stamp the right foot, but do allow it to make a light sound (don't land too softly). Do not pick up the left foot to stamp down – do a low shoveling step to come in with a sliding stamp.

263

99. **Close Off, Shut Down** (for the sixth time, alternate version)
rú fēng sì bì 　　　　　　　　　　　　　　　　　　如封似闭

<u>Overall Movement</u>: Step directly into Close Off with the right foot and do a follow in stamp with the left foot, timed with the push.

<u>Breakdown of Movement</u>:

Part One: Open the right palm, turning slightly right and starting an outer circle with the palm up. Photo 99a.

Part Two: Step the right foot forward. Turn left and do the usual arm actions of the opening block (see move 6). Follow-in step the left foot with a sliding stamp, timed with a low *fajin* push. Photos 99b and 99c.

<u>Direction of Movements</u>: Going west.

The sound made by the feet in moves 98 and 99 is "*tik tok tik tok.*"

The explanation for this is thus:

'1 horse' (*ma*) is written 马 . '2 horses' (*biao*) is written 马马 .

'3 horses' (*tik*) is written 马马马 . '4 horses' (*tok*) is written 马马马马 .

Stepping that makes the sound '*tik, tok*' suggests the sound of horses trotting. Moves 98 and 99 should flow smoothly together with a rhythmic '*tik, tok, tik, tok*' sound in the stepping: a light step, a heavier stamp, a light step, and a heavier stamp. Sifu was pretty pleased with himself when he wrote this out in my notebook, and he said that his sifu had told him the exact same thing. The written explanation doesn't make a whole lot of sense to me, since these characters do not actually exist, but of course I treasure his hand-written note. Maybe it makes more sense in Shanghaihua, where these sounds might exist. The idea works, and helps give a rhythm to your movement.

I loved those moments when sifu would sit me down and explain something. It didn't really matter if I understood it or not. Most of his teaching was physical transmission, that is, practice with occasional correction. Any art that can only be passed down from person to person is one thing that joins humans to one another and makes society worthwhile on some unexplainable level.

100. **Dantian Transforms** (for the seventh time) dān biàn 丹变

Overall Movement: This is done as usual, see move 7. Photos 100a, 100b, and 100c.

Direction of Movements: To the east, finished with the torso facing south.

Internal Connections: The shoulders are the key to transferring *qi* and blood circulation, energy, and power between the arms and the body. The bones of the upper arms must stay settled within the shoulder joints, which are depressions created by the entire shoulder structure. When the arms *shunchan* it is relatively easy to keep the shoulders sunken. You still must pay attention that the arm movement does not close off the chest. When the arms *nichan* you must pay attention that this action does not shrug the shoulders up. Keep the clavicles set down at all times, whether lifting the arms above the head or coiling the arm behind the body. This will help keep the entire shoulder structure set into the body. If the shoulder structure tilts or rises, all balance and power transfer is lost.

The arms are stretched like the hands are the head and tail of a snake, connecting to each other through the upper body to have the right feeling. You should feel that if one hand is attacked the other will react immediately, and if the centre is attacked both hands will come in immediately. The Dantian Transforms is essentially just two different ways of lining up a Single Whip, and the line of the arms through the body is the key.

Additional Comments: The chest is empty like an empty room, that is, it is upright and square with solid walls and a roof. It is not caved in.

The interaction between the hips, chest, and shoulders during Dantian Transforms is a good time to focus on their relationship. The push of the left foot into the body accentuates the close relationship, and the settling into the final stance accentuates the united structure.

> Don't get excited, careless, fatigued, or bored because you are almost finished the form. Pay attention to the process of doing each move. Every single movement is of equal importance to you.
>
> You would not be repeating a move the seventh time if it were not important.

Shadowboxing in Shanghai

101. **Spread A Quilt On The Ground**   pū dì mián   铺地绵

<u>Overall Movement</u>: Start out as if going to Pound With The Pestle, but stomp the right foot and lift the left, then drop, holding the arm posture.

<u>Footwork</u>: Move forward, lift the left knee, then drop fully onto the right leg, extending the left leg forward.

<u>Breakdown of Movement</u>:

Part One: Coil out of Dantian Transforms, pulling back and coming forward (east) as if going to Pound With The Pestle. But instead, once the right hand arrives in front, clench and lift it straight up. Bring the right foot in and lift the knee as the right hand lifts. Photos 101a, 101b, and 101c.

Part Two: Stamp the right foot and lift the left knee, foot tucked in and turned slightly. Drop the left fist onto the left foot, backfist on instep. Lift the right fist further, with the fist heart facing down, in a fairly tight position. Photos 101d and 101e.

Part Three: Squat on the right leg and extend the left leg to the front (east), dropping into a half split hurdler's stance. Keep the hands in the same position, so the left arm will be extended along the left leg and the right arm will be protecting the head. Or you can set in half horse stance and remember your glory days when you could do the half-split. Photo of Gilbert, 101f.

<u>Direction of Movements</u>: To the east.

<u>Possible Applications</u>: Move forward to a knee strike, bringing the opponent's arm up out of the way. If you get into trouble, drop quickly and

Yilu: The First Form

drive his supporting legs out from under him by shoving his feet with your left heel. If you hold onto him as you do this, you will spread him out on the ground like a quilt.

Do not think that you can drop down, get your leg and arm between your opponent's legs, and then come forward and pick him up on your shoulders. That is just crazy talk. It is possible to pick someone up on your shoulders scooting into a half-squat with your feet together and getting your shoulders into his hips. Trying it from a full drop stance you would need iron knees, back, and hips, and a fair bit of cooperation from your opponent.

<u>About the Name</u>: *Pu di* means to spread out on the ground. *Mian* means soft, with a secondary meaning of continuous, but it also very often means the cotton wadding in a quilt, coat, or shoes. The name suggests be that you cover the ground with your opponent like throwing out a quilt, or that you drop as if to spread out a large quilt.

Most Chen branches call this *pudijin*, which is essentially the same, but with brocade instead of a quilt. The two characters 绵 and 锦 look quite similar, so it is easy to see that they could become mixed up when copying, if the radical is not written clearly. I think that spreading a quilt to air in the sun is a more likely activity than spreading silk brocade, but it doesn't really matter. The image of the opponent going flying out, fully spread eagle, is the main thing.

In many Chen branches this move is called *que dilong*. This name is pure Chen village dialect – *que* means to drill or tunnel forward through something, and *dilong* is an earthworm. The image is drilling through the ground following the route of earthworms to collect them for fishing. The muddy ground at the riverside would be slightly drier where they were burrowing near the top, as it would be thinner, so the children could see where the worms were and burrow in to catch them. This description comes from Chen Zhenglei. It for some reason is always translated as 'Dragon On The Ground,' which doesn't mean much. It should actually be translated as 'Tunnel After Earthworms,' which is cool and descriptive.

<u>Additional Comments</u>: I was never great at moving forward directly from the half-hurdle stance. A trick is to do a very low drop stance, then put the knee down into the hurdler's stance, then bring it back up again, and then go forward as normal from a drop stance.

> You should always enjoy what you can do, because you never know when you are going to lose it. It seems so easy at the time. As you get older and have collected a few injuries and joint restrictions, a low drop stance doesn't seem so important in the grand scheme of things, and a hurdler's stance even less so.

> Chen Xin mentions (page 407) that this move is also called Rooster Spreads On The Ground. Because the quick tempered rooster tends to overheat, it will spread one wing on damp ground to cool down its skin.

Cai Yuhua's house was originally a suburban farmhouse, the neighbourhood was one of small lanes with houses, their courtyards walled for privacy, and the farmland out at the end of the lane. The train went by quite near, and there was a stream where Cai Yuhua used to go fishing. Gradually the nearby road got wider, housing spread out to the area, traffic on the main road got busier, and later a metro line reached out there and beyond. I rode my bike through a village marketplace on the way to training.

During the late 1990s the large scale urban renewal was reaching out to our area. When I went back in 2001, sifu's neighbourhood had gone, and I couldn't find him at home or in the park. I spent a fruitless morning wandering around Longhua park, searching through various new possible training spots. Cai Yuhua was preparing to leave for Switzerland (as usual I had just gone without getting in touch first) and didn't know how to find him either. He helped with phone calls to fellow students, to no avail. We spent a couple of days catching up, then he headed to Switzerland and I headed back up to Beijing.

Really, I was lucky that Cai Yuhua's house was still in the old place and the little lanes still there in 2001. By the next trip to Shanghai, almost fifteen years later, they had gone. In 2015, our home area was still recognizable on a map, but not in reality. So much new housing has gone in that I had no clue when Patrick was driving me back from Cai Yuhua's new place, and asked if I recognized where we were. We were 'home.' From an elevated expressway we looked out over a space-age dome of the new South Rail Station, towards an endless expanse of high apartment block complexes.

102. Seven Stars Fists   qī xīng quán   七星拳
or **Advance To Seven Stars**   shàng bù qī xīng   上步七星

<u>Overall Movement</u>: Move forward with the forearms crossed then curl to punch through.

<u>Footwork</u>: Shift forward and bring the right foot forward to a high empty stance.

<u>Breakdown of Movement</u>:

Part One: Move forward and up, stepping the right foot forward (east) and settling on the left leg in a high empty stance. Bring the right fist to the front, passing under the left fist, fist heart facing in. Both arms are *shunchan* with the fist hearts facing in. Photo 102a.

Part Two: Roll the fists in (*nichan*), curling the right fist around the left forearm. Extend the right fist out to the front, little finger side on top, with a short and light *fajin*. The left fist is again on top, on the right forearm near the elbow. Photos 102b and 102c.

<u>Direction of Movements</u>: Facing east.

<u>Possible Applications</u>: Come up prepared to strike with any surface. Finish with a punch to the solar plexus. The crossed arms can apply power upwards into the fists or downwards into the forearms, whichever is needed.

<u>Internal Connections</u>: Consciously join all of the seven stars together so that any one can be the effective attack. Swallow into the body to spit out the second punch.

<u>About the Name</u>: This type of posture is often called Seven Stars in traditional styles. The seven stars are those of the Big Dipper, which are neatly lined up like the legs, arms, and body.

The seven striking surfaces are traditionally considered the fists, elbows, shoulders, feet, knees, hips, and head. In Chen village they consider the seven stars of the Big Dipper posture the two hands, two elbows, two shoulders, and head.

The name points out that the posture sets the striking surfaces up neatly up so that any one of them could strike.

<u>Additional Comments</u>: Here are photos from the other side.

My last trip, in 2019, Patrick and his wife invited Cai Yuhua, his daughter Wen, and I to eat Shanghai's famous crab-filled *xiaolongbao* – Shanghai dumplings – in the private rooms upstairs at the Yuyuan Gardens. Cai Wen, now a mature woman with her own child, had as much trouble finding it as I did, but we managed eventually to sit down at a big round table laden with steaming baskets. Thirty-five years of friendship, and, as always, we all picked up as if we had just seen each other yesterday.

I should mention that Yuhua's wife, Xiaolan, was of course welcome, but not able to come. She has been fighting MS since 2001, and does not have the energy that going to a downtown restaurant meal demands. Transit in Shanghai is for the fit. Yuhua has kept her mobile and functional by hours of *tuina* therapy every day. She has learned to enjoy living with her limitations, and has become a gentler person. When we used to go shopping together, she was the hardest bargainer in the city. I used to feel bad for the vendors after a bout.

Yilu: The First Form

103. **Ride The Tiger**   kuà hǔ shì   跨虎势

     or **Step Back And Press Down With The Palms**   tuì bù àn zhǎng

                                                                                               退步按掌

Overall Movement: Step back and brush knees to both sides, to finish settled in horse stance with the left hook hand behind and the right palm upright in front.

Footwork: Step the right foot back and turn to horse stance facing south.

Breakdown of Movement:

Part One: Roll the hands through again, unclenching then pulling down. The left hand comes up inside the right hand then extends to the front (east). Start to step the right foot back during this roll. Photos 103a and 103b.

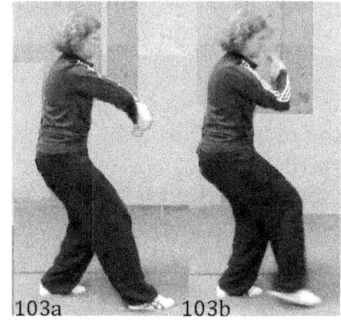

Part Two: Step the right foot back and turn to a horse stance, facing south. Sweep the palms to block the knees, alternately to either side, right, then left, palms facing down, tiger's mouth pointing to each knee. Maintain an expanding energy (*peng*) throughout. Photos 103c and 103d.

Part Three: Continue to coil and circle until the left hand is hooked behind the waist and the right hand is upright in front of the chest. The right hand has the thumb side in and the palm facing left. Sit in a horse stance and show a strong, calm presence. Photos 103e, and 103f.

Direction of Movements: Facing south.

Possible Applications: Quite the same as Brush Knee Counter Stance, but setting up for a bigger throw in the following move. The first sweep takes him (or a bale of hay) across the thigh. The rising move brings the bale of hay up to your shoulder. You probably wouldn't do that to an opponent.

Internal Connections: The horse stance briefly passes through a full horse stance, evenly weighted, torso upright, feet pointing forward and flat on the ground, knees pulled in to open the hip sockets.

About the Name: The use of '*kua*' always refers to a leg action of reaching to step over something, like fording a river or mounting a horse. Ride The Tiger makes the description more dynamic, of climbing onto a tiger, helping to give you a strong spirit.

In Chen village this is called *kua hong shi. Hong* means the thigh (it usually means the arm, but in the martial arts it also refers to the thigh). So the name means to stride the thigh in to the opponent's space to be able to roll him over it. This explanation comes from Chen Zhenglei. The action is like stepping and setting the leg into a bale of hay, then encircling it with the arm over the top and around to hoist it onto the shoulder.

Step Back And Press Down With The Palms is a straightforward description of the first action.

Additional Comments: Roll in the legs, never stopping the *chansi* power. The arms go along with the roll of the legs, do not stop or break the power at any time during this move. This posture and the beginning action of the following posture tests whether or not you have truly understood the coiling within the legs and body and the connection and coiling into the arms.

You can see in photo 103d the spread of the fingers of the left hand, as each finger hooks separately from smaller finger to index finger while passing the left knee.

Here also is photo 103b from the front.

Cai Yuhua, in addition to his martial and healing skills, is a traditionally trained and talented artist. He supplemented his income selling Chinese landscape paintings to an art store that paid him peanuts and sold them at quite high prices. As he made friends among foreign martial artists, the Swiss realised his talent, and started selling his paintings in Switzerland, and having him visit there to teach painting as well as Taijiquan and his martial skills.

Yilu: The First Form

104. **Turning Swaying Lotus**　　　zhuàn shēn bǎi lián　　　转身摆莲

or **Turning Double Swaying Lotus**　　zhuàn shēn shuāng bǎi lián

转身双摆莲

Overall Movement: Continue to turn, pivoting into a long cross-step and extending the arms. Then do an outside crescent kick.

Footwork: Turn the left foot in, then the right foot out, to turn gradually into a long cross stance. Then step and shift to the left leg and swing the right leg up and out in an outside crescent kick.

Breakdown of Movement:

Part One: Carry on the circle to bring the hands around, turning the body around to the right. Pivot on the legs, following the *chansi* coiling of the previous move, so that you first turn the left foot in then turn the right foot out. You end up in an extended cross-step with the body facing north. Continue the line of action of the hands, keeping the arms quite straight, until they end up with the right hand at the east in an upright palm and the left hand at the west in a hanging hook. Photos 104a and 104b.

Part Two: Continue the coiling of the legs, step the left foot to the left, and shift firmly to the left leg. Bring the left hand over to meet the right hand and pull with both hands until they are in front of the body, palms out, fingers turned to the left. Photos 104c and 104d.

Part Three: Bring the right foot directly up then swing it out. Bring both hands across and in to slap the outside/top of the foot with both hands. Keep the hand movement small and slap sharply. Photos 104e and 104f.

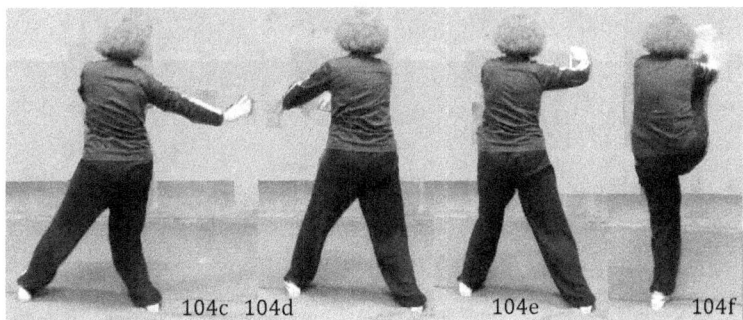

Direction of Movements: At the peak of the turn, the stance is on the east to west line, the body faces north.

Possible Applications: Come up under the opponent's arm, pull over and around, catching his elbow with the left hand. Then throw, using the crossing power of the arms and leg.

About the Name: This is a straight forward description, once you are used to this term for outside swinging kicks. The 1982 list name of <u>Double</u> Swaying Lotus refers to the double-handed slap.

Additional Comments: During the kick, bring the right leg up from behind, do not tuck it in beside the left foot before kicking. Swing the leg in full range so that it lands to the rear. Use power from the hips.

Here are photos of the turn (104b) and the kick (104e and 104f) from the side.

Cai Yuhua also supplemented his income by framing paintings in the traditional Chinese manner. Making a '*biao*,' or a silk rolled frame, for a Chinese painting is complicated, and Yuhua is an expert. I learned the steps, watching them, but can't really remember. They involved a lot of paste, a lot of different and special brushes, some volunteer labour from apprentices to trim the wooden hangers, and sticking the paintings to the wall. When he was working on a batch he took over the whole house, and we all helped in whatever way we could. I'm afraid that my biggest help was to stay out of the way.

Yilu: The First Form

105. **Seize The Heart**　　　　huò xīn quán　　　　　　获心拳

<u>Overall Movement</u>: Land the foot and double hit.

<u>Footwork</u>: Land the right foot behind then step the left foot forward (north). Drive forward and punch.

<u>Breakdown of Movement</u>:

Part One: Stomp the right foot as it lands to the rear. Step the left foot forward (North). The hands are still in front of the body after the kick, so draw them directly in and up the midline. Pull in with the palms down and the elbows tucked in. Massage the ribs with the elbows. Photo 105a.

Part Two: Do a *fajin* double hit, circling the hands up the body, clenching as they move. Then hit forward (North) and almost down. The fist hearts face in, the back fists obliquely forward and down. Photo 105b.

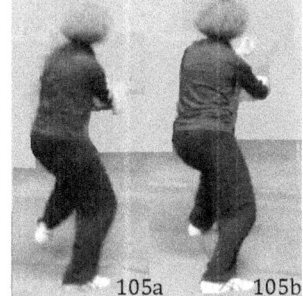

<u>Direction of Movements</u>: Facing north.

<u>Possible Applications</u>: Block and strike at the same time by rising and striking down with the fists.

<u>Internal Connections</u>: Swallow and spit the power to drive both fists at once.

<u>About the Name</u>: The name reminds you to keep the action down the centre of your body, the better to get into the heart of the opponent.

<u>Additional Comments</u>: Make the elbow 'massage' distinct, to get the power for the hit.

Here is the strike from the side.

106. **Rap On The Head With Cannon-Balls**   dāng tóu pào   当头砲

<u>Overall Movement</u>: Sit back, then come forward with a front swing kick and lifting strike, then drop the leg back, draw the hands in and double punch.

<u>Footwork</u>: Sit back on the right leg into a low pouncing stance, then shift forward to the left leg and swing the right foot straight up to the front (north). Drop the right leg back to the rear so you are in a bow stance for the punch.

<u>Breakdown of Movement</u>:

Part One: Sit down on the right leg with the left leg extended forward in a low pouncing stance. Thread the left fist, rolled over, along the left leg. Draw the right fist back to block up. Photos 106a and 106b.

Part Two: Shift forward and bring the right fist through. Swing the right leg straight up, dorsi-flexed. Do a right uppercut or elbow lift with the fist eye up. Place the left palm on top of the right forearm. Photo 106c.

Part Three: Drop the right leg back to the rear to go back into a bow stance. Draw the hands in together to the belly, the left palm on the right wrist. Bring the hands up the midline, massaging the chest up the centre. Punch with a double strike, the same as move 105. Photos 106d, 106e.

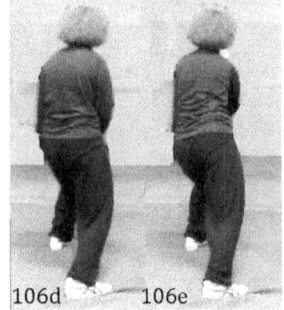

<u>Direction of Movements</u>: Facing north.

<u>Possible Applications</u>: Straight kick to the groin, using the hands to control the opponent's arms to prevent him from blocking. Then come up through the middle to strike to the head or down into his chest.

Internal Connections: Swallow and spit the power again to link the kick to the punch.

About the Name: In both the 1982 and 1990 lists, the word *pao* is written with a stone radical 砲 instead of the fire radical 炮. Usually, with the fire radical, *pao* means a double hit, which this is. *Pao* with the stone radical means "ancient ballista for throwing heavy stones."

Dangtou is a phrase used in Zen Buddhism, for when the monks are rapped on the head with a stick during meditation to keep them awake. So the overall implication of the name is to give a good solid rap on the head.

Additional Comments: Drop the leg with power, doing an axe kick. That is, applying force downward with the heel after the upward kick. The force of the downward kick takes the straight leg directly to the rear, into the bow stance.

Here is the final punch (106e) from the side.

I have two stone paperweight blocks that are always on my desk. One, made by a friend of Cai Yuhua, a professional carver, is one character, carved in offset, of a famous character for tiger that is written in one stroke.

The other, and my most cherished, was carved by Cai Yuhua himself. It describes Taijiquan and training all in one phrase 绵绵不断 'continuous without a pause.' This refers to the movements of and within your body while doing Taijiquan, and also your life of training.

Yilu: The First Form

107. **Temple Guard Pounds With The Pestle** (for the fourth time) jīn gāng dǎo duì 金刚捣碓

Overall Movement: The same as usual, but do not emphasize the twisting as much. Settle into the stance and allow the energy to sink fully.

Footwork: Drop back to low pouncing stance, then shift through the same as move 4, to *kaibu*.

Breakdown of Movement:

Part One: Sit back to the right leg, leaving the left leg extended to the front (north), in a low pouncing stance. Pull back with both hands, then through as usual for Pound With The Pestle. Photos 107a, 107b, and 107c.

Part Two: Continue on as usual with the Pound With The Pestle, but really sinking into the body and allowing the energy to fully relax. Photos 107d, 107e, 107f, 107g, 107h, and 107i.

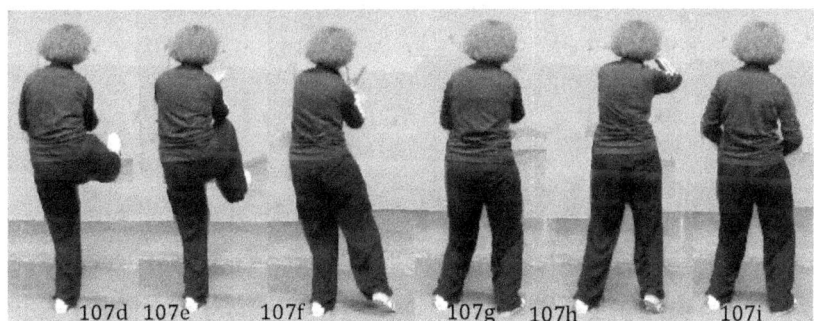

Direction of Movements: This form is traditionally completed facing north, that is, in the opposite direction that it faces at the opening stance. Finish the form, then if you want to face the other way, perhaps if your teacher is watching you from the other side, just turn around. If you are performing in a show, you may turn to face south within the movement, placing the right foot turned out as it lands, then stepping the left foot around to *kaibu*.

Additional Comments: Make sure to use the leg to drive out, the same as in the first Pound With The Pestle.

Here are photos from the side.

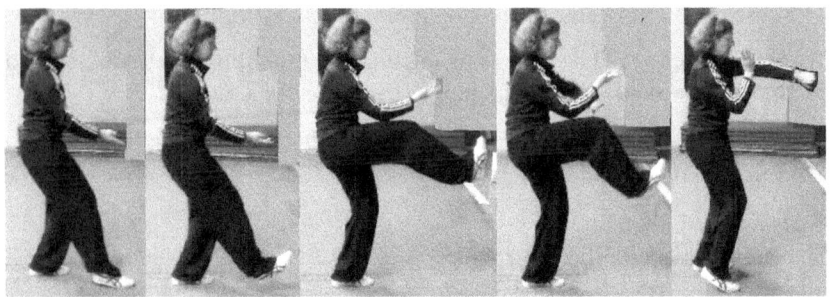

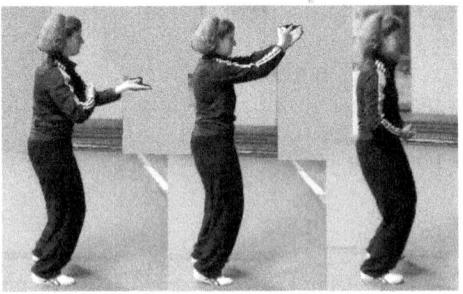

The best part of Shanghai is the friends. The food runs a very close second place. Yuhua's homemade meals are still better than any restaurant (and the restaurants are excellent), and the kitchen in his new home is spacious and coal dust free.

Cai Yuhua and Patrick in the new kitchen.

Yilu: The First Form

108. **Closing Posture**   shōu shì   收势

or **Three Openings And Closings Of The Dantian** prior to **Closing Posture**   dān tián sān kāi hé   丹田三开合

Overall Movement: Continue to roll and coil until you feel you are done, then close the form.

Footwork: Settle into the *kaibu*, rise up, then settle again. You may then turn the toes in and then heels in if you wish, to finish in a *bingbu* with the feet together. You may also stand up directly from the *kaibu*.

Breakdown of Movement:

Part One: Roll in the legs and roll the right fist around in the left palm to place the fist underneath. Photos 108a, 109b, and 108c. (See also photos 5a, 5b, 5c, and 5d, but finishing with the fist underneath.)

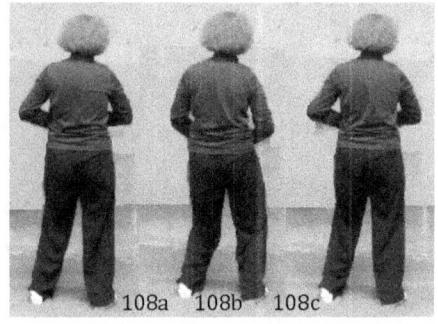

Part Two: Straighten the legs to stand up, still in *kaibu*. Open the hands to the side, palms down, then lift and turn the palms up. From shoulder height, turn the palms forward and sink down until the palms are beside the legs. Photos 108d, 108e and 108f.

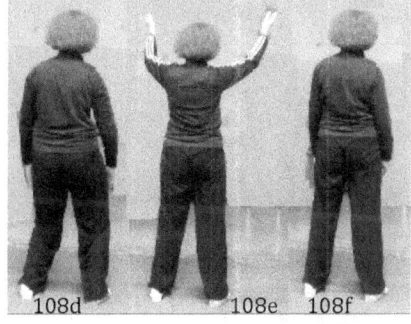

Part Three: Coil the palms up, circle in to the front, toes in. (optional)

Part Four: Coil the palms down, pressing out to the sides, bring the heels in so the feet are together. (optional)

Part Five: Place the hands on the thighs the same as in the Opening Movement.

Possible Applications: Practice getting your heart rate back to normal after a spurt of activity. The last moves are quick and powerful, and your heart rate may rise. Use the circles of the hands in part one to feel your heart beating. Circle and breathe until you are relaxed and settled. The ability to calm yourself quickly is necessary in a fight.

Internal Connections: Make sure to settle down the *qi*. Continue to roll and circle if your heart rate doesn't slow.

Shadowboxing in Shanghai

<u>About the Name</u>: This is the usual name for the closing of a form, meaning the posture that brings the form to its end. The 1982 also contains a name for parts one to four (Three Openings And Closings) separately from the actual closing posture, which is just part five.

<u>Additional Comments</u>: You may roll the right fist in the left palm once or twice, until you feel ready to 'put out the fire.'

You do not need to do the whole closing as described. You may close the form as you feel comfortable. You need to feel ready to stop. If you need to roll more, or prefer to settle into the *kaibu* instead of rolling to *bingbu*, that is fine.

Here are photos for move 108 from the side.

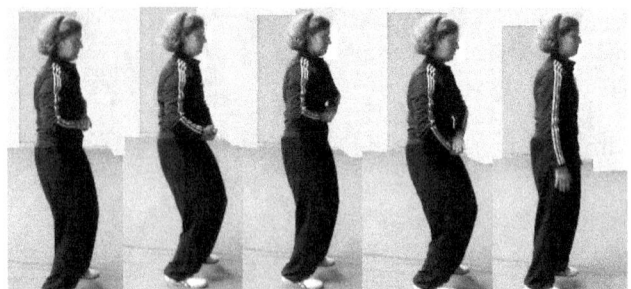

Done!

A cameraman in the broken mirror.

282

Shanghaihua, a language of the Wu kingdom

In China, different languages are called dialects, even though they are mutually unintelligible, which is the usual dividing line. This is because, should you want to write something down, most words can be written with characters held in common. When I was in Shanghai in the 1980s and 90s, people would start out talking in Putonghua, to try to include me, but gradually slide to Shanghaihua as they talked amongst themselves. I got to understand quite a lot, especially if they were talking about food or wushu, but never really had the nerve to try to speak it. I wish I had worked harder on learning Shanghaihua, I do like to listen to it, and the ability to speak it marks you as someone who belongs. Not speaking it marks you as an Outlander, whether foreign or Chinese.

Most early emigrants to Shanghai came into the city from the surrounding region in the developmental years during the 19th and early 20th centuries, so Shanghaihua is a dialect of the Wu language, of the southern Yangzi delta. People came in mostly from nearby Ningbo and Suzhou city areas, and from northern Zhejiang and southern Jiangsu provinces. Shanghainese are descendants of these migrants, and their language developed into the urban dialect of Shanghai. Migration in later years (such as the Anti-Japanese war of 1937-1945 and the Chinese civil war of 1946-1940), was into this established group, and incomers needed to learn Shanghaihua to be considered a Shanghainese.

I did some research for a linguistics course while I was in Victoria in the early 1990s, comparing the phonetics of Putonghua and Shanghaihua. I had a lot of fun with further research while writing up this book, so updated and improved on that work.

<u>Initials.</u> The Wu language dialects share a three-way obstruent distinction of aspirated, glottal stops, and murmur. An obstruent is an initial consonant that 'obstructs' the sound at first, like p, t, k. The three-way distinction means that there is an unvoiced aspirated class – p^h, t^h, ts^h, $č^h$, k^h, kw^h, and w^h – each of which also occurs without aspiration as a tense class with glottal stop – p, t, ts, č, k, kw, and 'w – and as a lax class with murmur –b, d, dz, j, g, gw, w.

The previous list is all the aspirated initial consonants, but there are twice as many in the unaspirated and murmur lists, so the more interesting distinction is between 'with glottal stop' and 'murmured.'

Murmur is a lax vibration of the vocal chords <u>throughout</u> the entire phonation process (but not before – that is, there is no initial obstruction). The vocal cords are less tense, more lax, than normal voicing, letting more air escape than normal voicing. This is why murmur is often called 'breathy voice.'

The glottal stop is a rapid closing of the vocal cords <u>prior to</u> articulation.

Both murmur and glottal stop affect more than the way the consonant is pronounced. Murmur depresses the following vowel and lowers the pitch register of the whole syllable. The glottal stop cuts the following vowel short, shortening the syllable. In addition, if the syllable starts with a glottal stop it also ends with a glottal stop.

<u>Tones</u>. Also characteristic of the Wu language are tonal contours that spread across words, which is called 'tone sandhi.' In Shanghaihua, a written character (one syllable) does not have a set tone. Syllables will change tone depending on the tonal context of preceding syllables. The tone of the first syllable spreads to the following syllables within a word, replacing their original tone.

I ran into trouble in my research o the 1990s when asking for the tones of individual characters. I would ask my friend, a native Shanghaihua speaker, to read a character for me, and he would quite often say, "I can pronounce it, but can't give you the tone without context." I finally found scholarly research that confirmed this.

In addition, the pronunciation of the syllable includes the tone in a way different from other Chinese dialects. While there are technically five tones, they are so closely linked with the syllable type that they are almost pitch rather than tone. Some consider the Wu languages to not have tones, only pitch that follows the structure of the vocalization.

Yilu: The First Form

Rough pronunciation guide to the sounds of Shanghaihua.

There is no definitive romanization, so I developed my own. For my romanization, I looked at other methods, and used my criteria of accurate, intuitively understandable (especially to an English speaker), and able to type of a computer keyboard (no longer stuck with just a typewriter).

For the pronunciation, I give English and French examples, since I am Canadian. I have used some Russian and Japanese as well, because their writing systems are remarkably consistent for the sounds, unlike English and French. I have also included the pinyin when Putonghua has an equivalent sound. I give the International Phonetic Alphabet symbol for clarity.

INITIALS
Aspirated, Voiceless Initials. The larynx is relaxed, making no stop or voicing. The pitch of the syllable will be medium to high.
Sounds are close to the examples, but with more of a puff than usually done in English. Apiration is often marked with /'/ in romanization, but I have kept the /'/ for glottal stops.

p^h	Eng: pin. PTH pinyin /p/. IPA /p'/. (Keyboard, superscript the h.)
t^h	Eng: top. PTH pinyin /t/. IPA /t'/.
ts^h	Eng: exaggerating the puff after cats. PTH pinyin /c/. IPA /ts'/
$č^h$	Eng: <u>ch</u>at with a puff of air, but with the front of the tongue raised and the tip on the lower teeth. PTH pinyin /q/. IPA approximately /tʃ'/.
k^h	Eng: cat. PTH pinyin /k/. IPA /k'/.
kw^h	Eng: quidditch, with an extra puff of air. PTH pinyin /ku-/, as in kuai.
w^h	Eng: which (when it is pronounced with the puff of air, different to witch). IPA /ʍ/.
h	Eng: ham, with an extra puff of air, like saying the letter h as 'haitch'. Jpn: は (ho). IPA /h/.
Unaspirated, Voiceless, Tense, Upper Series Initials. The larynx does a glottal stop at the initiation of the consonant, glide, or nasal. The pitch of the syllable will be medium to high. The examples are simply unaspirated, most languages do not have the initializing glottal stop.		
p	Eng: spin. Fr: paix. Russ: папа (papa). Jpn: ぱ (pa). PTH pinyin /b/. IPA /ʔp/.

f	Similar to Eng: fool. Fr: fort. Russ: фамилия (familija). PTH pinyin /f/. Shanghaihua tends a bit towards Jpn: ふじさん (Fujisan). IPA between /f/ and /ɸ/. The teeth touch lightly behind the lower lip, not over it.
t	Eng: stop. Fr: tarif. Russ: телефон (telefon). Jpn: たけ (take). PTH pinyin /d/. IPA /ʔt/.
s	Eng: see. Fr: sauter. Russ: себя (sebja). Jpn: さい (sai). PTH pinyin /s/. IPA /s/.
ts	Eng: it<u>s</u> raining. PTH pinyin /z/. IPA /ʔts/.
š	Eng: like 'she' — but the front of the tongue is raised and the tip is on the lower teeth. Russ: ш, romanized as /š/. PTH pinyin /x/. IPA /ʂ/. (Keyboard: press s and hold, then pick š.)
č	Similar to Eng: pi<u>ct</u>ure, or the English pronunciation of tune. The front of the tongue raised and the tip on the lower teeth. PTH pinyin /j/. IPA approximately /ʔtʃ/. (Keyboard, press c and hold, then pick č)
k	Eng: scan. Fr: coq. Russ: как (kak). Jpn: かく (kaku). PTH pinyin /g/. IPA /ʔk/.
kw	Eng: Sas<u>qu</u>atch. PTH pinyin /gu-/, as in guai.
'l	Eng: let. Fr: leur. PTH pinyin /l/. IPA /ʔl/.
'm	Eng: met. Fr: mère. Russ: мама (mama). Jpn: め (me). PTH pinyin /m/. IPA /ʔm/.
'n	Eng: net. Fr: nez. Russ: ночь (noč'). Jpn: の (no). PTH pinyin /n/. IPA /ʔn/.
'ñ	Eng: canyon. Fr: oignon. Spanish mañana. IPA /ʔñ/. (Keyboard press n and hold, then pick ñ.)
'ng	Eng: si<u>ng</u>. PTH pinyin ng (though never as an initial). IPA /ʔŋ/.
'w	Eng: we. Fr: oui. Jpn: わ (wa). PTH pinyin /w/. Sh: 'w', tending towards 'u'. IPA /ʔu/.
'y 'i	Eng: yes. Jpn: ゆ (yu). PTH pinyin /y/. Sh: /y/, tending towards /i/. IPA /ʔi/. Clearer to write /'i/ when with initial vowels – 'ie, 'iø, 'iå, 'ia.

Yilu: The First Form

'	Used when a syllable starts with a glottal stop vowel, such as /'a/, and when a syllable starts with a glottal stop liquid or nasal.

Unaspirated, Voiced, Murmured, Lower Series Initials. The larynx is lax and vibrating at the initiation of the consonant, glide, or nasal, causing a breathy voicing that carries into the following vowel. The pitch of the syllable will be low.

Examples are voiced, as few languages have murmur. You need to remember the murmur.

b	Eng: but. Fr: boule. Russ: бабушка (babuška). Jpn: ば(ba). IPA /ɦb/.
v	Eng: voice. Fr: vivre. Russ: вода (voda) (though voiced and murmured, with the same placement as the unvoiced f). IPA /ɦv/.
d	Eng: do. Fr: dent. Russ: дома (doma), Jpn: だけ(dake). IPA /ɦd/.
z	Eng: zoo. Fr: zèle. Russ: зоопарк (zoopark). Jpn: ざい(zai). IPA /ɦz/.
dz	Murmured and voiced ts. IPA /ɦdz/.
ž	Eng: not quite 'plea_s_ure' (though with the similar tongue placement as the unvoiced š). Russ: ж, Romanized as /ž/. IPA /ɦz/. (Keyboard, press z and hold, pick ž.)
j	Eng: joy. Fr: jazz. (though with a similar tongue placement as the unvoiced č). . IPA /ɦdẓ/.
g	Eng: go. Fr: gauche. Russ: говорить (govorit'). Jpn: がく(gaku). IPA /ɦg/.
gw	Eng: Gwen.
l	Similar pronunciation to l, with murmur. IPA /ɦl/.
m	Similar pronunciation to m. IPA /ɦm/.
n	Similar pronunciation to n, with murmur. IPA /ɦn/.
ñ	Similar pronunciation to ñ, with murmur. IPA /ɦñ/.

ng	Similar pronunciation to ng, with murmur. IPA /ɦŋ/.	
w	Similar pronunciation to w, with murmur. IPA /ɦu/.	
y i	Similar pronunciation to y, with murmur. IPA /ɦi/.	
Initials Used Alone		
tsʰ, ts, dz, s, z	Pronounced with the sound /ɨ/ in IPA. (Like Putonghua has the syllables ci, si, zi). I write them as tsʰî, tsî, dzî, sî, zî so that they look more natural.	
m, ng	Pronounced with no particular sound aside from their own – m like English cha<u>sm</u> and ng like ha<u>ng</u>er.	
FINALS.		
Nasal Finals: Nasalize the vowel to its nearest place of pronunciation.		
n	When a final, n nasalises the vowel rather than both being fully pronounced, and lengthens the vowel. Comes after the vowels a, e, ye, o oe. (pronounced ã, õ).	
ñ	Spanish mañana. When a final, ñ palatalizes the vowel rather than both being fully being pronounced. Comes after the front vowels i and e.	
ng	When a final, ng takes the vowel into the g pronunciation place, like French bo<u>n,</u> rather than both being fully pronounced. Comes after the vowels a, au, oo, u, and ya.	
Abrupt Finals		
'	A glottal stop after a vowel. A final glottal stop makes the tone short. Commonly used following i, e, a, å, o, œ, u, and ya.	

Open Vowel Finals	
\multicolumn{2}{l}{There are twelve distinct vowels in Shanghainese, plus long and short pronunciations of many of them.}	
\multicolumn{2}{l}{A characteristic of the Wu language are vowels with rounded and unrounded pairs. Rounded vowels are sometimes also called compressed vowels, but there is a distinction. Rounding is done by bringing the corners of the mouth forward and protruding the lip. The vowels ü, î, ø, u, o, and å are rounded. Compression is done by bringing the sides of the lips together by closing the jaw and tightening the corners of the lips. There is a gap in the centre, but the lips are not protruded. The vowel ò is compressed.}	
Close, or high, Front, Central, and Back Vowels	
i	When in open syllable, Eng: easy. Fr: ici. Russ: один (odin). Jpn: ひと (hito). PRH pinyin /i/. IPA /i/.
	Lengthened i, written /i:/. Long, open syllable keeps the same sound. Eng: seen. Fr: dire. Jpn: ひいらぎ (hiiragi). IPA /i:/.
	Before glottal stop or /ng/ final, Eng: sit. Quebecois: icitte. PTH pinyin /i/. IPA/ ɪ/.
ü	Fr: du. PTH pinyin /ü/. (keyboard, option u, u, or press u and hold then pick ü) (rounded version of i). IPA /y/.
	Lengthened ü, written /ü:/. Rounded version of /i:/, keeps close to its same sound. Fr: mur. IPA /y:/.
	With glottal stop. Fr: chute. (rounded version of /iʔ/) IPA /ʏ/.
î	A close, or high, central vowel, unrounded. Follows s, z, ts', ts, dz. (doesn't really need to be written, can just write the consonant alone) Russ: мышь, (myš') /ы/ is usually romanized as /y/. IPA /ɨ/. (keyboard, option i, then i. Or press i and hold, and pick î.)
û	Russ: чуть (čut'), the Russian /y/ is usually romanized as /u/. Rounded version of î. (keyboard, option i, then u. Or press u and hold, then pick û). IPA /ʉ/.
	Lengthened û, written /û:/. Keeps close to its same sound. The only example I can find is Catalan: ful. IPA /ʉ:/.
u	Eng: do. Fr: goût. PTH pinyin /u/. IPA /u/.
	Lengthened u, written /u:/. Eng: fool. IPA /u:/.
	With the glottal stop final, Eng: foot. IPA /ʊ/.

	Close, or mid, Front, Central, and Back Vowels	
e	Eng: prey. Fr: clé. Russ: шея (šeja). IPA /e/.	
	Lengthened e, written /e:/. Australian: there. Jpn: へいき (heiki). IPA /e:/.	
	Before glottal stop final. Eng: wet, Fr: metre. Russ: это (eto). PTH pinyin /e/. IPA /ɛ/.	
ø	Fr: deux. A rounded version of e. (keyboard, option o. Or press o and hold, and pick ø.)	
	Lengthened ø, written /ø:/. Fr: neutre. IPA /ø/.	
ê	Eng: about. Fr: de. In many languages, more of a lazy pronunciation of an /e/ or /a/ than anything else, taking the vowel to a central-mid place. IPA /ə/. (Keyboard, option i, e. Or press e and hold, and pick ê)	
œ	In Shanghaihua, a compressed, rather than rounded, version of /ə/. Jpn 空気 (kūki). IPA /ɯᵝ/.	
	Examples of a similar, but rounded, /ə/ are Russ: тётя (tjótja), the Russian ё usually romanized as ó. German: Goethe. (Keyboard option e, o. Or press o and hold, and pick œ.)	
o	Eng: though. Fr: eau. Russ: вошь (vošʼ). Jpn ぼだん (bodan). PTH pinyin /o/. IPA /o/.	
	Lengthened o, written /o:/. Fr: jaune. Jpn: ぼうりょく (bōryoku). IPA /o:/.	
	Before glottal stop final. Eng: put. Russ: м<u>у</u>жчина (mužčina). IPA /ʊ/.	
å	Eng: hot. Fr: bonne. IPA /ɔ/. (Keyboard, option a. Or press a and hold, and pick å.)	
	Lengthened å, written /å:/. Eng: August. Fr: or. IPA /ɔ:/.	
Open, or Low Vowels		
a	Fr: ânes. Russ: палка (palka). PTH pinyin /a/. IPA /ɑ/.	
	Lengthened a, written /a:/. Eng: far. Fr: pâte.	
	Before glottal stop or /n/ final. Eng: cat. Fr: lac. Russ: маленький (m<u>a</u>lenʼkij). Jpn: か (ka). IPA /a/.	

For a very good online resource to find the pronunciation of all these sounds, do a search for Wiktionary: IPA pronunciation key.

Yilu: The First Form

TONE OR PITCH?	
DESCRIPTION	VOCAL RANGE (lowest is 1, highest is 5).
High falling. Begins with voiceless initial (glottal stop or aspirated), ends in open vowel or nasal. If vowel is prolonged, the fall is more pronounced.	53
Moderately high, level. Begins with voiceless initial, ends in open vowel or nasal. If vowel is prolonged, tends to rise.	34
Begins with voiceless initial, ends in glottal stop, this is high and short.	5
Begins with murmur, low. If vowel is prolonged, tends to rise slightly.	13
Begins with murmur, low, level, short, ends in glottal stop.	2
Words with an initial glottal stop are medium to high in pitch. They may be normal, prolonged, or shortened.	
Words said with murmur are low in pitch. They may be normal, prolonged or shortened.	
Words cut by glottal stop are shortened. They may be high or low in pitch.	
Open vowels or velar nasal endings are said with a contoured tone, and may be normal or prolonged.	

Rather than indicate 'tones,' romanization needs to clarify pronunciation. A high normal syllable can be written /'pa/ and /pʰa/. The exact height of the high tones (start at 3 or 5) is the only indicator that is missing. A high, prolonged syllable /'pa:/ can be written /pʰa:/. In prolonged syllables, if the starting height is 3, there is a slight rise, if 5, a fall. A high shortened syllable can be written as /'pa'/ and /pʰa'/. A low normal as /ba/, a low prolonged as /ba:/, and a low shortened as /ba'/. Following syllables follow the tonal changes of tone sandhi, so multi-syllable words need to be hyphenated.

Some words and phrases in Shanghaihua – Zǎng-he œ-wo

(Please note that this is not written in pinyin – pronunciations of Putonghua written in pinyin are at the back of this book, to help with pronunciation of the names of the forms' moves.)

No:ng-zǎ	Good morning. (greeting, general)
Tsǎ-'a	Good morning. (greeting, place name before)
Ya li ho	Good evening. (greeting)
Wo 'a	Good night.
Tse-we	Goodbye. (see you later)
Sǎ be no:ng	Goodbye. (said by person leaving)
Man-čʰi	Goodbye. (said to person leaving)
No:ng hǎ va	How are you?
Ngu-ma-ho	I'm fine.
Zia-zia	Thank you.
Ve čʰê gu va'	Have you eaten? (greeting)
Čʰê-gu-le	I've eaten.
E	Yes.
Ve'-zi'. Ve'.	No (as in, it's not so). Not.
Mê'	No.
Te-vê'-či'	Sorry.
Wu vê' šio-tʰê'	I don't know.
No:ng la 'a li	Where are you?
Ngo: sa-do:	I'm tired.
Kê-šin	Happy (I also continued to say a Putonghua-ised, version of this, saying kaixin instead of gaoxing)
So dêng	Wait a moment.
Tang-sing	Take care.
Sa ku' mǎ-bing?	What is the matter?
Čung-tsǎ man ñi'	Its hot today.
Zǎ'-ñi'	Yesterday.
Ming-tsǎ	Tomorrow.
Ña-di-nin	Outlander.
Bang-iø	Friend.

Yilu: The First Form

Ga-di'	How much is this?
Di-ku' sa ka-jen	How much is this?
Ka-dien tʰa' ču	That's too expensive.
Tung jo	Boil water for tea.
Pʰå jo	Pour the water to make tea.
Kʰe sî	Boiled water.

De-tsî A table. Zång A bed. Yü-tsî A chair. Mo-do:ng A commode. Ya'-dzî A key. Mien-bung A basin. Ngå-bung A frying pan. Så-tsø A broom.

Mo-kwo A jacket. Pe-sing A vest. Či-tsî A tie. Do:-i An overcoat. Kʰo:-tsî Trousers. Jün A skirt. Bå-kwo A cloak. 'Œn-san A shirt. Ñø-tsî Buttons.

Ng Fish. So:-tsʰe Vegetables. Či Chicken. A' Duck. Ngo: Goose. Ño' Meat. Čœ'-tsî Orange. Bing-ko: Apple. Dø Beans. Tå-dø String beans. Čœn-sing-tsʰe Cabbage. Po:-tsʰe Spinach. Wʰo-tsʰe Cauliflower. Mi Rice. Mi -fung Flour. Kʰa-fi Coffee.

Numbers 1 to 10. 1. I', 2. Lian, or Ñi, 3. San, 4. Sî '. 5. Ng, 6. Lo', 7. Tsʰi', 8. Pa', 9. Čø, 10. Ze'.

I'-pa' One hundred. I'-tsʰien. One thousand. I'-ian Ten thousand.

The classic book, Useful Phrases In The Shanghai Dialect, by Gilbert McIntosh (American Presbyterian Mission Press, 1908) has an excellent description of the sounds, and a well organized phrase book (including a number of word lists, and forty-three measure words). It also gives us a taste of the expats' life in Shanghai in 1908, including business conversation, shopping, visiting the tailor, taking the rickshaw, taking trips to the countryside, cooking, and dealing with your servants. The driving section includes necessary phrases such as "Bring the carriage round," "Are there candles in the lamps?" "The collar doesn't fit, it will hurt the horse's shoulder," "Those wheels are loose, put new washers on," and "Be careful with that horse, he may run away."

The servant sections are a real cry from the heart. "Sweep this floor," "This is not clean, do it again," "You must scour the table," "Use a cloth to dust the room," "This cloth is dirty; you must wash it," "If you want to go out, first tell me," "Why do you work so very slowly?" "I think you smoke opium," "If you go home, you must get me a substitute," "If you want to go, you must wait till I find a new man,' "If you go now I will cut your wages."

And one thing that never changes in shopping. Di-ku' ve'-zî tsung-ku' "This is a fake."

When I was there in the 1980s and 90s, all that you heard in the streets was Shanghaihua, whether downtown or out in our suburban area. Returning in 2015, I heard much less in the streets, though when I trained in Kangjian Park, most people were still speaking Shanghaihua, and switched to Putonghua to talk to me.

With economic growth, and the changing of residency rules, naturally there are more people arriving who speak other dialects and Putonghua. But there is more going on than that. Two measures are eliminating Shanghaihua as the language of the city. The first is the government's policy on Putonghua. The second is the dispersal of the urban Shanghainese.

All children are taught in Putonghua in school throughout China, so, more and more, tend to use it amongst themselves. Shanghainese born before the 1990s often spoke only Shanghaihua. Those born in the 1990s often spoke Putonghua at school and Shanghaihua at home. Those born in the 2000s can understand it, but are more comfortable in Putonghua. Those born in the 2010s are often monolingual, but in Putonghua. It is almost normal for Shanghainese now to speak to their parents in Shanghaihua and to their children in Putonghua.

New emigrants to Shanghai, into the managerial positions that became available in the 21st Century, speak Putonghua. Unlike emigrants of the 20th Century, they do not have to or want to learn Shanghaihua. Signs in public offices throughout Shanghai exhort the readers to 'please speak Putonghua.' Public announcements are given in Putonghua. Before, not speaking Shanghaihua made you feel a bit awkward. Now, Putonghua is the go-to language. Shanghaihua, instead of being the dominant prestige language, is becoming marginalised, even looked down on as a local dialect.

The policy of the government is that speaking Putonghua shows patriotism and loyalty to the Party. Dialects are 'low culture' and backward. The Party much prefers a population that is culturally homogenous and politically loyal, and a standard language does a long way in managing this.

Homogenity and uniformity are not part of what Shanghai has ever been about. Even with Putonghua in all schools, Shanghaihua continued to be widely spoken in informal settings into the early 21st Century. But it is quickly losing ground.

The urban renewal has separated the Shanghainese from each other, and intensified the loss of their language. Over a million Shanghainese in the old style *lilong* neighbourhoods have been involuntarily relocated to the fringes of the metropolis, their neighbourhoods torn down to make room for the metro, elevated expressways, high-end malls, and high rise apartments. They were not moved together, but dispersed, into areas where people spoke other dialects, with Putonghua as the language held in common. Shanghainese identity, so firmly attached to the neighbourhoods and language, was displaced, dispersed, and destroyed. Parents need to speak their native dialect at home to keep it alive. And language needs to be spoken in the neighbourhood, not just the household, to survive. The shared kitchens, the life spilling out into the alleys, the kids playing together outside, all kept the language alive. Put into mixed speaker communities, they don't feel that they can initiate conversations in Shanghaihua. It is almost considered rude, as a larger and larger part of the population does not understand it.

Loss of a language leads to loss of a culture, as our province of Québec in Canada reminds us constantly. On the bright side, most studies talk about the inner city dispersal, while I know that the areas of Chabei, Hongkew, out past Xujiahui, our old area south of Longhua, were Shanghainese, speaking Shanghaihua. Shanghaihua was spoken throughout the metropolis, not just in the downtown core. New housing, such as the empty fields with the roads already built near our home, if people were relocated there, are well within still being Shanghainese. A lot of initially relocated people came out to our Caohejing area, so were able to maintain cohesion. But then the Caohejing area was cleared and rebuilt, displacing the original residents further out, so I am not sure what is happening there. The people in Kangjian park spoke a mix of Shanghaihua and Putonghua when I last visited.

Shanghaihua was the prestige language of the city through the 20th Century. Now, even though all dialects are seen as backwards, many Shanghinese still want to speak it amongst themselves, and do not care what the national policy is, or what other people think of their language. The ability to speak Shanghaihua has, up until now, given Shanghainese a sense of superiority, of belonging to the city, of excluding the Outlanders. Before, there was an insider prestige to speaking Shanghaihua. Migrant workers, especially small business people, worked hard to converse with their customers in Shanghaihua, to belong, to show that they were not Outlanders. (Outlanders were blamed for anything that was not quite right, from trash in the street, to robberies, to cats disappearing. When our white cat went missing, I was told that locals don't eat cats, Outlanders do, so it was obvious that Outlanders had stolen it.)

As late as the early 21st Century, Shanghainese would converse together, and newcomers would feel uncomfortable and excluded. But now, if you exclude newcomers in the workplace by chatting in Shanghaihua, you are creating an awkward situation for yourself. Newcomers don't want to learn it. Conversations with strangers need to be initiated in Putonghua, and only if you see that both people are Shanghainese, can you switch.

Shanghai is on its way to becoming a global city, with homogenous architecture, culture, and language. There may soon be nothing left to make being a Shanghai citizen special. Instead of identifying with Shanghai, new residents will identify with the state-sanctioned identity of being Chinese.

Shanghai's close-knit communities destroyed, the prestige of living in a villa in the French Quarter (even though you are a whole family in one room) gone, there remains only the stubborn pride of being a Shanghainese. Although the prevailing attitude now is that only old, or uneducated, people can't manage Putonghua, speaking Shanghaihua is becoming an act of defiance and showing local pride. If anyone has enough defiance and pride to keep a language alive, the born-in-Shanghai Shanghainese just might.

SANLU, THE THIRD FORM   sān lù   三路

ABOUT SANLU

The third form, *Sanlu*, is also called *Dasi Taochui* 大四套捶, the Big Four Sets Of Pounding. Its characteristics are: most moves have a small and compact framework, their applications are mostly to the four corners, and most moves have a corresponding balanced move to the other side. To perform it, you need the foundation of the first and second forms. The whole form uses small opening and closing bodywork, coordinated with the characteristic smooth and counter coiling silk power of the hands. The form is short and compact, with solid *fajin* moves, and clean hand techniques. The hand techniques are mostly short range, the footwork small and skillful, and the bodywork lively. It is done relatively quickly, with a lot of stamping and *fajin*, making it an athletic form.

I learned this form from my martial brother Cai Yuhua in Shanghai, in 1990, at home. I showed him the Taiji Changquan that I was probably not supposed to show him, and he showed me the third form that I probably wasn't ready for yet. Cai Yuhua corrected this form for me in 1996, 2001, and again in 2015. He gave me the name list and verses in 1996. The verses have gaps because I always thought there would be a good time to go over them again to clarify some characters that I couldn't read clearly.

Dasi Taochui is a form that is sometimes mentioned in lineages, but I have never seen it written up. Although I don't do it well, since I never seem to practise it enough, I have good notes, so can present I here with a bit more information than is usually given. I filmed it for the photos in Québec City on a warm and sunny day in October, 2022.

NAMES OF THE MOVEMENTS OF SANLU

1. 预备式, 懒扎衣   Preparation, to Tuck In The Robe Casually
2. 单鞭   Single Whip
3. 翻花砲   Overturn Flowers Punch
4. 望门攒   Watch The Gate Strike
5. 掩手肱拳   Hide The Hand And Punch
6. 卧弓射虎   Shoot The Tiger From A Prone Position
7. 拗步下击   Reverse Stance Low Strike
8. 拗步上击   Reverse Stance High Strike
9. 披身压肘   Drape The Body And Press With The Elbow

10.	指裆势	Point To The Groin
11.	金鸡独立	Golden Rooster Stands On One Leg
12.	护心拳	Protect The Heart
13.	六封四闭	Six Sealings, Four Closings
14.	纵横劈击	Chop The Length And Breadth
15.	耳环跟打	Kick The Earrings
16.	削转左右七星	Pare And Turn To Seven Stars Left And Right
17.	翻花孤雁出群	Overturn Flowers, Lone Goose Leaves The Flock
18.	下扎式	Stab Downward
19.	翻花舞袖	Overturn Flowers By Flourishing The Sleeves
20.	分门一脚	Break Open The Door With One Kick
21.	转身一拳	Turn And Throw A Punch
22.	穿梭两脚	Thread The Shuttle With Two Feet
23.	舞袖推山	Flourish The Sleeves And Push The Mountain
24.	转身当头砲	Turn To Rap On The Head With Cannon Balls
25.	收势	Closing

1. **Preparation, to Tuck in the Robe Casually**   yù bèi shì, lǎn zhā yī

   预备势，懒扎衣

Verse for the Move: 揽扎衣立势高强。 Tuck In The Robe Casually is an upright stance that is tall and strong.

Overall Movement: Sanlu starts the same as Yilu. Face south in Preparation. Photo 1.1.

Continue on with moves two and three of Yilu – Three Openings And Closings Of The Dantian. Photos 1.2a, b, c, d, e, f, g, h, i, and j.

Sanlu: The Third Form

Continue on with move four of Yilu – Temple Guard Pounds With The Pestle. Still facing south. Photos 1.3a, b, c, d, e, f, g, h, I, j, k, l, m, n, o, p, and q.

Shadowboxing in Shanghai

Then do move five of Yilu – Tuck In The Robe Casually. Photos 1.4a, b, c, d, and e.

Note: All of these opening moves are done as normal in Yilu. Perhaps don't take quite so much time as in Yilu, but do not move noticeably quicker at this point.

2. **Single Whip**   dān biān   单鞭

<u>Verse for the Move</u>: 拉下单鞭鬼爷怕。 When you pull out to Single Whip, even demons are afraid.

<u>Overall Movement</u>: Continue on with move six of Yilu – Seal Off, Shut Down. Photos 2a, b, c, d, e, f, g, h, i, j, k, and l.

Then do Single Whip posture. Do not roll into Dantian Transforms. Photos 2m, n, o, p, q, and r.

Sanlu: The Third Form

3. **Overturn Flowers Punch**   fān huā pào   翻花砲

<u>Verse for the Move</u>: 出门先使翻身砲。 Starting out, first use the rolling hit.

<u>Overall Movement</u>: Roll over with an elbow strike, land and punch.

301

Shadowboxing in Shanghai

Breakdown of Movement:

Part One: Hook the left foot in and turn around to the right. Roll the left shoulder under to roll the left hand so the palm faces up. Curl the right elbow upwards. Photo 3a.

Part Two: Turn completely around to the right, lifting the right knee and striking up, over, and down with the right elbow. Then stamp the right foot and land the left foot to bow stance distance. Set the right fist in the left palm, then punch to the front in bow stance. The punch is to the south. Photos 3b, 3c and 3d.

4. **Watch The Gate Strike**   wàng mén cuán   望门攒

Verse for the Move: 望门？。 Watch The Gate…

Overall Movement: Strike to the ear with the palm rolled over, turning the body away to get more reach.

Breakdown of Movement:

Part One: Roll back slightly, opening the arms, keeping the elbows down, turning the fist hearts out, to do an outward pressure with the forearms. Roll the arms with a closing power, bringing the right foot in quickly, stepping across up to or in front of the left foot. Photos 4a and 4b.

Part Two: Step the left foot out to a left bow stance. Hit the right palm out to ear height, palm turned as if hitting the side of the ear, with the thumb side down. Do a short, sharp, *fajin* to hit. The body is turned away from the hit (stance is east to west, body faces almost east, the palm is extended to the south). This is a palm strike to the west, not a backhand to the east. Photo 4c.

5. **Hide The Hand And Punch** yǎn shǒu hóng quán 掩手肱拳

<u>Verse for the Move</u>: 反堂压，后带着掩手肱拳。Turn over the chest and press down, then continue on to Hide The Hand And Punch.

<u>Overall Movement</u>: Two kicks, then punch.

<u>Breakdown of Movement</u>:

Part One: Roll back slightly, opening with outward pressure of the forearms. Cross the forearms and kick sweep to someone standing to the south of you. This is a scraping kick – hit the heel on the ground then lift the foot slightly to the north. Do not land the foot. Photos 5a and 5b.

Part Two: Low back heel kick to the same spot (kick the groin of the person just swept if he is still standing). Open the left hand to the North and slap the outside edge of the heel with the right hand. Photo 5c.

Part Three: Turn to face south, then stamp the right foot and pound the right fist into the left palm. Step the left foot out to land, then punch. Make sure to turn first, turning the leg with the knee up. The punch is to the south. Photos 5d and 5e.

6. **Shoot The Tiger From A Prone Position**

wò gōng shè hǔ 卧弓射虎

<u>Verse for the Move</u>: 骑马势，下连着窝弓射虎。From a horse riding stance, continue on to Shoot The Tiger From A Prone Position.

<u>Overall Movement</u>: Close in then double punch.

<u>Breakdown of Movement</u>:

Part One: Open, then close in the power, shifting in the stance but not stepping. Photos 6a and 6b.

Part Two: Double hit with the left fist out, around, and in, down to the left. Hit with the right fist up and to the right. The left is a bit of a hook punch, moving inwards on the final snap. The punch is to the south. Photos 6c.

7. Reverse Stance Low Strike   ǎo bù xià jī   拗步下击

Verse for the Move: 左拗步，十面埋伏。 Left Reverse Stance ambushes from all sides.

Overall Movement: Step and push to the west.

Breakdown of Movement:

Turn to face west, open the right foot to a right bow stance, brush the knee with the right hand and push with the left hand. (The left hand is forward, so the verse calls the posture a left reverse stance.) Photo 7.

8. Reverse Stance High Strike   ǎo bù shàng jī   拗步上击

Verse for the Move: 右拗步，谁敢争锋。 Who dares go against the Right Reverse Stance.

Overall Movement: Step forward and push.

Breakdown of Movement:

Step the left foot forward to the west into a left bow stance. Brush the knee with the left hand and push with the right hand. (The right hand is forward, so the verse calls the posture a right reverse stance.) Photo 8.

Sanlu: The Third Form

9. **Drape The Body And Press Down With The Elbow** pī shēn yā zhǒu 披身压肘

Verse for the Move: 庇身拳，势如压印。The body shielding posture is like pressing down with a seal.

Overall Movement: Step forward, drop and roll, coming up with the body draping technique. See also move 24 of Yilu, where this move is called Bend And Hit With The Back, *beizhekao*.

Breakdown of Movement:

Part One: Step the right foot forward to the west, sit on the left to a drop stance. Roll the right shoulder under to thread the right hand along the right leg, palm turned over to face up. Extend the left hand to the rear, palm facing back. Photo 9a.

Part Two: Turn the body fully to the right without moving the feet. After the right palm goes around the right knee, take it fully to the rear, following the turn of the body. Bring the left hand in around the back of the head and reach it forward, extending it to the front (in front of the right foot). Photo 9b.

Part Three: Turn well to the left without moving the feet. Draw the left hand in to the body and bring the right hand all around to the left in a vertical circle. Then roll to Drape the Body. Do a short *fajin* at the end. Photo 9c.

10. **Point To The Groin** zhǐ dāng shì 指裆势

Verse for the Move: 指裆势，高推底掤。Point To The Groin, push high and press low.

Overall Movement: Turn and punch.

Breakdown of Movement:

Part One: Turn towards the right elbow. Lift the right knee, curl the right elbow, then punch the right fist low and the left fist high, to the west. The left fist is above the head, hitting with the fist surface. The right fist is about face height, hitting with a backfist. Photo 10a.

Part Two: Land the right foot with a stamp, step the left foot forward to a bow stance, and do a low punch to the west with the right fist. Photos 10b and 10c.

11. Golden Rooster Stands On One Leg   jīn jī dú lì   金鸡独立

Verse for the Move: 金鸡独立且留情。Golden Rooster Stands On One Leg leaves no mercy.

Overall Movement: Two jump double stamps. This is the same as moves 81 and 82 in Yilu, except that both moves remain facing the same way.

Breakdown of Movement:

Part One: Thread the right palm through the left and up, raising the right knee, pushing the left hand down to the side. Facing west. Photo 11a.

Part Two: Push off the left foot to do a jump double stamp, landing left then right. Hit up with the right hand then press down with both hands. Still facing west. Photos 11b and 11c.

Part Three: Thread the left palm up, raising the left knee, pushing the right hand down to the side. Facing west. Photo 11d.

Part Four: Push off the right foot to do a jump double stamp, landing right then left. Hit up with the left hand then press down with both hands. Still facing west. Photos 11e and 11f.

Sanlu: The Third Form

12. **Protect The Heart** hú xīn quán 护心拳

<u>Verse for the Move</u>: 护心拳八面？？。 Protect The Heart takes care of all eight sides.

<u>Overall Movement</u>: Three backfists in front of the chest. Still facing west.

<u>Breakdown of Movement</u>:

Part One: Step the right foot back, extending the left palm forward with a chop. Then gather the left hand in to give power to the following hit. Settle into an empty stance.

Part Two: Backfist the right fist, bringing the left fist in. Don't move the feet.

Part Three: Backfist the left fist, bringing the right fist in. Don't move the feet.

Part Four: Backfist the right fist, bringing the left fist in. Don't move the feet. (In 2015 I noted, just do two backfists, right and left.)

13. **Six Sealings, Four Closings** liù fēng sì bì 六封四闭

<u>Verse for the Move</u>: 六封四闭势难客。 Six Sealings, Four Closings makes it hard for the adversary.

<u>Overall Movement</u>: Jump forward into a low up-lifting push. Still moving west.

<u>Breakdown of Movement</u>:

Jump forward onto the right leg, bring the left foot up to a T stance, touching down behind. Open the palms, circle them up and in to the face, then push out at abdomen height. Follow through higher, as in Yilu. The push is to the northwest.   Photos 13a, 13b, and 13c.

14. Chop the Length And Breadth   zòng héng pī jī   纵横劈击

<u>Verse for the Move</u>: 转身劈打纵横。 Turning, chop the length and breadth freely.

<u>Overall Movement</u>: A Travelling Hands type action, stepping to each cardinal point.

<u>Breakdown of Movement</u>:

Part One: Turn the upper body left, start a Travelling Hands sort of action with the left hand up and the right down, going across to the left, going east. (This is very similar to Xingyiquan's alligator form, or else I have changed it slightly.) Photo 14a.

Part Two: Step the right foot around to the North, body facing west, bring the hands across to the right with the horizontal chopping strike. Bring the left foot in to touch down by the right. Turn the body well into the action. Photo 14b.

Part Three: Step the left foot to the south and do the horizontal chopping strike action to the left. Photo 14c.

15. Kick The Earrings   ěr huán gēn dǎ   耳环跟打

<u>Verse for the Move</u>: 上一步二换跟打。 Step forward and switch-over to kick.

<u>Overall Movement</u>: A jump front slap kick, dropping back to pull.

<u>Breakdown of Movement</u>:

Part One: Start the Travelling Hands to the right, then pull the right palm in, rolling it over, then press down with the back of the hand. As you press the right hand down, bring the left over, step the right foot forward and push off to jump up. Do a jump front slap kick, slapping the right foot with the right hand. Photos 15a, 15b, 15c, 15d, and 15e.

Part Two: Land on the left foot and step the right foot back, crossing in front. The hands are up, so leave them up and bring them to the right side, palms facing up, fingers pointing back. Pull the hands in a circle to the right, then down, dropping low onto the right leg. Photos 15f and 15g.

Sanlu: The Third Form

16. **Pare And Turn To Seven Stars Left And Right**   xiāo zhuǎn zuǒ yòu qī xīng   削转左右七星

<u>Verse for the Move</u>: 倒回来左右七星。Go back with Seven Stars to left and right.

<u>Overall Movement</u>: Go through a drop stance and pull through to Seven Stars. This is similar to move 102 in Yilu, but in bow stance.

<u>Breakdown of Movement</u>:

Part One: Come through a drop stance and pull the hands through. Then shift to a left bow stance and punch the right fist through under the left forearm. Both fists have the fist eyes up. Photo 16a.

Part Two: Roll the right fist over, then under to punch forward again, fist reversed. Photos 16b and 16c.

17. **Overturn Flowers, Lone Goose Leaves The Flock** fān huā gū yàn chū qún
翻花孤雁出群

Verse for the Move: 翻花炮，打一个孤雁出群。Hit with a Roll Flowers, then hit with a Lone Goose Leaves The Flock.

Overall Movement: Switchover steps to roll in then strike out with a double strike (similar to Xingyiquan's horse form punch). There are three 'horse form' punches. The first roll in is within the Seven Stars, the second and third are rolling draw-backs.

Breakdown of Movement:

Part One: Roll as part of the Seven Stars, rolling the fists and forearms together and drawing the fists into the waist. Punch in a sixty-forty stance with a double punch. The left fist is forward, the right fist is tucked at the left elbow, both fist hearts in. Photos 17a and 17b.

Part Two: Roll left then right, rolling the fists and forearms together. Draw back to the right side with the left forearm vertical. Bring in the left foot to stamp and step forward the right foot into a sixty-forty stance. Do the same double punch with the right fist forward, the left tucked at the right elbow, both fist hearts in. Photos 17c, 17d, and 17e.

Part Three: Roll back to the left, then right side, left forearm vertical. Draw in the right foot to stamp then step the left foot forward to sixty-forty stance. Punch in smooth 'horse form.' The left fist is forward, right tucked at the left elbow, both fist hearts in. Photos 17g and 17h.

Sanlu: The Third Form

18. **Stab Downward** xià zhā shì 下扎式

Verse for the Move: 下插势，谁敢来攻。Downward Stab Posture, who dares to attack against it.

Overall Movement: A rolled low stab in a high tucked empty stance.

Breakdown of Movement:

Step the right foot forward to touch it down in front in a tucked in high empty stance. Extend the right fist over the left forearm, then punch down the fist to the right knee, rolling the body. Photo 18.

19. **Overturn Flowers By Flourishing the Sleeves** fān huā wǔ xiù
翻花舞袖

Verse for the Move: 翻花舞袖如长虹。Overturn Flowers By Flourishing The Sleeves is like a long rainbow.

Overall Movement: A jumping turn to a double chop.

Breakdown of Movement:

Hook in and land the right foot, and turn around to the left. Lift the left knee and do a strike with the left elbow as turning. Jump off the right foot to turn completely around to the left. Land in a sixty-forty stance on the left leg and do a double chop. Photos 19a and 19b.

20. **Break Open the Door with One Kick** fēn mén yī jiǎo 分门一脚

Verse for the Move: 分门压之震残生。Break Open The Door and flatten it to shock your opponent's remaining years.

Overall Movement: Two piercing palms with two kicks.

Breakdown of Movement:

Part One: Thread through the left hand, palm up, from the throat. The actions are going west. Photo 20a.

311

Part Two: Thread through the right hand together with a left heel kick, foot turned out. Kick to the west. Photo 20b.

Part Three: Land the left foot forward and do a right heel kick to the west. Press both palms out to either side. Photo 20c.

21. **Turn And Throw A Punch**   zhuǎn shēn yī quán   转身一拳

<u>Verse for the Move</u>: 转身一锤打做。 Turn and strike with a hit.

<u>Overall Movement</u>: Stamp and punch.

<u>Breakdown of Movement</u>:

Part One: Land the right foot with a stamp, turning to face south. Pound the right fist into the left palm. Photo 21a.

Part Two: Land the left foot and punch with the right fist. The punch is to the south. Photo 21b.

22. **Thread The Shuttle With Two Feet**   chuān suō liǎng jiǎo   穿梭两脚

<u>Verse for the Move</u>: 两脚穿压难打。 Two feet with a thread and a press down are hard to hit (defend against).

<u>Overall Movement</u>: A shovel kick, then a side kick.

<u>Breakdown of Movement</u>:

Part One: Hook the left foot around, hitting the ground to the south to swing it up to the North, hooking the foot up. Be sure not to swing too high, but to land fairly quickly. At the same time, punch the left fist upside down out to the south. Do not do a sweep hook with the hand as you usually do with this kick, but punch out from the waist. Photos 22a and 22b.

Part Two: Land the left foot to the North and do a right side kick to the south. Keep the left hand back in a hooked position. The right forearm is across the lower chest, hand at the left side. Photo 22c.

Note: In 2015 I learned this as a *koubu* landing with the left foot, stepping the right foot on the spot, then a step with the left foot, so there is just the one kick, which is a side kick, but I prefer to do the little sweep hook kick that I remember from before. I have done a straight heel kick instead of a sidekick in the photo. If you do a sidekick, keep the body turned away.

23. **Flourish The Sleeves And Push The Mountain** wǔ xiù tuī shān
舞袖推山

Verse for the Move: 舞袖一推往前攻。 Flourish The Sleeves and attack pushing to the front.

Overall Movement: Stamp and roll to a snapping punch.

Breakdown of Movement:

Part One: Stamp the right foot, turning to face south. Step the left foot to the south and circle the hands around with the turn. Photo 23a.

Part Two: Loop the left hand up inside the right, using the right elbow to roll over. Trap the left hand inside the right, then snap the left fist out. This is a double roll over, using the back. Photo 23b.

24. **Turn To Rap On The Head With Cannon Balls** zhuǎn shēn
dāng tóu pào 转身当头砲

Verse for the Move: 回头当阳砲冲。 Turn the head and charge to strike the temples.

Overall Movement: Roll back, kick, roll and double punch.

Breakdown of Movement:

Part One: Roll back, still facing south. Come forward and do a right hit uppercut with the right straight swing kick up (the same as move 106 in Yilu). Photo 24a.

Shadowboxing in Shanghai

Part Two: Land the right foot behind and double punch the fists (the same as move 106 in Yilu). Photo 24b.

25. **Closing** shòu shì 收势

Overall Movement: Temple Guard Pounds With The Pestle, then Closing.

Breakdown of Movement:

Part One: Still facing south, do Temple Guard Pounds With The Pestle (the same as move 107 in Yilu). Photos 25a, 25b, 25c, 25d, 25e, 25f, 25g, and 25h.

Then do Closing (the same as move 108 in Yilu). The only difference is that you finish facing the same direction as the opening move in Sanlu. Photos 25i, 25j, and 25k.

Shanghai in the Future?

Shanghai was well on its way to becoming a post-Socialist city. The events of the 'covid years' show that this is not going to happen. While I worked on the final of this book, the citizens of Shanghai spent over two months in complete lockdown of all housing compounds and businesses, with daily swab testing. Shanghai has been through a lot over the years, and the Shanghainese always managed to bounce back. There is no repressing their love for their city, which, of course, is part of the perceived problem – they identify with the city more than with the Party. In one of life's ironies, it is, of course, where the Party was able to start out, due to the rules of the French Concession. You can visit its old headquarters, just off Huaihai East Road.

The old Chinese City is the next in line for demolition. From the beginning, when the wall was taken down in 1911 as 'not modern,' it didn't really count, and somehow escaped urban renewal. It is now too seedy to represent the downtown core of modern Shanghai, and is not seen as its beating heart. Much like London's Dockyards, development of such prime land is inevitable. It is now being demolished to make way for modern (read expensive) housing, and commerce. Most residents have already been moved to 'nicer' places in the suburbs.

Photos of the old Chinese City as it was being cleared out, June 2022. Photos courtesy of a friend.

The last time I went, in 2019, this fascinating old neighbourhood was still a maze of alleys, with distinctive sights and smells, though it was gradually being surrounded by high-rises. The northern part, with Yuyuan Gardens and shopping/eating streets, will stay as it is now, as it has already been refurbished for tourism. The area around Yuyuan Gardens used to be surrounded by an amazing free market that spread out like a maze. I remember in the 1980s one table with more buttons than I ever imagined possible. In the 1990s there were lots of stalls with Socialist kitsch, and you could pick up Mao buttons on the cheap. Now I can't help thinking it looks all a bit generic when crossing from Lao Xi Men.

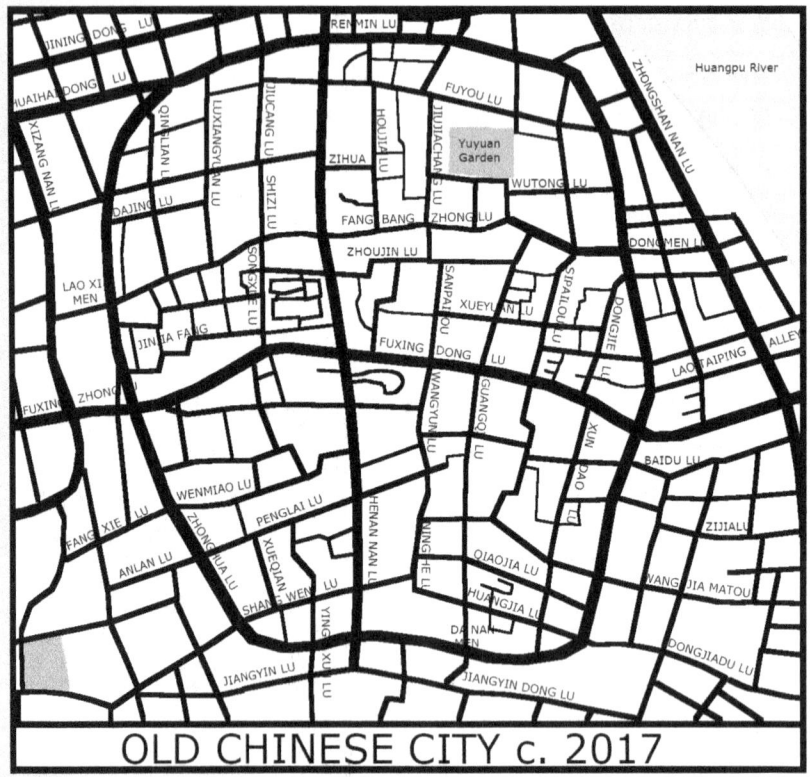

OLD CHINESE CITY c. 2017

The map of Shanghai issued by the city doesn't manage to name all of the alleys and passageways in the old Chinese city. Google maps gives a maze of lanes and alleys that are not on the city map. No surprise I got lost every time I wandered through there. I wonder how it would have fared if the wall had been kept, like in Quebec City and York.

This image of modern Shanghai and socialist culture clash is just too good to not put in the book. Taken at the Hongqiao train station Enquiry Desk in 2015, Lei Feng assures us that it is there to serve the people. What I found funny is that the service was, actually, quite good.

The last time I met with my friends, in 2019, we didn't realise it may be the last time. The covid-19 worldwide pandemic travel issues that stopped my training and teaching trips through 2020, 2021, and 2022, and all the difficulties that arose during that time, made me realise that I may not return to China.

I miss my training with Cheng, and really want to learn the rest of Jiang Rongqiao's seventy-two hidden kicks. There is nothing worse than knowing two-thirds of something. Except not being able to visit friends during a global pandemic. Even worse is getting news, or not getting news, from friends who are under unreasoned lockdown. Not knowing all the hidden kicks is put into its proper place of non-importance.

My Shanghai years gave me, in addition to a very cool Taijiquan form, an extraordinary bagua style, and a magnificent Taiji Changquan form:

A bronchial sensitivity that means I have to be very careful at the hint of a cold, to make sure it doesn't work its way down and settle in. Though I may have Beijing's coal haze to thank for that.

The ability to sweat from every pore, which gives me a tolerance, even enthusiasm, for heat and humidity.

A recognition that if you have enough to eat, you don't need much more to have a good life. If someone else is doing the cooking, that is a bonus. If you also have a bicycle and the time and health to do martial arts or something else that you love, then that is outstanding.

A fascination that takes me down rabbit holes online, gives me many happy hours in libraries, and adds to my book collection. Having lived in and experienced one of the world's great cities on different levels and in various neighbourhoods, I have become more and more intrigued by it. And I am not alone here – there is a continual supply of research on, books about, and stories based in Shanghai. Even if I don't make it back, I won't lose touch.

SOME CHINESE TERMS THAT I MAY HAVE USED IN THE BOOK (IN PUTONGHUA)

an	to press down, or press down and away
ao bu	a reverse stance, different foot and hand forward
bai bu	a turned-out step, placing the foot turned outward
cai	to pluck, grasp with both hands, pushing and pulling in a balanced way
cai bu	a trampling step, foot turned out
cha bu	a back insertion step, foot steps behind the other, legs crossed
chan si	coiling silk power, spiraling power through the body
chou shen	to draw into the hip joints and torso
dan tian,	the body core within the pelvic girdle
ti dan tian	to raise the core, lifting inside the hips and through the spine
fa jin	a power release, to throw a punch
ge	a transverse block, cutting across with the forearm vertical
gen bu	a follow-in step, bring the rear foot up near the front foot
gong bu	a bow stance, facing front, front knee bent and over the foot, rear leg pushing, but not straight.
han xiong	to relax the chest, leave it naturally settled
he jin	a gathering power, closing-in power
ji	to press, crowd, jostle, squeeze with the arm or trunk.
ji bu	a skip step, pushing off with the front foot and tapping the rear foot to the front foot in the air
kai bu	1. standing with feet parallel, legs straight, and apart about shoulder width. 2. a short, high horse stance with the feet parallel about shoulder width apart.
kao	to lean, strike with the torso
kou bu	a tuck-in step, placing the foot turned inward
liao	slice up with the arm quite straight
liao quan	to slice up with the arm quite straight, holding the hand in a fist
lü	to stroke, pull without grabbing
ni chan	counter-coiling power, coiling that results in internal rotation of the arm (thumb towards palm), and usually movement towards the body.
peng	elastic, resilient power, expanding outward

pu bu	a drop stance, sitting on one leg, extending the other to the side
shun bu	smooth stance, same foot and hand forward
shun chan	smooth coiling power, coiling that results in external rotation of the arm (thumb away from palm) and usually movement away from the body.
song kua	to release tension in the hip joints, allow the thigh bones to move easily in the joints
xie bu	a resting stance, legs crossed and sitting, rear knee tucked into the hollow of the front knee
xu bu	an empty stance, sit on one leg and place the other lightly in front

PRONUNCIATION OF PINYIN, THE CHINESE NATIONAL PHONETIC ALPHABET FOR PUTONGHUA (WITH INTERNATIONAL PHONETIC ALPHABET EQUIVALENTS)

INITIALS (words can start with these consonants, or have a zero initial)		
PINYIN	IPA	ROUGH PRONUNCIATION GUIDE
p	pʰ	Like English <u>p</u>et with a considerable puff of air.
b	p	Similar to the *pinyin* "p" but without the puff of air (unvoiced, neither English <u>p</u>et nor <u>b</u>et).
t	tʰ	Like English <u>t</u>ag with a considerable puff of air.
d	t	Similar to the *pinyin* "t" but with no puff of air (unvoiced, not <u>d</u>og).
k	kʰ	Like English <u>k</u>ill with a considerable puff of air.
g	k	Similar to the *pinyin* "k" but with no puff of air (unvoiced, not English <u>g</u>et).
c	tsʰ	Like exaggerating English ca<u>ts</u>.
z	ts	Like the *pinyin* "c" but without the puff of air (unvoiced).
ch	tʂʰ	Somewhat similar to English <u>ch</u>at with a puff of air, but with the tip of the tongue rolled back.
zh	tʂ	Like the *pinyin* "ch" but with no puff of air (unvoiced).
q	tɕʰ	Somewhat similar to English <u>ch</u>at with a puff of air, but with the front of the tongue raised and the tip on the lower teeth.
j	tɕ	Like the *pinyin* "q" but without the puff of air (unvoiced).
m	m	Like English <u>m</u>et.
n	n	Like English <u>n</u>et.
f	f	Similar to English <u>f</u>at, but with the teeth just touching lightly behind the lower lip.
s	s	Similar to English <u>s</u>et.
sh	ʂ	Somewhat similar to English <u>sh</u>ow, but with the same tongue placement as the *pinyin* "ch" and "zh."

321

x	ɕ	Somewhat similar to English <u>sh</u>ine but with the same tongue placement as the *pinyin* "q" and "j."
h	χ	Raise the back of the tongue and let the breath come through the obstructed passage without vibrating the vocal cords.
l	l	Like English <u>l</u>et.
r	ɹ	Like the *pinyin* "sh" but with voicing.
FINALS		
n	n	Like English pi<u>n</u>.
ng	ŋ	Like English si<u>ng</u>.
VOWELS		
a	A a ɛ	Usually close to English f<u>a</u>ther (not p<u>a</u>t). Like y<u>e</u>t when written "-ian" or "yan."
e	ɤ e ɛ ə	Usually similar to English p<u>e</u>t, can tend towards a mid vowel.
i	i ɭ ɪ	Usually similar to English b<u>ee</u>. Similar to w<u>e</u>t when written "ui." After c, z, s, ch, zh, sh, and r it is similar to s<u>ir</u>.
o	o u	Usually close to English r<u>o</u>ll. Similar to c<u>ow</u> when written "ao," and <u>ow</u>e when in "ou."
u	u y	Usually similar t English o b<u>oo</u>t. After the *pinyin* "x", "q", and "j" and in the vowel groups starting with these consonants, it is pronounced "ü."
ü	y	Similar to French <u>ü</u>. It is written after "n" or "l," because these are the only positions where both "u" and "ü" are possible
y	i	Partially like an English 'y', tending towards i.
w	u	Partially like an English 'w', tending towards u.

TONES IN PINYIN			
NUMBER	PINYIN	NAME	RANGE
1	ˉ	high level	55
2	´	high rising	35
3	ˇ	dipping	214
4	`	high falling	51
none	° or blank	neutral	in context

With tone sandhi, tones may change according to the preceding or following tone.

The tone marking is put over the main vowel when there are two vowels written together (usually involving the pronunciation of y or w).

Shadowboxing in Shanghai

About the Author

Andrea Falk has practised external and internal Chinese martial arts since 1972. She has studied Chinese art, geography, history, language, linguistics, literature, philosophy, politics, religion, and sociology since then, as well. Andrea received a Bachelor of Arts majoring in Chinese (1978), a Bachelor of Physical Education (1980) and a Master of Physical Education with an emphasis on coaching science (1990) from the University of British Columbia. She trained in wushu full time on scholarship from 1980 to 1983 at the Beijing Physical Culture Institute (Beiti), earning an Advanced Studies Diploma in  Wushu under the tutelage of Professor Xia Bohua and instruction from Men Huifeng and others. There she learned the basics of Yang and Chen style Taijiquan, Baguazhang, Xingyiquan, Chaquan, Tongbeiquan, and modern Longfist (Longfist included barehand and four standard weapons forms). Andrea spent two further extended summers at Beiti in 1984 and 1986.

Starting in 1984, Andrea gradually changed over to learning traditionally, visiting China on extended trips as often as possible to learn in parks, parking lots, and courtyards. She has trained and/or is training Chen style Taijiquan, Baguazhang, and Taiji Changquan as an inside apprentice of the late Huan Dahai (1924-2015) and elder martial brothers in Shanghai, Xingyiquan and Baguazhang as a close student and friend of Di Guoyong in Beijing, and Baguazhang from friends Li Baohua and Lu Yan. When not in China or travelling to teach, she is usually in Québec City, or at a cabin in the Laurentian hills.

Andrea has taught and translated books about Chinese martial arts since 1983. She founded *the wushu centre* in Montreal in 1984, in Victoria in 1992, and in Québec City in 2007. Andrea has taught Chen Taijiquan, Baguazhang, and Xingyiquan around the world, but mostly in Canada and England.

For years, Andrea translated books for her own students. In 2000, *tgl books* and the website www.thewushucentre.ca were established to bring these translations to a wider audience.

trois gros lapins traversent le chemin

ISBN 978-1-989468-29-6

www.ingramcontent.com/pod-product-compliance
Lightning Source LLC
Chambersburg PA
CBHW061931220426
43662CB00012B/1869